Presented to

_____

From

_____

Date

_____

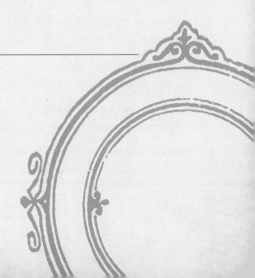

Published in Nashville, Tennessee, by Thomas Nelson. Thomas Nelson is a registered trademark of Thomas Nelson, Inc.

Thomas Nelson, Inc. titles may be purchased in bulk for educational, business, fundraising, or sales promotional use. For information, please email NelsonMinistryServices@ThomasNelson.com.

All Scripture references are from The New King James Version® (NKJV) © 1982 Thomas Nelson, Inc. Used by permission. All rights reserved.

ISBN-13: 978-1-4041-7428-3

Printed in China

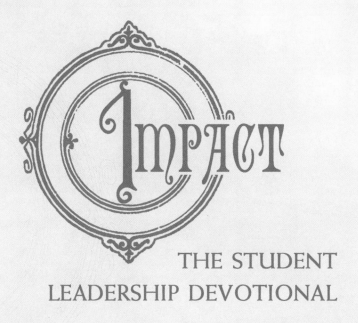

THE STUDENT
LEADERSHIP DEVOTIONAL

A Division of Thomas Nelson Publishers

THOMAS NELSON
Since 1798

NASHVILLE   DALLAS   MEXICO CITY   RIO DE JANEIRO

Contents

Contents

IMPACT: Student Leadership Devotional

Contents

IMPACT: Student Leadership Devotional

Week 1, Monday
Divine Purpose

*To them God willed to make known what are the riches of the glory of this
mystery among the Gentiles: which is Christ in you, the hope of glory.*

Colossians 1:27

Students whom I encounter in the classroom are often wondering: *Why are we on Planet Earth?* While this is a complex, esoteric question, perhaps we are here for a Kingdom purpose.

The Kingdom to which we have been called is a Kingdom of God's glory. Our calling is directly related to His presence. We are here to make His glory known—to express the presence of God. He wants to "move around" and be seen and known through us, just like He moved around and was seen and known in the Tabernacle of the Old Testament.

In fact, until this time, God's glory has been in a burning bush, on the face of Moses, in a cloud by day and a fire at night, in a tabernacle, and in a temple. But God's glory is now in a new home. If we have a personal relationship with Jesus Christ, then the hope of God's presence on earth now rests inside you and me. God's hope of making His presence known down here is placed inside us—Christ in us, the hope of glory.

Just imagine, you are the "home" for God's glory! What an incredible honor, blessing, and privilege. You are to bear and express the glory of God wherever you go! "Whether you eat or drink, or whatever you do, do all to the glory of God" (1 Corinthians 10:31). The Creator has a hope and desire for your life. His heart is longing to engage you in divine purpose.

What thoughts and feelings do you have about being trusted as a "bearer" of God's glory? What does it do to your heart to know that God is longing for you to extend His presence and express His glory?

*Father, what a wonder it is that I can express Your presence—Your life
and love—in my world; make me ever mindful of this privilege. Might Your
Spirit stir me often with gratitude, wonder, and praise? Amen.*

David Ferguson, The Great Commandment Network

Week 1, Tuesday
God's Unmerited Favor

For by grace you have been saved through faith, and that not of yourselves;
it is the gift of God, not of works, lest anyone should boast.

Ephesians 2:8, 9

A social trend among students in America is an attitude of entitlement, a belief that they deserve certain privileges. If God is hoping that we will express His glory wherever we go, how are we to consistently live this way? What had Moses done to earn the privilege of God's glory being displayed to him? What had the people of Israel done to earn or deserve the privilege of God's glorious presence among them?

A better question: What have *we* done to be worthy of this divine favor? The answer to all these questions is, "Absolutely nothing!" Our lives will only express the glory of the Lord as we come to experience gratitude for His grace. It is only by God's grace that we can hope to become an expression of God here on earth.

Grace is God's unmerited favor toward us. Grace means He initiates loving us and showering us with privileges, blessings, and purpose. Grace means that God takes this initiative simply because He loves us and longs to show us grace (Isaiah 30:18) in order to display His glory through us. It was His grace that enlisted Moses and delivered and guided Israel. It was His grace that persevered in Israel's unfaithfulness. It was by His grace that He returned the glory outside of Bethlehem. It was His grace that embraced us: "*For by grace you have been saved . . .*" (Ephesians 2:8).

Pause to reflect upon your own experience of the glory of God's grace. Be still before the Lord and ask His Spirit to stir up remembrances, perhaps of times when He unexpectedly provided for you or accepted you in the midst of failure. Perhaps the Spirit will remind you of a time when God healed you of a physical or emotional pain or when He restored a broken relationship. Give Him thanks for His unmerited grace!

Lord Jesus, thank You for granting me forgiveness. May I release my anger toward others. I'm grateful for Your acceptance and wish to be a person who embraces the differences in others. I appreciate Your healing touch and hope to extend restoration to other people. Amen.

Week 1, Wednesday
It's About Him

*As each one has received a gift, minister it to one another,
as good stewards of the manifold grace of God.*

1 Peter 4:10

The more we realize that the Kingdom is "about Him," not us, we will come to realize that He has a heart, a passion, a love for people. The more we understand that the Christian life is "about Him"—bringing glory to Him—then evangelism, missions, discipleship can't just be religious activities that we do in order to feel better about ourselves or to earn God's approval. Instead, these activities—all ministries—become opportunities to express and expand His glory!

As we express the glory of God, His Spirit is at work to challenge people to notice and "turn aside," just like Moses did when he saw the burning bush (Exodus 4:1–3). They want to know, "What is that? Where did you get that love, that acceptance, and that grace? Where did you get that compassion?" Our only explanation is that we got it from Him. As you experience more of His acceptance, His love, and His compassion, you will then be able to extend the same to others. These will become demonstrations of God's glorious grace in your life. He will then want to send people your way who will want to know, "What is that?"

One of the most important callings God has on your life is telling others about the grace He has extended.

How could you express God's grace to others today? How might you accept others when they have failed (Romans 15:7)? How might you encourage others when they are down (1 Thessalonians 5:11)? How might you support others when they are struggling (Galatians 6:2)?

Dear God, may I stop and notice opportunities to point people to Your grace. May I go looking for people who have experienced failure, being eager to show them Your acceptance. May I listen for those who are expressing words of struggle, being ready to offer words of encouragement or practical support. Amen.

David Ferguson, The Great Commandment Network

Week 1, Thursday
Always Be Ready

But sanctify the Lord God in your hearts, and always be ready to give a defense to everyone who asks you a reason for the hope that is in you, with meekness and fear.

1 Peter 3:15

We live in a culture in which people seem hostile toward someone "preaching" at them, and yet they seem open and curious about hearing someone's story. Everyone has a story. What is the story that God is cultivating in your life?

As others around us "turn aside" like Moses did at the burning bush (Exodus 4:1–4), having noticed His glory expressed through our life, we must be ready! The testimony of the first century was that people "realized that they had been with Jesus" (Acts 4:13). Living out the glory of His grace will draw others around us to notice that we also have been with Him.

First comes our "walk" with Him and then our "talk" with Him. Being prepared to talk "of Him" can begin with our personal testimony of coming to know Him at our new birth. Reflect on the time when you came to receive Him as Savior and submitted to Him as Lord by writing how you would complete the following sentences:

- My life before receiving Christ can be described as . . .
- Some of the events leading up to my salvation included . . .
- Some of the people God used in my life to draw me to Himself included . . .
- Changes God's Holy Spirit began to make in my life over time were . . .
- I am thrilled to describe my relationship with Him today as . . .

Consider how "ready" you are to tell others about the changes Christ has made in your life. Be ready to tell others about your relationship with Him, to the praise of His glory!

Dear God, I'm grateful that my life in Christ had a beginning point, a time when I realized that I needed Your presence. And You have continued to provide for me and protect me. I'm glad that You've placed key people in my life to encourage and support me, as the Holy Spirit has helped me become more like Christ. May I be a person who brings others into a deeper, more thrilling relationship with You. Amen.

David Ferguson, The Great Commandment Network

Week 1, Friday
Sharing the Glory of His Grace

Therefore receive one another, just as Christ also received us, to the glory of God.

Romans 15:7

Faced with the realities of a prolonged era of economic stagnation, we may have a tendency to hold on to resources and become stingy. Millennials can feel that nobody has any natural or general responsibility to help other people.

Imagine being given a multifaceted diamond with many aspects to its brilliance and worth. God's grace is just such a priceless, multifaceted gift!

Picture that one facet or "side" of His grace is His acceptance, and we have the opportunity and privilege to share it with others. "Receive one another, just as Christ also received us, to the glory of God" (Romans 15:7).

Who are some of the people in your life who might need a measure of God's acceptance shared through you? Maybe someone recently rejected? Someone who recently "failed" in some way? Someone struggling with relationships?

Acceptance might look like: giving another chance when something has been done wrong; allowing the other person to think, act, or feel differently from you; loving that person anyway, in spite of offenses. Acceptance might sound like: *"What you did was wrong, but I still love you and want a relationship with you.... We do think differently on that issue, but I still want to be your friend.... No matter what you do, I'm always here for you.... We all mess up at times and you can count on me as you work through this."*

Consider several practical ways that God might want you to express His acceptance to others around you. Share at least one of these demonstrations of His grace to another person today.

Dear Lord Jesus, please lead me to someone today who is feeling rejected, or to a person who feels like a failure, or to someone who is experiencing conflict in a relationship. May I take initiative to embrace that person unconditionally and sacrificially, expressing Your acceptance toward him/her. Amen.

David Ferguson, The Great Commandment Network

Week 1, Weekend
Gratitude for His Grace

Blessed be the God and Father of our Lord Jesus Christ, who has blessed us with every spiritual blessing in the heavenly places in Christ, just as He chose us in Him before the foundation of the world, that we should be holy and without blame before Him in love, having predestined us to adoption as sons by Jesus Christ to Himself, according to the good pleasure of His will, to the praise of the glory of His grace, by which He made us accepted in the Beloved.

Ephesians 1:3–6

Because of the influence of materialistic values and mass consumerism, we can easily become focused on that which we do not have or will not be able to possess.

Could you pause and pray a prayer to God, praising Him for the wonderful things that have happened in your life, all because of the glory of His grace?! Let your heart be filled with praise as you worship Him today.

Pause now and let the Spirit move your heart with gratitude. Write about some of the goodness of His grace toward you: *Father, as I reflect on the countless blessings of . . . my heart is moved with . . . ,* then pause and pray.

Heavenly Father, I pause to consider the wonder that Your glory has taken up residence in me and the privilege I have to reflect Your glory. These are expressions of unmerited favor, unmerited love, and incomprehensible grace. Thank You for blessing me in this way, in order that my life might be an expression of praise to You.

It is only through the person and power of Your Holy Spirit that I have the potential to express Your presence so that others around me would wonder, What is that? I want my only explanation to be: "It came from You."

Finally, Lord, would You so impact my heart and life with Your grace that I am empowered and equipped to express Your glory to others? Thank You for how You accomplished that in my life this week. Amen.

Week 2, Monday
God's Loving Initiative

*And the L*ORD *God formed man of the dust of the ground, and breathed*
into his nostrils the breath of life; and man became a living being.

Genesis 2:7

As products of "Generation Me," many people tend to default into waiting to be served In contrast, God always initiates. His initiative is a significant expression of His love. Last week, we were reminded of God's initiative to reveal His glory; He desires for us to become an expression of His presence here on earth.

God's initiative to love us actually began in Genesis—in the beginning. The book of Genesis tells us that "the L*ORD* God formed man of the dust of the ground, and breathed into his nostrils the breath of life; and man became a living being" (Genesis 2:7). "God ... breathed ... and man became ..." With these few words we find the first reference in Scripture to God's relationship with mankind. Only on this sixth day of creation do we find reference to God relating. He previously spoke and creation was born, but now He relates. The Creator breathes, initiating the Spirit's activity, and it follows that man "becomes." This passage not only reminds us of the cycle of God's initiative and man's responsiveness, but it also reveals how we were created with the capacity to relate intimately with the Creator!

We can also see His loving initiative as we reflect on the kind of love that "goes first" to extend grace and mercy for our salvation. In fact the good news of the Gospel is that even though sin entered the world and we became separated from God, Christ came to restore the intimacy of relationship with God that was lost in the Garden. This restoration began His initiative " ... not by works of righteousness which we have done, but according to His mercy He saved us, through the washing of regeneration and renewing of the Holy Spirit" (Titus 3:5).

Allow these truths of God's initiative to stir your heart toward gratitude and love. What does it do in your heart as you reflect on God's initiative on your behalf? What feelings do you have as you consider a God who always "goes first" to show His love?

Lord, change my default mode to "giving first." Amen.

David Ferguson, The Great Commandment Network

Week 2, Tuesday
A God Who Reveals

For the perverse person is an abomination to the Lord,
but His secret counsel is with the upright.

Proverbs 3:32

In our culture, vulnerability is often viewed as weakness; for if we reveal ourselves to others, they may use it against us—and gain power and control over us.

Throughout Scripture it is God's character to reveal. It is a part of His nature to disclose Himself to those who love Him. In fact, the book of Proverbs explains that we have the awesome privilege to become true friends of God as "His secret counsel is with the upright" (Proverbs 3:32).

Genesis 18 records an account of Jehovah God coming to earth to visit His friend Abraham. This passage reminds us that we have a God who longs to relate to us as a friend. As the Lord God is about to leave to destroy the wicked cities of Sodom and Gomorrah, Jehovah pauses and asks Himself, "Shall I hide from Abraham what I am doing?" (Genesis 18:17). In this story, God seemed to want to let Abraham in on what He was about to do.

In the book of James, Abraham "was called the friend of God" (James 2:23). Likewise, God seemed to have a similar intimate relationship with Moses: "So the Lord spoke to *Moses face* to *face*, as a man speaks to his friend" (Exodus 33:11, emphasis mine).

Just as God deeply desired to relate to His friends Abraham and Moses, God longs for a similar friendship with you and me. He wants to reveal His ways, His thoughts, His heart, and His character to each of us. He longs to disclose Himself to us and relate in meaningful ways.

Consider now what a wonderful blessing it is to have a God who shows His love by revealing Himself to us! Pause and allow your heart to be stirred with gratitude that God longs for you to know Him!

Write out a special prayer of thanksgiving to God for the wonder that His nature is to disclose Himself to you. Ask Him to "take you into His confidence." And then . . . be sure to listen!

Dear God, please speak to me. I wish to listen to You as I would a dear friend. Amen.

Week 2, Wednesday
His Abundant Gifts

*As His divine power has given to us all things that pertain to life and godliness,
through the knowledge of Him who called us by glory and virtue, by which have been given
to us exceedingly great and precious promises, that through these you may be partakers of
the divine nature, having escaped the corruption that is in the world through lust.*

2 Peter 1:3, 4

Consider your relationship with Christ. Reflect upon how you have been given everything you need for life and godliness, enabled to participate in the divine nature, and became a joint heir of Christ.

When you became a follower of Christ and accepted His gift of salvation...

- You were adopted (placed as an adult heir) into the family of God (Romans 8:15; 8:23; Ephesians 1:5).
- You were forgiven all your sins (Ephesians 1:7; 4:32; Colossians 1:14; 2:13; 3:13)—they have been removed "as far as the east is from the west" (Psalm 103:12).
- You have been brought near and made a citizen of God's Kingdom (Ephesians 2:13, 19; Philippians 3:20; Colossians 1:13).
- You are no longer a slave to sin—you are free by His Spirit to yield to God, obeying Him out of a desire to love Him (Romans 6:17–18).
- You have been purified and made eager to do what is good (Titus 2:14).
- Jesus prays for you and the concerns of your heart (Romans 8:34; Hebrews 7:25).

What does it do to your heart to realize that not only did God love you so much that He did all the above for you, but that He delighted in it? That He was eager and passionate in His love for you to give these blessings to you that you could never have gained by your own efforts? Express your heart to God.

*Dear God, as I consider these truths revealed to me by You in Scripture—
all that You have done for me when You saved me, how You have blessed me
through Your Holy Spirit with so many different blessings because of Your
infinite love for me, my heart is stirred with . . . Please continue to reveal
who I am in Your eyes and how You have blessed me and want to continue
to bless me. Amen.*

Week 2, Thursday
Nourished by the Word

As newborn babes, desire the pure milk of the word, that you may grow thereby.

1 Peter 2:2

One of the Millennium Development Goals of the United Nations is to reduce malnutrition, a condition that occurs when the body doesn't get enough nutrients.

Christ-followers are nourished into spiritual health as we receive and yield to God's Word. To be nourished by God's Word, we must take full advantage of every opportunity to encounter God in His Word and experience its nourishing benefits and blessings.

- As we HEAR the Word of God taught, preached, and shared, our faith will be strengthened: "Faith comes by hearing" the message (Romans 10:17).
- As we READ the Word, we will be blessed: "Blessed is he who reads . . . the words of this prophecy" (Revelation 1:3).
- As we STUDY the Word, we will be approved by God as ". . . a worker who . . . [is] rightly dividing the word of truth" (2 Timothy 2:15).
- As we MEMORIZE it, we will be less vulnerable to sin: "Your word I have hidden in my heart, that I might not sin against You" (Psalm 119:11).
- As we MEDITATE upon it, our yielding to it will be increased: "This Book of the Law shall not depart from your mouth, but you shall meditate in it day and night, that you may observe to do according to all that is written in it" (Joshua 1:8). Our meditation on the Word will also produce spiritual prosperity, health, and fruitfulness (Psalm 1:1–3).

Consider these five opportunities for nourishment from God's Word. How many have you taken advantage of this week? Sadly, too many of God's children remain "babes" in their faith as they come to hear God's Word preached or taught by others, but rarely take advantage of other avenues of nourishment.

Pause now and take a moment to express your gratitude to God for providing so many different ways for us to be strengthened by His Word. Decide which one of these opportunities you will take advantage of today. Will you memorize the suggested Scripture passage for this week? Will you spend time meditating on particular passages or stories of Christ? Will you spend time, allowing God's Spirit to impress you with particular insights?

Week 2, Friday
Encounters with Jesus

"But the Helper, the Holy Spirit, whom the Father will send in My name, He will teach you all things, and bring to your remembrance all things that I said to you."

John 14:26

Members of the so-called EPIC Generation are experiential, participatory, image-driven, and connected. The Christian life is about relating to this One who lived, died, and rose again. Christianity and life transformation will only occur when we come to truly relate to and encounter Jesus Christ. The Father's love-filled hope for our encounters with Jesus is that they will transform us into His very image. Faithful disciples diligently pursue fresh encounters with Jesus with yielded hearts, confident that such encounters will make them a little more like Him!

If events could sanctify the saints, Western world Christians would surely be among the Kingdom's most sanctified. If exposure to the Christian message and media could produce fully devoted followers of Christ, we would turn the world upside down for Christ, as did the first-century Church. If camps, conferences, and concerts could instill the faith in the next generation, we would not be struggling to make disciples of our own children. In spite of all of these well-intentioned events, vast segments of God's people have come to think that a relationship with Christ is only about being able to claim, "I believe and I obey."

Pause now and ask the Lord to lead you into a deepened relationship with Him. Ask His Spirit to help you go beyond the important set of Christian beliefs for the moment. Ask Him to help you move beyond the all-important commands to obey. Ask the Lord to lead you into more of a relationship with Him. Pray that you will come to know the Savior more intimately and be able to express His love more clearly.

Your prayer might sound like the following:

Lord, I long to encounter Jesus in deep, life-changing ways. I yield my life and heart to being transformed—whatever that may mean. I want Christ's promise to be real for me, that the Counselor, the Holy Spirit within me, will teach me all things. Speak now, Lord. I long to hear You and yield to You. Amen.

David Ferguson, The Great Commandment Network

Week 2, Weekend
He Delights in You

"The LORD your God in your midst,
The Mighty One, will save;
He will rejoice over you with gladness,
He will quiet you with His love,
He will rejoice over you with singing."

Zephaniah 3:17

Since this is an image-driven generation, imagine the "facial expression" that was on the face of Jesus as you woke up this morning. In your mind's eye, picture the face of Jesus. Imagine His bearded face, eyes that are kind and gentle, a smile that is warm and tender. Imagine that as you awoke this morning, God looked down and smiled at you, His precious child.

The Real God smiled, and with joy in His heart announced, "I am looking forward to sharing the day with you!" The Real God, who knows you intimately, could not wait to care for you today. The Creator of the Universe, who knows every hair upon your head and sees every tear that you have cried, cannot wait to show you how much He loves you. The Holy God of Heaven knows your darkest secrets and deepest failures, and yet, because of His grace, He cannot wait to have a relationship with you.

What does it do to your heart to consider a God who is acquainted with all your ways and longs to be caringly involved in your life? How does your heart respond to know that God takes great delight in you and rejoices over you?

As I reflect upon my God who can't wait to care for me, I feel . . .

As I consider how God rejoices over me and looks forward to spending the day with me, my heart is filled with . . .

Pause now and say a prayer that communicates your gratitude, humility, and wonder over a God who knows you and rejoices over you.

Heavenly Father, I feel . . . as I reflect upon your heart toward me. My heart is filled with . . . as I consider how You can't wait to care for me. I feel . . . as I consider how You delight in me and rejoice over me. Thank You for being the kind of God who . . . Amen.

Week 3, Monday
God Spoke

In the beginning God created the heavens and the earth.

Genesis 1:1

Have you ever wondered about the universe? Try to imagine what's out there. How does it all work? What was God's master plan when He created the universe? God created it all by His mighty power. He spoke, "Let there be"... and there was! Did He speak with a thundering voice or a whisper? Did He wave His hand, much like a conductor would direct an orchestra, or did He spread out His arms in an all-encompassing gesture? No matter, He's the Creator! God spoke ...

- "Let there be light!" Day and evening! Night and day!
- "Let the firmament divide!" Sky above! Oceans below!
- "Let the waters under the heavens be gathered together into one place, and let the dry land appear!" Earth and oceans!
- "Let the earth bring forth ... greenery!" Grass, herb and fruit trees!
- "Let there be lights in the heavens!" Sun, moon and stars! Winter, spring, summer and fall!
- "Let there be an abundance of living creatures in the air and in the sea!" Electric eels and eagles! Doves and deepwater stingray!
- "Let the earth bring forth ...!" Grasshoppers and gorillas! Red kangaroo, White rhinoceros and blue whales!

God's Word comes with such power and authority that His command is immediately fulfilled.

The Bible declares that God stretched out the heavens into limitless expanse that can never be measured and filled it with stars as numerous as the sands upon the seashore. The Bible also says the earth is suspended over nothing (see Job 26:7)—the mysterious force of gravity that no one even yet understands. All this is in preparation for God's greatest and best creation yet to come—human beings—you!

Lord, I praise You as the Creator and Sustainer of all things. From the very beginning of time, You have not changed, and I am grateful to know You as the One who has made all things. I thank You that all things are held together by the power of Your hand and I am secure in You. Amen.

Week 3, Tuesday
God Formed

The Lord God formed man from the dust of the earth …

Genesis 2:7a

God spoke all of His creation into existence, except one. He "formed" man from the dust of the earth. In previous creation activity, God spoke, "Let there be" and it was. Now God says, "Let Us make man in Our image and after Our likeness." "Let **Us** make man …" To whom was He speaking? We are introduced to the fellowship and unity of the Trinity—Father, Son, and Holy Spirit.

God first made man from dust of the earth and Eve from one of Adam's rib. But mankind is more than a body. What separates us from the animals, birds, and fish is our ability to reason, our emotion, and our will—the soul of man. We are body and soul!

Creation got up close and personal. No doubt God loved the rest of His creation—He said it was good. But the creation of man took on a personal and intimate tone. Can you imagine God stooping down to the ground and gathering up dust, piling it up together, and carefully and thoughtfully forming the father of the human race? What was He thinking? No one knows exactly.

Take time today to reflect on Psalm 139:13–16 "For You formed my inward parts; you covered me in my mother's womb. I will praise You, for I am fearfully and wonderfully made; marvelous are Your works, and that my soul knows very well. My frame was not hidden from You, when I was made in secret, and skillfully wrought in the lowest parts of the earth. Your eyes saw my substance, being yet unformed. and in Your book they all were written, the days fashioned for me, when as yet there were none of them."

It is remarkable that God would create a being with the ability to choose not to accept His gift of unconditional love and companionship. But such is the nature of true love. It must be freely received and freely given.

Father, I thank You that I am fearfully and wonderfully made. May I be reminded each day that I carry Your image and likeness, that I am a reflection of Your glory. Show me ways to demonstrate Your unconditional love and grace to everyone I meet. Amen.

Week 3, Wednesday
God Breathed

. . . and breathed into his nostrils the breath of life; and man became a living being.

Genesis 2:7b

One thing in life we take for granted is breathing. It is so natural that we barely give it a thought—breathe in; breathe out. When there's no life in someone, life is breathed into that person by blowing into their mouth. This require a very intimate contact between the two persons—the one without life and the one giving the breath of life.

This breath of life that came from God, however, is not a face-to-face resuscitation of what was once alive and is now dead. It is the impartation of the breath of the Spirit that caused Adam to become a living being. This is the third dimension of man—spirit. Human beings reflect the image of the triune God in that He created us a three-fold being in body, soul, and spirit.

Most of us don't think much about our breathing. The average person takes about fifteen breaths a minute, or 21,600 breaths a day. We do it unconsciously. This life-giving process goes on from our first gasp of air as a newborn until our dying breath.

God continues to breathe His life into us by the Holy Spirit. This wind of the Spirit is described for us in Genesis 1:2 and Job 33:4. As it relates to people, we see in Ezekiel 37:5, "Thus says the Lord God to these bones: "Surely I will cause *breath* to enter into you, and you shall live." Similarly, Job described to his friends "the *breath* of God" in his nostrils (Job 27:3). As followers of Christ, we have the Spirit of God in us (John 14:16–17). We are reborn in Christ of the Spirit (John 3:3–8). He breathed His life into you. Your Creator's breath of life is what empowers you to live an abundant life.

Take time today to become aware of every breath you take. Take time in the presence of the Lord. In that moment of stillness, listen to the sound of your breathing and ask God to breathe His life into you again—life-giving power to become who He wants you to be.

 Father, thank You for the precious gift of life. May I never take one breath for granted. Help me to live a bold life of faith because I am empowered by Your Spirit. Amen.

Week 3, Thursday
God Related—Communicated

No longer do I call you servants, for a servant does not know what his master is doing; but I have called you friends, for all things that I heard from My Father I have made known to you.

John 15:15

God came down in the cool of the day to spend time with Adam. I wondered what they talked about. Did they discuss the activities in the Garden or did they talk about things more mysterious—things beyond human comprehension? Do you think they told jokes to each other? Can you imagine the almighty Creator of the universe laughing at Adam's jokes? It is very clear that from the very beginning, man was to be set apart from fish, monkeys, zebras, elephants, and other animals. Could it be that God wanted a friend, a companion—someone who would choose to be friends with Him?

God spoke to Moses "face to face as a man speaks to a friend" (Genesis 33:11). Abraham was called "a friend of God" (James 2:33). Jesus puts it this way, "No longer do I call you servants, for a servant does not know what his master is doing; but I have called you friends, for all things that I heard from My Father I have made known to you" (John 15:15).

Would it surprise you to hear that God delights to be with you? Would it touch your heart to hear that God is calling you by name and seeking you out—just to be with you? He knows your name and He longs to be with you. Would it surprise you to hear the Creator of the universe call you friend? Would it surprise you to know that God is not waiting for you to earn His love, but that He's passionately pursuing you with His love?

Take time to consider that God longs to be with you—just to be with you because He loves you. Let that thought capture your heart and spend time in His presence today without fear of condemnation or judgment.

Father, thank You for Your unconditional love for me. Thank You for sending Jesus Christ to pay the penalty for my sins as the most loving act You could ever have done for me. Thank You for the Holy Spirit who always brings me into Your presence that I may be loved and healed. Amen.

Week 3, Friday
God Covered

Also for Adam and his wife the Lord God made tunics of skin, and clothed them.

Genesis 3:21

"You got yourself into this mess, now get yourself out!" How many times have you heard those words from a parent or from a friend when you land in some type of trouble? Adam and Eve were in serious trouble—and the consequence of the trouble they were in would change the course of human history. They disobeyed God's explicit instructions for living in paradise—the Garden of Eden.

God came down for His daily visit with Adam only to find him hiding—physically and spiritually. God's response was "Adam, where are you? What have you done?" Can you hear the sadness and regret in God's voice? He didn't abandon Adam and Eve. He went searching for them. From that day until now God passionately pursues us—not to expose our sin and shame, but to lovingly cover them.

As a result of their disobedience, they discovered they were naked and were ashamed. God shed blood to cover Adam's and Eve's nakedness. God made clothing from animal skins, and therefore those animals had to be sacrificed to cover them. This is a wonderful picture of "the Lamb of God who takes away (who is continually taking away) the sin of the world" (John 1:29). The time would come when the Lamb of God—Jesus Christ—would lay down His life for the world. This is what God wants to do for us. He searches for us and finds us in our failure, our estrangement, our guilt, our sense of nakedness, shame, and loss, and immediately He moves to cover us and bring us to repentance. Ultimately, it is God Himself who bears all of our pain, suffering, and shame.

When we willingly acknowledge that what we have done is contrary to what God wants, our sin is covered, we become the righteousness of God in Christ Jesus (2 Corinthians 5:21), and we are accepted in the Beloved (Ephesians 1:6).

Is there any area of your life left uncovered by the grace of God's greatest sacrifice? Readily admit it to Him and ask for His loving forgiveness.

Father, thank You for sending Your Son, Jesus, to pay the ultimate price, death on a cross, so that I may be forgiven of my sins. Lord, teach me to continually repent. Thank You for clothing me in the righteousness of Jesus. Amen.

Week 3, Weekend
Great Things

Consider what great things He has done for you.

1 Samuel 12:24

Isn't it amazing that God could have created you in any way that He pleased, but He chose to create you in such a way that allows you to have a relationship with Him? No other part of God's creation gets to relate to Him, but we do! Because God wanted a relationship with you, He created you with the capacity to love and relate. He didn't demand that you have a friendship with Him. He didn't control that possibility or manipulate a relationship with you. He simply created you in love and invites you to love Him back.

Take the next few moments to live out 1 Samuel 12:24: Consider some of the great things God has done for you. Listen to His voice as He relates to you.

I am the Lord, God in heaven above and on the earth beneath there is no other (Deuteronomy 4:39). I fashioned the earth and all there is in it, but I created my masterpiece when I created you (Ephesians 2:10). I thought carefully about you and just how you would be different from all other things that I created. Only you would be able to talk with Me, hear from Me, and relate to Me. I have no other agenda, but to share life and love with you (Psalm 139:13–18). Finally, My created one, once you accept the gift of a personal relationship with Me, there is nothing that can separate us (Romans 8:39). I will never leave you or abandon you. You never have to be alone (Hebrews 13:6). Look around you. There is evidence of Me and My love for you everywhere. I am here for you. Be still and consider the wonderful works of your God! (Job 37:14).

How do you feel as you reflect on God's heart and how He wants a relationship with you?

I feel _____ as I reflect on God's heart and how He wants a relationship with me. His words make me grateful that …

God, thank You for being the kind of God who wants a relationship with me. I am especially glad that You want this type of closeness with me because … Amen.

Week 4, Monday
Open Arms

Therefore the Lord will wait . . .

Isaiah 30:18a

Would it surprise you to know that our heavenly Father patiently waits? What is He waiting for? you might ask. The answer is *you*! He patiently waits for you!

Luke 15:20 paints a vivid picture of a father waiting—waiting patiently for a son to return to the security of his arms and home. As you read through this passage, do you get the sense that the father was longing to see his son—desperately wanting him to come home? Do you see the exuberant joy when the son finally did return home? Do you get a sense of the father's relief—finally! "I've been waiting a long time to hold you in my arms, to see your beautiful face again."

There were many reasons why the son should have been written off by the father. He had squandered his inheritance. He lived a life of rebellion and disobedience. He'd hit rock bottom. These are the same reasons the son could have stayed away from his father. He'd blown it. Why should his father welcome him home? The son could have concluded that there was no reason to go home again.

The young man did come to his senses. Do you think he was nervous about going home? What would his father say? What would he do? In humility, he recognized his foolishness and decided to return to his father and ask for forgiveness and mercy. The father, who had been watching and waiting, received his son with open arms of compassion. He was overjoyed by the return of his lost son!

This is a picture of the heavenly Father. God waits patiently, with loving compassion, to restore us when we return to Him with humble hearts. He offers us everything in His Kingdom, restoring full relationship with joyful celebration. He doesn't even dwell on our past mistakes—even when they are willful and rebellious.

Where do you find yourself today? Take time to reflect on those moments when you're most tempted to hide or run from God. Your heavenly Father is patiently waiting to have mercy on you and to bless you. His arms are wide open . . . waiting!

 Father, I am so grateful that no matter how far away from You I find myself, how desperate my situation, or how lost I become, You're always waiting for me with open arms. Amen.

Palma Hutchinson, The Great Commandment Network

Week 4, Tuesday
Good Things Come

Blessed are all those who wait for Him.

Isaiah 30:18d

Many times the thoughts we entertain can be a barrier to being in the presence of the Lord. If we see God only as a harsh judge or ourselves as unworthy, we are putting up road blocks that will keep us from the mercies of God. Learn to see God as the loving Father He is and learn to recognize yourself as a person who is greatly valued by Him.

So often we wait upon the Lord for answered prayers, for provision, for healing, for wisdom to make right decisions, and for direction. Waiting is difficult. Imagine a person waiting and becoming impatient—pacing, toes tapping, pacing—agitated. This impatience causes us to take matters into our own hands or we give up waiting altogether.

Are you at a place of waiting on God? Even though it's difficult to wait, be patient, be encouraged, because He also waits for you with benefits when you wait on Him. Your strength is renewed (Isaiah 40:31). God will be gracious to you (Ephesians 1:7–8). He will show mercy to you (Psalm 18:50). He will give you justice in the unfairness of life (Romans 2:2). He longs and delights to bless you. "Blessed be the LORD your God, who delighted in you . . ." (2 Chronicles 9:8).

Consider what you're waiting on God to do in your life.

When I have to wait on God for _____ ,
I feel _____.

I feel _____ *to know that God is also waiting for me.*

The vision of our loving Father waiting on us will give us courage and strength to continue to persevere. It will give us confidence that our waiting is not in vain. The Lord rejoices to see those He has been waiting for. Would you patiently seek Him now?

Heavenly Father, I thank You that my waiting is not in vain. Thank You for the strength that comes from waiting on You. I'm grateful that You are a Father who also waits for me. Please give me the courage and patience to wait upon You. Thanks for all the benefits that come from patiently waiting for You. Amen.

Week 4, Wednesday
Chill Out!

Be still, and know that I am God;
I will be exalted among the nations,
I will be exalted in the earth!

Psalm 46:10

Busy! Busy! Busy! It seems that even the youngest among us live busy lives. How often have you heard phrases such as "not enough hours in the day," or "too much stuff on my plate," or "wearing too many hats," used to describe our daily activities? When are we still? Even if we are able to be still physically, it is more difficult to be still spiritually.

We have a standing invitation from our heavenly Father to come into His presence, be still, quiet our minds, and know Him—the I AM!

Let go! Relax! Be still!

Don't you just love that "Be still" part of Psalm 46:10? Wow! That requires slowing down, doesn't it? Look at the benefits. In the stillness we will know God. Taking time to reflect on God—His greatness, His love, and His power—will help us know Him. God initiates! "Be still and know Me." We come into His presence, and in the stillness and the knowing we find mercy. Even in the midst of all the noise and the busyness around us, we need to spend time with the Lord. The world is full of commotion and chaos, but we have confidence that in the presence of the Lord we can find peace and rest.

When was the last time you came into the Lord's presence and listened to His voice? Take time today to slow down, step away from the activities of your day, and be still in His presence. Hear His invitation to: "Be still! Know Him!"

 Heavenly Father, in this busy, chaotic world, help me to slow down long enough to see Your greatness and hear Your voice. Let me know that You are God. Amen.

Week 4, Thursday
Here's Hope

Many, O Lᴏʀᴅ my God, are Your wonderful works which You have done;
and Your thoughts toward us cannot be recounted to You in order; if I would
declare and speak of them, they are more than can be numbered.

Psalm 40:5

Disappointment is part of life! Everyone has experienced it at one time or another. We live in anxious anticipation, only to be disappointed. People we depend on fail us. We're disappointed! We wait patiently for a lunch date we looked forward to all week, only to be stood up. We're disappointed! Life takes an unexpected, drastic, and tragic turn, and we lose our bearing. We're disappointed! Disappointment turns into a downward spiral until we find ourselves in what the Psalmist calls "the horrible pit." Disappointment leads to anger; anger to bitterness; bitterness to hatred; and hatred to a cold heart that shuts out the only thing that can bring hope and healing—the love of our heavenly Father. In times of disappointment, we need hope!

The hope we need and the hope we read about in Scripture is not vague, flimsy optimism. This hope is a strong and confident expectation that God will save and bless us. Disappointments, troubles, and problems are often the catalyst that produces perseverance, character, and finally, hope (Romans 5:3–4).

David found himself in a desperate situation. He was disappointed. Out of his disappointment and troubles he cried to God for help. God "inclined" His ears to hear him. God leaned forward and intently listened. God heard! God delivered! God saved! (Psalm 40:2).

David's disappointments turned into a song of praise. His life became a reflection of the One who loved him—a reflection of His glory (Psalm 40:3). "Many, O Lord my God, are Your wonderful which You have done; and Your thoughts toward us cannot be recounted to You in order; if I would declare and speak of them, they are more than can be numbered" (Psalm 40:5).

Disappointment turns to hope, and hope is realized in a Person—our Lord and Savior, Jesus Christ.

Father, I thank You that I can hope in You and that hope is not in vain.
I'm so grateful that You intently listen and readily hear me when I cry for
help. Today, I surrender every disappointment to You and ask that hope
would come alive in me. Amen.

Week 4, Friday
Seeing Is Believing

"You cannot see My face; for no man shall see Me.... Here is a place by Me."

Exodus 33:20

"Show me...!" These are the famous last words of the skeptic. When something is too good to be true or too hard to believe, we want to see the evidence for ourselves.

This was Moses' request to God. *Show me!* He'd seen a lot of indescribable, impossible-to-believe events—a burning bush, Egypt's plagues, a highway through a sea—too incredible for mere humans. Even though God had given Moses the promise of His presence, it was not enough. Moses wanted more than a presence. He wanted a Person. "Please, show me Your glory" (Exodus 33:18). Because of God's great desire to be known, He is always willing and ready—anxiously waiting—to reveal Himself to us (1 Corinthians 13:12).

As Moses made his way up the mountain, the Lord came down, stood with Moses, and proclaimed His name and His character. He introduced Himself as the "Lord." Then God described His character. He is compassionate, gracious, patient, loving, and faithful. Those were words Moses needed to hear. Those are words we need to hear.

Stop and ask God to show you His glory. He will reveal Himself and his character. Think of how you've experienced God's compassion, grace, patience, love, and faithfulness in your life.

I experience God's compassion when _____.

I experience God's grace when _____.

God is most patient with me when I _____.

I am most aware of God's love when _____.

I know God is faithful because _____.

Father, thank You for who You are and what You do for us every day. Thank You for Your attributes revealed to us in Your Word. Help us to live a life that is marked with gratitude because we have the chance to know You. Amen.

Week 4, Weekend
He Loves to Love Us

I will be glad and rejoice in Your mercy.

Psalm 31:7

Think back to some of the mistakes you have made. Remember any of the ways in which you have messed up or fallen short. Reflect on the times when you thought that you knew best, only to find out that you were wrong or mistaken. Have there been particular times when you've been disciplined or suffered consequences because of the choices you have made? Remember those circumstances and the difficult feelings of those situations.

Now imagine that in the pain of these moments, you have left your house and gone for a walk. You're trying to clear your head and heart of the guilt, regret, hurt, or anger that you're feeling. Just as you round the corner and see your house, you notice that Jesus is waiting for you. When He sees you in the distance, He is moved with compassion. He doesn't even wait for you to arrive. He runs to you! He leaps quickly and anxiously off the front steps because He can't wait to see you. He hugs you and whispers in your ear.

Jesus doesn't give a lecture or criticism. He doesn't fuss at you or remind you of how you've messed up. He acknowledges your behavior; Jesus knows the consequences of your sin. He's fully aware of how things have gone wrong, but His voice is filled with care. Christ's eyes are kind and His body language is gentle and relaxed as He talks with you. Jesus tells you He loves you and that His mercy is fully available to you.

Scripture reminds us that the real Jesus, the real God, waits to be gracious to us and longs to be merciful to us. Although we may suffer consequences as a result of our sinfulness, God's chief desire is not to punish or humiliate us, but to restore and bless us. How does this truth move your heart? "I will be glad and rejoice in Your mercy" (Psalm 31:7).

Take a moment to live out this Bible verse. Express your gladness for God's mercy.

As I imagine Christ, and think about how He can't wait to welcome me and have mercy on me in spite of my failures, my heart is glad because . . .

God, I am grateful You are a God who longs to be merciful because . . . Amen.

Week 5, Monday
He's with You

"The LORD your God [is] in your midst...."

Zephaniah 3:17

One of the basic needs of every human being is the need for security. We need to feel secure in our relationships—*am I loved and cared for?* We need to feel secure at home—*are the doors locked and the alarm set?* We need to feel secure at our place of employment—*will I lose my job?* We need to feel secure at school—*do I fit in?* We need to feel secure in our peer groups—*am I accepted for who I am?*

As a child growing up, the safest and most secure place was in my dad's presence—by his side or in his arms. When I was with him, I had every confidence that even the scariest monster could not come near me. My hero was by my side. He was braver than any superhero—stronger than Superman himself. I was secure!

Without a sense of security, we feel fear. Fear paralyzes. Fear robs us of the ability to trust. We don't have to be afraid. Our Abba Father gives us the spirit of power, love, and a well-balanced, disciplined mind—never fear (2 Timothy1:7).

Our heavenly Father is with us! He is all-powerful, and He promised never to leave us on our own. God encourages us to be bold and courageous (Joshua 1:9). Don't allow the challenges you face to overwhelm and discourage you. Take courage! You can do all things through Christ who gives you the strength (Philippians 4:13).

What challenges are you facing today that might bring fear into your heart? What's one thing you can do differently today as you take steps to trust the Lord with your fears?

Father, You know the things that cause me to fear. Please help me to be strong and courageous when I'm faced with life's challenges. May I face those things that terrify and discourage me with confidence, relying on Your promise that You will never leave me alone. Amen.

Week 5, Tuesday
Mighty to Save

"The Lord . . . the Mighty One, will save."

Zephaniah 3:17

I read a story once about a man who was drowning and a lifeguard who stood by and watched. The story tells of a man who got swept away by the current and started to drown. The people witnessing this called for the lifeguard to go and save him. The lifeguard grabbed his gear, ran out to the edge of the water, and stopped. As the drowning man struggled to stay above water, the lifeguard swam out a little farther and stopped. Needless to say, the onlookers were becoming worried and agitated with this lifeguard's seeming lack of response to a drowning man. After long, anxious moments, the lifeguard finally swam out to the man, pulled him from the water, pulled him to shore, and pumped his chest a few times. The man sputtered water and was saved.

"Why did you take so long to rescue him?" the people demanded. "He could have died out there!" The lifeguard responded, "As long as he was trying to save himself, I could not save him. I had to wait until he was totally helpless or he would have drowned both of us."

We have the tendency to want to save ourselves. We work hard at it. No matter how hard we try, however, we will never accomplish our own salvation, whether it is salvation from our sins or salvation from the challenges we face in our lives. *Jesus* means "Savior." Jesus came to earth to save us because we can't save ourselves from sin and its consequences. Jesus didn't come to help us save ourselves; He came to be our Savior from the power and penalty of sin.

Read the story of the woman who had a flow of blood for twelve years in Mark 5:25–35. Read it again slowly. She secretly touched Jesus and was immediately healed. Jesus, sensing her touch and knowing she was healed, still insisted on seeing her and hearing her story. Why was it so important for Jesus to see her, to hear her? She was already saved from her affliction. Jesus wanted to do more than save her. He wanted to know her. He wanted to be with her—even in the middle of a large crowd pressing in on Him.

Jesus can mightily save you from your sins and afflictions, but He also wants to see you, to know you, and to be with you!

Thank You, Jesus, for dying on the cross for my sins. Thank You for saving me from the consequences of my sins. I give up my feeble attempts to save myself. Please take complete control of my life today. Amen.

Week 5, Wednesday
Precious in His Sight

"The LORD . . . will rejoice over you with gladness. . . ."

Zephaniah 3:17

What a wonderful thought . . . the Lord delights in you! Can you imagine God clapping His hands and jumping up and down with glee at the thought of being with you? Does God clap and jump up and down? I don't really know. But when I'm delighted that's what I do! However God chooses to express His delight, that's exactly what He's doing at the thought of being with you.

I live in another state, miles away from most of my family. Christmastime is special because that's when we all get together. It's a whole, long year since I've been in the presence of my family. I start counting down the days around December 1. The closer Christmas gets, the more excited I get. I can hardly wait for the moment when I'll be with the ones I love most. I get pleasure when I'm in their presence. I'm excited and full of joy. We love and enjoy each other. That's how it is with our Father.

Why does God do all the things He does for us—our salvation, our healing, our comfort, our deliverances, our countless blessings? We certainly don't deserve them. Could it be it's because He delights in us? Could it be that we are precious to Him?

God comes to our rescue and willingly delivers us because He delights in us! God does not care for us out of a sense of duty. It is a joy for Him to be with us, to care for us, and to bless us. He calls us His treasured possession and the apple of His eye! He delights in our worship! (Psalm 37:4). He delights in our accomplishments! He delights in our victories! (Proverbs 11:20). But most of all, He delights to be with us! We are a pleasure to Him and He enjoys our friendship!

Take a moment to consider the joy and pleasure you get when you're with someone special in your life. Now imagine that God's delight to be with you is thousands times greater. Would it encourage you to spend time with the Lord knowing that you give Him pleasure and joy? Would your worship of Him and service to others be more joyful knowing that God is pleased with you?

Heavenly Father, thank You for Your great love for me. I'm grateful for the fact that my life brings You joy. May I never hesitate to accept Your invitation to come into Your presence. Thank You for the opportunity to worship You in spirit and truth and serve others with joy. Amen.

Week 5, Thursday
Quiet My Soul

"The LORD . . . will quiet you with His love. . . ."

Zephaniah 3:17

Our world is noisy and chaotic! The noise of our world is very loud—wars and threat of war, terrorism, global economic meltdown, environmental meltdown, violence, moral and ethical failures of leaders, massive unrest and confusion, and on and on. The noise grows louder every day!

The noise in our community is very loud—lawlessness, poverty, injustice, brokenness, materialism and secularism, abandoned children, broken homes, and on and on. The noise grows louder every day!

The noise in our church is very loud—judgment and condemnation, no grace living or grace giving, conditional love, and on and on. The noise grows louder every day!

The noise in our personal life is very loud—guilt and shame over past sinful behavior, loss and sorrow, disappointment with life, unfulfilled dreams, fear of the future, fear of being alone, distress and anxiety, and on and on. The noise grows louder every day! No wonder the suicide rate is so high. No wonder people suffer heart attacks and strokes. No wonder people are stress-filled and anxious. But . . .

Those who trust in the Lord will be quieted by His love. Like a mother gathers up her distressed and anxious child onto her lap, holds him close to her, and stills him with love, so does our heavenly Father bring us into His presence and quiet our soul and mind. He will still the noises of the world so that you can hear His voice and receive His comfort. When we are confident of His never-failing love, we can escape the noise and turmoil of life and find quiet and rest in His arms.

"He makes me to lie down in green pastures; He leads me beside the still waters. He restores my soul" (Psalm 23:2–3). Take some time today to find a quiet place. Acknowledge all the noises you are hearing right now—those in your own mind and those around you. One by one begin to eliminate each sound. Direct your mind to focus on your loving Father and let His peace fill your heart. He is quieting you with His love!

Father, I confess all my anxious fears to You today. Please quiet my mind of the noises of life. I long to hear Your voice but sometimes it is drowned out by the cares of life. I quiet my soul in Your presence. May I find rest and peace. Amen.

Week 5, Friday
His Theme Song

"The LORD . . . will rejoice over you with singing."

Zephaniah 3:17

I grew up in a household where there was a song for every occasion. My dad loved to sing. My mom had a song that encouraged us to clean up—"bits of paper lying on the floor makes the place untidy, pick them up." There were songs of warning when we were nearing the boundary line—"yield not to temptation." There was a song that went with discipline. (That song was not my favorite.) There were songs of victory and praise when we behaved and did something well. There were many songs of praise and worship to God. We sang prayers and scripture verses. We heard hymns as our parents worked. Of course, there were the nursery rhymes and our ABCs. My favorite songs of all were the bedtime songs—the lullabies. I felt such warmth and comfort being tucked into bed and listening to my mom sing as I drifted off to sleep. The song would usually end in a humming whisper. Even now my sister and I spontaneously break into songs of our childhood on any given occasion.

Your heavenly Father is singing over you! He doesn't just sing; He rejoices as He sings! I wonder what God's singing voice sounds like. Is it booming like thunder or soothing like a running brook? Both? Or, maybe neither! Doesn't matter! I also don't think we have to worry about the style of music He sings. What matters is that He rejoices over you with singing!

What song is God singing over you today? I believe He's singing love songs. He's singing His promises. He's singing victory songs. He's singing songs of peace and blessings.

One of the blessed joys of listening to your Father sing over you is the pleasure of joining Him in song and dance. With exuberant joy we return songs of love and praise to Him!

Take some time today to listen for the songs of your heavenly Father. Hear His love song for you. Hear His soothing, calming lullaby and let it quiet the chaos of the world around you. Relax in His loving arms and let His songs fill your soul.

 Father, thank You for rejoicing over me with singing. Quiet my mind and my heart that I may hear clearly the sound of Your voice. Amen.

Week 5, Weekend
You Make Him Smile

Give thanks to the LORD, for He is good!

Psalm 136:1

Have you ever thought about the way God views you? What do you think goes through God's mind when He sees you? What kind of expression is on God's face when He considers your life? What emotions does He experience? You might be surprised to know that the real God is a God who rejoices over you. He smiles when He sees you. God is pleased when He considers your life. He beams with pride when He watches you go about your day!

A key ingredient for coming to truly know and love the real God is gaining an accurate understanding of how He sees us. If we believe that God is distant and not particularly concerned with our lives, it will be difficult to feel that we can truly come to know Him. If we think that God is constantly inspecting us or disappointed with us, we will find it hard to love Him. It is only when we experience God's delight in us, as His children, that we are freed to truly experience delight in Him in turn.

Think about your own relationships with friends for a moment. How do you show that you are happy about knowing someone? How would it be evident that you were proud to be someone's family member, friend, boyfriend, or girlfriend? How might we tell that you were glad to be in relationship with them?

Would you talk about this person a lot? Would you have their picture as a screen saver? Would you get excited when they called or sent you a message?

Zephaniah 3:17 reminds us that God is happy about knowing you. He is proud of you and delighted to be in relationship with you. He thinks about you a lot. He would have your picture as His screen saver! And He gets excited when you talk to Him because He is delighted when we relate to Him!

"Give thanks to the LORD, for He is good!" (Psalm 136:1).

Take a moment to live out this verse: Give praise to the Lord for being the kind of God who rejoices over you.

 God, I feel _____ as I reflect on Your heart toward me. Thank You for being the kind of God who delights in me. Although it's sometimes hard to believe, I praise You for Your goodness to me. Amen.

Week 6, Monday
Will the Real God Please Stand Up?

*"Can a woman forget her nursing child, and not have compassion on the son of her womb?
Surely they may forget, yet I will not forget you. See, I have inscribed you on the
palms of My hands; your walls are continually before Me."*

Isaiah 49:15

What kind of God do you have? How do you view Him? We all have different perceptions of God's character, a slightly different view of Him and how He relates to us. Some of us see God as more of a policeman, a guiding shepherd, a school principal, a well-meaning doctor, a dictator, a stern but loving father, or a disinterested spectator. What's your view of God?

Do you have an *inspecting* god? It's almost as if he has a heavenly tally sheet and carefully records everything we do. This kind of god inspects our every move and then relates to us according to how many good marks or bad marks we've been given.

Do you have a *disappointed* god? He looks down at us and never likes what he sees. He notices our attempts at living a good life, but ultimately shakes his head in disappointment. This kind of god might shrug his shoulders because he's given up on us; he's just sure we won't get it.

Do you have a *distant and uninvolved* god? This kind of god is often too busy to notice our small concerns. He hears us as we talk to him, but he sits behind that big desk in heaven and gives us his half-hearted attention. He's nice to us, but he often seems detached or maybe too distracted to care.

The real God is much different. He is attentive and caring. He doesn't sit in heaven with a tally sheet or sit behind a desk. The real God's care is so deep and so strong that even a mother's love pales in comparison. He thinks of you so often and is so excited about the possibility of a relationship with you that He's "tattooed" your name on the palm of His hand. He's not inspecting; He's admiring His creation in you. God is not disappointed in you; He is excited to love you. God's not uninvolved; He is with you every moment of every day.

God, help me to see the real You. I want to know You more so that I can sense Your love for me. Amen.

Terri Snead, The Great Commandment Network

Week 6, Tuesday
Can You See Me?

Behold what manner of love the Father has bestowed on us,
that we should be called children of God!

1 John 3:1

Can you imagine falling in love with someone who constantly pointed out what you did wrong or sent the message that you were never good enough? Can you imagine trying to love someone who barely noticed you, never seemed to pay attention to you, or was always too busy to talk with you? It would be hard to love anyone in a relationship like that. The same is true in our relationship with God. It's extremely difficult to love a God whom we believe is examining us, disappointed in us, or whom we believe is not interested in our lives or doesn't seem to notice.

God wants us to have an accurate view of Him because He loves us and wants us to see Him clearly. He wants us to see Him clearly so that we'll be free to love Him and others. One of the ways we can see God more clearly is by reflecting on Christ's encounters with people. Because we know that He is the same yesterday, today, and forever, we can rest assured that Jesus relates in the same ways with us.

Imagine the scene in Mark 10 when Jesus interacted with children. The news had spread about the Teacher's amazing miracles, so crowds of people flocked to see Jesus on this day. Groups of parents had even brought their children to Jesus. When the disciples dismissed the children as unimportant, Jesus spoke up for them, defended them, and prioritized the children. The passage tells us that Jesus took them in His arms and blessed them. And what was also amazing . . . the One who was most qualified to talk to the kids about their behavior, didn't. The Master Teacher didn't have a sermon and didn't share a lesson. He simply accepted and affirmed the children for who they were at that moment. He smiled at the children. His eyes glistened with approval and then reached out, put His arms around them, and spoke words of blessing for their future. Aren't you glad we have a God like that?

God, thank You for prioritizing me just like You did the children. Thank You for accepting me, affirming me, and praying for my future. Help me to see You more like the children saw You that day. Amen.

Week 6, Wednesday
In Circulation

Oh, that men would give thanks to the LORD for His goodness,
and for His wonderful works to the children of men!
For He satisfies the longing soul, and fills the hungry soul with goodness.

Psalm 107:8, 9

One of the ways that we can learn to see the real God is by looking in His Word. Psalm 107 reminds us to give thanks to the Lord because of His unfailing love and His wonderful deeds for men. This passage of Scripture reminds us that God's love will never fail. He makes wonderful things happen for us. Sometimes God shows His love directly, and sometimes He makes wonderful things happen through people around us.

Think about a time when you experienced God's love through another person. Remember a time when you encountered God's love, but it was expressed through a human. Think about a time when you were confident that this person wasn't distant from you. Perhaps they were attentive, listened well, were sensitive to your needs, or noticed when you were upset. Was there a time when a friend or family member was excited to see you, seemed especially glad to be with you, or told you they were proud of you? Has there been a time when a friend or loved one accepted you unconditionally, forgave you, or loved you even though you messed up?

I remember a time when I felt especially loved by another person when . . .

Those times were God's wonderful works on your behalf. Since God *is* love, He's the source of love. And when those friends and family members loved you well, they were simply keeping God's love in circulation. (See 1 John 4:7–8, 12.)

Could you now take a few moments and do what the Psalmist suggests? Could you give thanks to the Lord for His goodness?

God, I am thankful that You are a loving God. Thank You for revealing Your love to me through other people. I'm especially grateful for the times when . . . Amen.

Terri Snead, The Great Commandment Network

Week 6, Thursday
Face-to-Face

But You, O Lord, are a God full of compassion, and gracious,
longsuffering and abundant in mercy and truth.

Psalm 86:15

Take the next few moments to imagine the character of the real God and how He might relate to you. The Psalmist tells us that the real God is overflowing with compassion for you.

Imagine one of your most difficult days. Think about one of those days when conflicts with parents, school pressures, or relationships with friends were at their hardest. Imagine a day when nothing seems to go well; you're overwhelmed and feeling very alone.

At the very moment, when things seem their worst, imagine that you come face-to-face with Jesus. Are you afraid He'll lecture you or tell you how you could have done things better? Are you afraid He'll shake His head in disappointment and say, "How many times have I told you . . ." Are you worried that He'll walk past you and not even notice the stress on your face or the sadness in your eyes? Or perhaps you're scared that He might notice those things, but just not take the time to care.

The real Jesus would be full of compassion. He would look at you with the kindest eyes and warmest smile. He would give you a warm embrace and ask about your day. Jesus would listen as you tell Him about your struggles. He would be attentive and genuinely want to know how you feel. Jesus would reassure you, "I'm not going to inspect you or tell you what you've done wrong. I want to provide for you. I want to give you strength and encouragement for this day. I'm not distant or uninvolved. I care deeply about what you're going through. I was with you every moment of today—laughing when you laughed, crying when you cried. My heart hurt each time you experienced something difficult. I was present with you then and I am here for you now. I'll never leave you because I love you. I'm not disappointed in you, I feel great compassion for you. I want My compassion to give you the stamina to face the day. My compassionate love for you is unwavering, unchanging, and never ending."

 God, thank You for Your compassion. Help me sense Your love for me every moment of the day. Amen.

Week 6, Friday
The Source

Let us love one another, for love is of God; and everyone who loves is born of God and knows God. He who does not love does not know God, for God is love.

1 John 4:7, 8

We see daily evidence that people are having trouble loving. Gang violence, the increase in divorce, racial tensions, and hate crimes all point out that loving one another is often harder than we think.

How about you? Are you having trouble loving? Do you have difficulty showing love to any particular person or type of person? Is it hard for you to love your parents, your sister, brother, family member, or friend?

First John tells us that love is from God. He's the source of all love. It comes from Him. So if we're running out of love, we have to look to Him for the supply. Secondly, the verse tells us that if we do not love, we have not come to know God. If we're having trouble loving someone, then we haven't come to truly know God or deeply experience His true love. Here's what that might look like:

If we view God as a stern, inspecting dictator, we may tend to inspect other people. We might have a hard time giving grace to others, giving second chances, or offering forgiveness.

If we view God as one who is always disappointed, then we may come to believe that others can never measure up. We might have trouble seeing the positive attributes in ourselves and other people. We might have trouble being grateful for God's blessings or appreciative of others' care for us.

If we view God as distant or uninvolved, we may come to believe that God didn't notice our needs—so it may be hard to notice anyone else's. We may find it hard to trust other people. We may have trouble getting close to other people.

In contrast, if we view God as One who looks forward to being with us and is excited to love us, then we can respond to others in the same way. We can be free to notice others' needs. We are able to give care, love, grace, and forgiveness because we have experienced those attributes in our own relationship with God.

 God, please help me to experience more and more of Your love so that I am free to love others well. Amen.

Terri Snead, The Great Commandment Network

Week 6, Weekend
In Good Hands

I will also meditate on all Your work, and talk of Your deeds.

Psalm 77:12

What was God's heart toward you when you woke this morning? Was He upset to see you? Did He even notice? Or could He have been excited and thrilled to know that you started your day?

Many of us may have never even considered our view of God. We have believed certain things about Him and have never questioned them or been challenged with an alternative. The truth is: The real God is a God who protects us and provides for us. As we come to know the real God as He truly is, we will be able to love Him as He has loved us.

How has God protected you? Think about the times when He has kept you from harm, healed you from illness, or prevented pain in your life. Has God rescued you, spared you from trouble, or heard your cry for help? Remember how He has saved you, protected you from eternal separation from Him, and paved the way for you to live with Him forever.

I can see God's protection for me when . . .

How has God provided for you? Remember the times when God has acted on your behalf and lovingly met your needs. Think about His provision of family, friends, and loved ones to care for you. Consider the ways in which He has ultimately given every good thing that's in your life.

I can remember God providing for me when . . .

When we get to know the real God who protects and provides for us, we can't help but love Him back! And then as we learn to love Him, we will be better equipped to love others.

How could you protect other people in your life this week? Could you help protect a friend and discourage them from making wrong choices? Could you protect a friend by refusing to listen to gossip or slander?

How could you provide for others this week? Could you provide support, encouragement, or compassion? Would your family member benefit from your respect, appreciation, or concern?

Lord, help me to see You as One who provides and protects so that I will be better able to love others around me. Amen.

Week 7, Monday
Brag About It

And my God shall supply all your need according to His riches in glory by Christ Jesus.

Philippians 4:19

Has there ever been a time when you've announced the accomplishments of a friend or told the great news about a family member? You "bragged" about your friend or family member because you care for them and wanted others to know it.

Paul must have felt that way about God. Paul's words, "my God," are unusual in the New Testament, but they show that Paul was bragging about "his" God. He was excited to announce that his God is a God who meets needs. That's great news for you and me. It's good news for us because:

- God notices when we're in need—He pays attention. Jesus' response to the woman with the issue of blood reveals God's true heart (Mark 5:25–34). He wasn't too busy to notice and was sensitive enough to stop and express His care.

- The real God meets our need even when others don't—He gets it. Jesus felt compassion on the multitudes. He was sensitive to their hunger (unlike the disciples), not just because He was all-knowing but because He, too, knew what it was like to feel hungry (Mark 6:30–44).

- The real God takes initiative to respond to respond to our needs—His love takes action. Jesus noticed the woman at the well. He noticed her "heart need" and went out of His way to meet that need. Jesus was the first to speak—an unheard-of custom in that day. "Give Me a drink" (see John 4:5–26).

Think about a time in your life when you sensed God's special care. Try to think of a time when He noticed your need and met that need directly. He might have met your need through a time of prayer with Him, through a sermon, through one of your devotional times, through a song, or just through a peace that could only come from Him. Ask God to reveal a time when He was with you, caring for you and meeting your need . . . even if you weren't aware of it at the time.

I remember sensing God's special care just for me when _____ *and God* _____
_____ .

 God, I'm grateful that You notice, that You are sensitive, and that You take action. Thank You for the time when You cared especially for me . . . Amen.

Terri Snead, The Great Commandment Network

Week 7, Tuesday
I See You

And He looked around to see her who had done this thing.

Mark 5:32

Jesus was a busy guy. He was always involved in lives of people. On one particular day, He was hurriedly moving through the crowd because of the impending death of a religious leader's daughter. Jesus was occupied—He was taking care of "important" business. But if we were able to look closely, we would see that Jesus didn't miss a thing. The need of just one simple, unassuming lady got His attention and His lavish provision.

There she was, on the outskirts of the crowd. She was someone who hadn't been noticed. She was outside all the hustle and bustle of life, but was still overwhelmed by the weight of her need. She'd tried to fix the crisis. She'd tried to solve the problem. She'd tried all that she could, but her need, her pain, and her struggle had only gotten worse.

Sometimes we try to solve things on our own. We try to fix the crisis, but things only seem to get worse. Some of us, like the lady in Mark 5, are on the periphery of the crowd. We're spectators, watching Jesus take care of the "big things," and wonder if He notices *our* need.

Picture yourself in the scene of Mark 5. You're the one who's tried to fix things. You've tried to solve the challenges of life, but things have only gotten worse. You're the one who is surrounded by people, but those people haven't been sensitive to your needs. You might be standing on the edge of the crowd, and have a growing sense that people in your life haven't noticed your needs, much less been a part of meeting them.

Now imagine, in the midst of that scene, the crowd suddenly stops. And Jesus, who's been heading in another direction, turns around and looks at you. He looks into your eyes, looks deep into your heart, and then speaks with tender words: "Dear one, you just touched Me. Your pain, your needs, the weight of your struggles has just touched Me." Jesus takes the next few moments to speak to the issues of your heart. He comforts the pain you feel. He calms every fear. He soothes every disappointment and addresses every need.

 Jesus, thank You for noticing me and my needs. Thank You for not being too busy. I love You. Amen.

Week 7, Wednesday
Creative Supply

*But I rejoiced in the Lord greatly that now at last
your care for me has flourished again.*

Philippians 4:10

God has lots of creative ways that He meets our needs. Sometimes He meets our needs with abundant supply even before we're aware we have a need. Take your need to breathe, for example. God uniquely designed the human body to need oxygen. He also creatively designed all plants on earth to produce oxygen. You were born needing oxygen. God creatively provided oxygen—even before you were aware of your need. And because God is also a generous God, we'll never run out of what we need!

One of God's other creative ways to meet your needs is by including other people in the process. God designed relationships like family, friends, and the Church to keep His abundant supply in circulation. So perhaps you need some encouragement today. God's put you in relationships with people who can deliver some of God's encouragement, just for you. Maybe you need some support today. God's provided friends, family, and sometimes even people you don't know who can be a part of meeting that need.

Reflect for a few moments on how God has done that in your life. You may have been unaware of God's creative supply, but how has God provided for you through other people? When do you remember sensing some of God's special care, delivered through another person?

I remember experiencing another person's special care when . . .

I know now this was God's provision for me and a demonstration of His . . .

Next, take the time to thank God for His provision. The apostle Paul rejoiced greatly in the Lord because of how He provided through other people. Can you do the same?

*God, thank You for meeting my needs through the people around me. You
delivered Your special care through the lives of others. I'm especially glad
about the time when . . . Amen.*

Week 7, Thursday
Just for You!

As each one has received a gift, minister it to one another,
as good stewards of the manifold grace of God.

1 Peter 4:10

Imagine a beautiful, many-sided diamond, brilliant in color and clarity. This is the image that Peter has in mind when he speaks of God's grace having many forms. Just as a diamond has many facets that reflect light in a unique and stunning way, God's grace has many aspects. Each side of His grace becomes visible when we experience His love in our lives and then share His love with others.

God offers this multifaceted diamond to you as a gift, with each side of the diamond representing the grace you need at various times in your life. He offers you loving acceptance when you're feeling unlovable or different; affection and care when you're lonely or need reassurance; appreciation for your efforts; approval as His beloved child; and comfort when you are in pain. He wants to give you the gifts of encouragement when you are down, respect for you as an individual, security in the midst of uncertainty, and support for when you are overwhelmed. These gifts are lovingly offered to you. You've done nothing to deserve them and nothing to earn them. That's God's grace!

Take the next few moments to remember a time when you were discouraged and God encouraged you through His Word, a song, a family member, or a friend. Or remember a time when you were overwhelmed and He gave you a sense of peace and security or brought someone along to support you.

God, I remember a time when I felt _____ and You offered your grace to me by . . .

Be sure to thank Him for this gift. It was given just for you.

God, thank You for Your grace. Your love and grace has so many facets. I am thankful that You freely share them with me. Thank You for being a God who is generous to meet my needs. Amen.

Week 7, Friday
One Who Gives

Serve the Lord with gladness.

Psalm 100:2

The real God is fundamentally a need-meeting God. God's very nature is One who gives. Think about the simple act of enjoying a steak for dinner. In order for us to enjoy a steak, God must first provide life for the cow, as well as oxygen, grain, and water to sustain that life. Then the cow must be butchered using metal instruments and the meat must be packaged, refrigerated, and transported—all processes that require the use of God-created, natural elements (such as iron, timber, ice, and petroleum), as well as modern technological innovations that were only made possible through God-given creativity and inspiration. Finally, we must have either fire or electricity (both God-created phenomena) with which to cook the meat, and of course a properly functioning digestive system with which to consume it. If God failed to meet any one of the dozens of individual requirements that make up this chain, the need would remain unmet. Yet amazingly, God is both willing and able to continually perform the infinite number of acts necessary to provide billions of people with everything they need on a daily basis.

Think about a time when God provided for you and your family by meeting a physical or material need (such as a need for food, shelter, clothing, or finances) in a special way. What do you feel toward God as you remember His provision?

I remember God meeting my need when _____ and I feel _____ now because _____.

God not only meets our physical needs, He also meets our emotional and spiritual needs. Reflect on a time when God met one of your spiritual or emotional needs in a special way. What do you feel toward God as you remember this provision?

I remember God meeting my need when _____ and I feel _____ now because _____.

Take a few moments to live out Psalm 100:2. God feels loved when we share our gladness for the ways that He gives to us.

 God, thank You for being a need-meeting God. I am especially glad for how You . . . Amen.

Week 7, Weekend
Better Than the Birds

"Consider the ravens, for they neither sow nor reap, which have neither storehouse nor barn; and God feeds them. Of how much more value are you than the birds?"

Luke 12:24

When we remember God's special care for us and embrace the truth that He is a need-meeting God, at least two things can result:

• We increase our ability to see Him work in our lives. We can see God more easily because we know He is trustworthy.

Jesus reminded us of God's care on our behalf when He described the Father's care for birds and flowers. Jesus described God's care of the ravens and how God feeds the birds and carefully provides for them. In Jewish culture, this would have been particularly significant because ravens were considered unclean creatures that were the least respected birds of the day. Jesus pointed out that if God cared enough to provide for the ravens, He certainly will provide for you and me.

• Our faith in God increases. We come to believe in God, count on Him, and look to Him to meet our needs for the future. And consequently, we get to please God. Our demonstrations of faith in Him actually make God smile. He loves it when we trust Him. Without faith it is impossible to please God.

Take the next few moments to reflect on the many ways that God has provided for you. Remember the ways He has noticed your needs and been sensitive to you and what you're going through. Reflect on the ways He has responded to you and acted on your behalf. Remember the ways He has given you acceptance, comfort, encouragement, forgiveness, and peace. Remember the people God has brought into your life. Remember the special care Christ demonstrated on the cross. Now, because you know the truth that He is a need-meeting God, declare your faith in Him for future needs.

God, as I remember Your special care for me, I can now trust You to . . . Amen.

Week 8, Monday
Been There

For we do not have a High Priest who cannot sympathize with our weaknesses,
but was in all points tempted as we are, yet without sin.

Hebrews 4:15

It's sometimes hard to get our heads around the truth that Jesus could be both completely human and completely God. That's one of the mysterious truths of the Gospel. While Jesus was here on earth, He lived for thirty-three years as a "regular guy." He felt the same feelings that you feel and experienced the same needs. Jesus was both physically human and supernaturally divine.

Here's the big deal about this mystery for us. Because Jesus knows what it's like to be human, we can take comfort in the truth that He understands our world.

He knows what it's like to feel:
- The hurt from a friend: "Most assuredly, I say to you, one of you will betray Me" (John 13:21).
- Frustration with those who are supposed to be closest to Him: "Have I been with you so long, and yet you have not known Me, Philip?" (John 14:9).
- Feelings of joy: "These things I have spoken to you, that My joy may remain in you, and that your joy may be full" (John 15:11).
- Sadness because of a broken relationship: "My God, My God, why have You forsaken Me?" (Matthew 27:46).
- Rejected: "If the world hates you, you know that it hated Me before it hated you" (John 15:18).

I've been feeling a great deal of _____ lately because . . .

Take the next few moments and consider the truth that Jesus understands when you feel hurt, frustration, joy, or sadness. You have a God who has felt these feelings, too. He's ready to listen. He's ready to care if you're hurt, frustrated, or sad. He's ready to celebrate with you and share your joy. He just wants you to share what's on your heart. Talk to God about your life. Tell Him what you're feeling and relax in the truth that He's been there, too.

Jesus, I am grateful because You know how it feels to experience _____. I am glad I have a God who understands and who has been there, too. That helps me know that . . . Amen.

Terri Snead, The Great Commandment Network

Week 8, Tuesday
Just Like You

Your testimonies also are my delight and my counselors.

Psalm 119:24

Jesus understands. The real God is One who came to earth and lived among us in the person of Jesus. And because He did that, Jesus is able to understand and relate to all of our human experiences and emotions. The Bible clearly reveals that Jesus knew what it was like to be hungry, thirsty, and tired. He knew what it was like to be criticized, misunderstood, betrayed, and abandoned. Jesus was frequently ridiculed by crowds of people, and He faced unimaginable physical pain on the cross. He knows what it's like to hurt, both physically and emotionally.

This particular truth can be comforting for us, especially when we are in the midst of painful circumstances ourselves. During these times, it's often helpful to realize we have a Savior who is praying for us and the One who is praying for us understands our world. Just like you, Jesus has experienced:

- Rejection: by His own people (Luke 4:14–30; Mark 6:1–6).
- Abandonment: by His disciples (Mark 14:43–50, 66–72).
- Disappointment: by people closest to Him (Matthew 17:1–5).
- A lack of acceptance: by family and friends (Matthew 13:57).
- Criticism: by the religious leaders (Luke 20:17–20; 22:1–6).
- Great loss and sadness: after losing a friend/loved one (Matthew 7:1–5).
- Feeling unappreciated: even after meeting others' needs (Luke 17:11–19).

It can bring comfort and delight to us to know that we have a God who understands. He rejoices with you during your successes and sympathizes with you during your struggles.

Take a few moments to live out Psalm 119:24. Let the testimony of Christ be your delight.

It means the most to me that Jesus experienced _____ *because I . . .*

Now, express your wonder and gratitude to the One who understands.

Jesus, I feel grateful/hopeful/amazed and filled with delight when I think about how You experienced _____.
Thank You for being the kind of God who lived here on earth so that You can identify with me. Amen.

Week 8, Wednesday
He's Ready to Join Us

Jesus wept.

John 11:35

What is your picture of Jesus when you imagine Him? Close your eyes and think about Jesus. Picture Him in your mind's eye. What does He look like? What does His voice sound like? When we use our imagination to reflect on Jesus, it's important to remember that Jesus experienced life like we do. Jesus knew joy and knew pain. He knew disappointment and loss. This means that the God-man, Jesus, is able to come alongside and help us with *our* life struggles because He has been there, too.

We see the human-ness of our Lord most vividly at the death of His friend Lazarus. The divinity (or God-part) of Jesus is clear in the passage, because only God can raise the dead! But it is His humanity that touches our lives and helps us experience Christ as He really is.

As Jesus stood before His friends, He knew they were upset with Him. "Why didn't You come sooner? If You would have been here, my brother wouldn't be dead!" Martha cried. At these words, Jesus was moved with sadness. As Jesus stood watching His friends struggle with the death of Lazarus, Jesus had an emotional response that was like a "deep sigh and a groan" from within Him. It was a deep emotion of pain and sadness that sympathized with Mary and joined in mourning alongside His friends.

Mourning was a very important ritual act in Jesus' day. Whenever people experienced the death of a loved one, they enacted a mourning ritual. In this ritual, people of the community would mourn with the family. This was very important because the process of mourning could, in fact, *never* be completed until someone came alongside the bereaved, shed tears, and sat with them while they grieved.

The truths of Christ's humanity in this passage are astounding. First, it's incredible to know that we have a God who understands our pain. He knows what it's like to lose a loved one. He understands what it's like to feel great sadness and loss. And secondly, Christ's humanity reassures us that He wants to be a part of our mourning ritual, too. Jesus wants us to know that He is available to come alongside us, shed tears with us, and sit with us while we grieve so that healing can occur.

God, I'm especially grateful for these truths because . . . Amen.

Terri Snead, The Great Commandment Network

Week 8, Thursday
Family Life

*But when he was still a great way off, his father saw him and had
compassion, and ran and fell on his neck and kissed him.*

Luke 15:20

For many of us it's hard to believe in or accept the love of God that Jesus reveals. Perhaps you feel as if God's love is a nice, spiritual thought, but when it comes to "real life," God's love may have never worked out for you. You might even feel as if God doesn't understand your needs and what you've been through. After all, divorce, abuse, and hurt are prevalent realities for many students today. The hurtful experiences are all too real, and the stories of God's love can seem to be simply that: *stories*.

Sometimes it's hard to believe that God truly understands what life is like, especially life in families. But take another look at the parable of the lost son in Luke 15:11–32. It reveals God's realistic picture of family.

Luke 15 describes a very realistic picture of family relationships. The parable shows the hard aspects of family: selfishness, jealousy, rebellion, regret, patience, celebration, unhealthy wants and needs, and ultimately love. If there were ever a picture painted that accurately reflects the dysfunction present in families today, this is it! What does this tell us? Because it comes from Christ's own lips, we see that Jesus really does understand the realities of families. He doesn't "whitewash" the challenge of family relationships . . . rather He reflects the brokenness with a clear eye and unnerving insight. Jesus knows, as God knows, the hurt and brokenness present in family relationships. God is aware and feels our unmet needs in family life.

Here's the good news: while He recognizes and understands the brokenness of family life, Jesus gives a vision of a loving heavenly Father, whose extravagant love can heal us and "bring us to our senses" to restore health and vitality in all our relationships.

I have found it difficult to believe that God understands my family life and my family relationships. But as I reflect upon the parable of the lost son, however, I see . . .

 Jesus, thank You for demonstrating the love of God in Your life and in this parable. I open my heart to You and want You to help me experience more of Your love even in the midst of sometimes difficult relationships with family or friends. Amen.

Terri Snead, The Great Commandment Network

Week 8, Friday
Radical Love

He had compassion on her.

Luke 7:13

The widow of Nain doesn't get a lot of attention. In fact, I don't think I've ever heard one lesson taught on this Bible story. But I've come to believe that it's one of the purest, most telling pictures of the heart of Jesus. The funeral procession began at her home and then wound its way through the dusty streets of Nain. Just as the widow and the mourners came to city gate, another crowd of people was entering. This crowd was following Jesus. The two crowds converged. One group followed the coffin. The other followed the Christ.

And as the two crowds converged, Jesus saw the widow. Because He was God, Jesus would have looked deep into her heart and known that she was alone. She was a widow who had just lost her only son. That meant no husband to provide for her, no one to take care of her, no security, and no guarantee of safety.

Jesus would have also seen the woman's future. She had no one to grow old with, no one to cook for, and no one to share life with. No son to lean on. No one.

The Savior was so moved by compassion for this woman that it welled up inside of Him: "Dear one, please don't cry." Then Jesus did something radical. He touched the coffin! To touch a coffin meant that Jesus would be required to be a part of ceremonially washings, a huge investment of time and sacrifice. Jesus was apparently so moved by the woman's hurt that He didn't care. He stopped the funeral and raised her son from the dead!

Amazingly, the widow made no request; there was no desperate plea. Jesus simply acted because He saw her hurt and it moved Him to do something. Her pain moved His heart with compassion.

Take the next few moments to rest in the truth that Jesus is moved by what He sees in your heart. Even during the times when you're too confused or too sad to pray, God sees what's in your heart and His heart hurts. He's also ready to do something. Be sure to look for His working in your life.

 Jesus, sometimes I can't always sense that You are with me, but help me to know You are there for me. Thank You that You see what's in my heart and are moved with compassion for me. Amen.

Terri Snead, The Great Commandment Network

Week 8, Weekend
Can You Hurt for Jesus?

That I may know Him and the power of His resurrection, and the fellowship of His sufferings.

Philippians 3:10

The God we serve is not a god who's high in the clouds, far away from human pain and struggle. Rather, He is GOD, who suffered the pain of sorrow ... to the point of His death. The real God longs to have a close relationship with us, and that closeness will mean a greater understanding and heart connection with the feelings of Jesus. We've spent the last few days exploring the truth that Jesus understands your pain. Now, can you understand His? Can you hurt for Jesus?

Put yourself in His shoes while He is in the Garden of Gethsemane for the last time. (Read Mathew 26:36–56). He is praying to God and knows the suffering He is about to endure. He knows that the decision to come to Jerusalem means a terrible and painful, humiliating, and embarrassing death. He knows the things that have enraged the religious leaders of the day. They want His life ... they want to humiliate Him. And so He prays. Do you feel the pain that Jesus is going through? Do you hurt as He is hurting? This is the humanity of our Lord.

Next, replay the rejection Jesus experienced. His closest friends see His pain, and He invites them to pray for Him through the night. Perhaps Jesus thinks that if only His friends can go through this with Him, they might strengthen and support Him (v. 38). Jesus trusts His friends to help Him, sustain Him. But instead of helping, He comes back to find them sleeping. Jesus is distraught and hurt: "Couldn't you keep watch with Me for one hour, Peter?" Jesus says. Imagine the hurt in Jesus' voice as Peter looks up at Him blankly. Feel the sense of loneliness that begins to creep into Jesus' heart. And feel the loneliness grow as He comes back *again* to find them asleep! He has no words for His friends. Jesus feels rejected and alone.

When you consider the rejection, loneliness, and betrayal of Jesus, how does this make you feel toward Him? Do you hurt with Him? Can you fellowship in His sufferings? Tell Him about your care.

Jesus, I am sad when I remember how You went through ...

It hurts my heart to know that You experienced ...

Thank You for Your sacrifice. Thank You for going through all of that pain for me. Amen.

Week 9, Monday
Moment by Moment

From that time many of His disciples went back and walked with Him no more.

John 6:66

Have you ever heard the phrase "lost in the moment"? It's easy to get lost in the moment and make a foolish decision or, due to peer pressure, do something we will always regret. The "moment" is one of the hardest places to live. When you are faced with a decision "in the moment," it really comes down to two options: will the next second of your life represent Christ and His character, or will it represent the world and its downfall?

Living for Christ moment by moment can be one of the hardest things to accomplish in your life, but it is what true followers of Christ do. Anyone can live for Christ at church, during a Bible study, at a camp or retreat, or even when you are with all your Christian friends. What about when that is all gone, though? When everyone is looking at you, expecting you just drop the "God thing" and join in their fun? Those moments are when a true follower of Christ is defined.

John 6 speaks about how Jesus is the Bread of Life. All of His followers are given a challenge in verses 53–59. The result of this challenge was that some of His disciples said in verse 60, "This is a hard saying; who can understand it?" Then in verse 66, "From that time many of His disciples went back and walked with Him no more."

There was a moment when following Jesus was "cool" or "accepted." But when push came to shove and the disciples had to make a decision, they quit. I wonder how many of you are like the disciples and in the moment quit following Jesus! Have you stopped having faith that God can move mountains? Galatians 3:3 asks, "Are you so foolish? Having begun in the Spirit, are you now being made perfect by the flesh?" How do you answer that question? Have you stopped following and trusting in your Lord because of the moment you are in? I challenge you today to follow Jesus moment by moment and never give up on Him!

Dear Lord, I pray today that You will give me the strength to stand for You moment by moment. I never want to take a challenge out of Your Word like some of the followers did in John 6 and turn from that challenge simply because it was too hard. I pray You will be my wisdom in all decisions I make in choosing to follow You moment by moment. Amen.

Brian Mills, Longhollow Baptist Church

Week 9, Tuesday
No Excuses—Just Follow

And when Jesus came to the place, He looked up and saw him, and said to him,
"Zacchaeus, make haste and come down, for today I must stay at your house."

Luke 19:5

Have you ever let your circumstances keep you from following Christ? There are always opportunities to use negative situations as an excuse.

In the story of Zacchaeus, there are several things to learn of how not to let circumstances become excuses. First, don't let your spiritual condition stop you. Zacchaeus was basically considered a thief and could have held himself back as unworthy. Have you ever held yourself back from following after Christ because of what you know about yourself or what you have done in the past?

Second, don't let your physical limitations keep you from following. Zacchaeus was short and had no access to even see Jesus. It took extra effort to put him in a position to see past the people who were blocking his view of Jesus. There are many physical limitations that you can claim as excuses for why not to follow, but they don't hold water.

Third, don't let what others say keep you from following Jesus. As a tax collector Zacchaeus had the worst of reputations and could have let what others had to say, mumble, or mutter about him stop him from responding when Jesus called to him. Zacchaeus spoke up in faith under great pressure and negative peer influence. When was the last time you felt pressure to ignore the call of Christ because of what others said or thought about you?

The truth is that the Lord loves you no matter what and He is calling you to follow Him regardless of your circumstances. No excuses—just follow.

Thank You, Father, that You are calling me to follow You. Thank You that You love me no matter what and that You are seeking after me. There are so many times when I am guilty of finding excuses for why I can't follow. Please forgive me for giving in to those excuses and show me the areas in my life where I need to run to You like Zacchaeus did. I want my life to be an example of how to follow after You regardless of what my past is, what my present is, or what others have to say about me. I trust You. Amen.

Week 9, Wednesday
Friends Forever

So He Himself often withdrew into the wilderness and prayed.

Luke 5:16

Each fall my father drives to his reunion. This is not his high school class reunion. This reunion is of college friends who were involved in the same church *over* sixty years ago.

Why does my father drive hundreds of miles each year? He has friends for life. Do you want to know how to have a lifetime of friendships? The Bible provides examples of the skills needed to help develop friendships for a lifetime.

Friendships should be focused on our heavenly Father. "So He Himself often withdrew into the wilderness and prayed" (Luke 5:16). Jesus drew strength from His Father. You can also find the strength, grace, and guidance you need by spending time with your heavenly Father.

Friendships center on accountability. "As iron sharpens iron, so a man sharpens the countenance of his friend" (Proverbs 27:17). We all have blind spots, so it is helpful to have friends who are close enough to you to lovingly point them out.

Friendships involve fellowship. "Flee also youthful lusts; but pursue righteousness, faith, love, peace with those who call on the Lord out of a pure heart" (2 Timothy 2:22). If you are a part of a small group or Sunday school class at your church, these friends can give you both the encouragement and challenge you need.

Friendships gather for worship. "And let us consider one another in order to stir up love and good works, not forsaking the assembling of ourselves together" (Hebrews 10:24–25). When you worship with your friends, you have an opportunity to be exposed to the character and activity of God. Joining with God and your friends in His movement can be life altering.

Dear heavenly Father, I pray that You will allow me the blessing of having great friends. I pray You would send friends into my life whom I can worship You with and serve You together. I pray You would surround me with others who love You as much and more than I do so that my walk can be stretched and strengthened. I pray that my relationship with You will continue to grow. Help me to hear Your still, small voice so that I may walk humbly, in obedience, and by faith. Amen.

John Steen, Longhollow Baptist Church

Week 9, Thursday
Who Am I?

If the Spirit of Him who raised Jesus from the dead dwells in you, He who raised Christ from the dead will also give life to your mortal bodies. . . .

Romans 8:11

In our lives there are a lot of people with opinions about who we are. Many of them have never even met us. They take one look at us and think they have us all summed up. Unfortunately we listen to some of these people. The problem is, they don't know us. Today let's look at Someone's opinion who counts, Someone who really knows us, the One who created us. Take a few minutes and read Romans 8. Here are just a few things out of Romans 8 that God says about us.

Verse 1: We don't have to carry guilt with us all day long.

Verse 3: He values us enough to send His Son to the cross as a payment for our sin.

Verse 9: He gave us His Spirit (the Holy Spirit) to live in us.

Verse 10: He calls us righteous (without guilt or sin).

Verse 14–17: He calls us His children, tells us we can call him Abba ("Daddy"), and says we are co-heirs with Jesus. (We get what He gets. That makes no sense, but this is who He says we are.)

Verse 26: The Holy Spirit goes to God on our behalf and prays for us. (Wow!)

Verse 28: God works out ALL things for the good of those who love Him.

Verse 31: He says He is for us. NO ONE can stand against us.

Verse 34: Jesus also cries out to God on our behalf.

Verse 35–36: NO ONE can separate us from Him.

Verse 37: In ALL things we are MORE than conquerors.

Verses 38–39: Nothing can separate us from His love.

This is how He sees us. This is who we are.

So why is it that when we look in the mirror we don't see the same things He sees? Too many times we are bombarded with the world's view, and what God thinks falls to the side.

God, help me to hear Your voice over the noise of the world. God, help me to see what You see in me. The world tells me I have to have a certain look, or status, or ability in order to have worth. You say because I have YOU, I have all the worth I will ever need. Teach me to be more than a conqueror. Amen.

Shane Sisk, Longhollow Baptist Church

Week 9, Friday
Faith to Follow

Immediately Jesus made His disciples get into the boat and go before Him to the other side, while He sent the multitudes away. And when He had sent the multitudes away, He went up on the mountain by Himself to pray. Now when evening came, He was alone there.

Matthew 14:22, 33

The disciples were in a tough spot, a dangerous spot and here comes Jesus walking out to them on the water. Can you imagine what they were thinking? The Bible tells us that they were shocked and scared for their lives. Then Jesus did what He does so perfectly—He spoke to them.

He wasn't worried about the storm, He was focused on the learning experience for His disciples. When Peter spoke up, Jesus told him to come on out of the boat. That was a test of faith. When Jesus calls us to follow Him, He also calls us to have faith in Him.

Notice where the other disciples were-in the boat. They were focused on the circumstances and the dangers to the point that they missed out on the opportunity to do something miraculous. Peter chose to step out and trust. To follow in faith, and that made the difference.

Who do you tend to be more like? The disciples in the boat who are looking at all the reasons why not to have faith or Peter who took the call to follow to the next level of faith? Notice that Peter did waver when the waves continued to roar around him. His faith wasn't perfect but at least he showed some faith. Don't miss what happened when Peter's faith was shaken—Jesus reached out and grabbed him. Peter had the opportunity to get even closer to Jesus than ever before.

Jesus is calling you to follow Him. To have faith. Are you going to stay in the boat and be afraid of your circumstances? Or are you going to step out in faith? When you choose to step out, the circumstances won't always change but you will. Remember Jesus is right there to pick you up when you are following Him in faith.

Father thank you that you are bigger than my circumstances and that you never leave me alone in the storms of my life. Strengthen my faith and help me choose to follow no matter what. I want to be a man who follows in faith and doesn't stay in the boat.

Jeff Lovingood, Longhollow Baptist Church

Week 9, Weekend
The Perfect Plan

Let all those who seek You rejoice and be glad in You; and let those who love
Your salvation say continually, "Let God be magnified!"

Psalm 70:4

Broken relationships are at the root of many of the world's problems. A broken relationship with God and broken relationships with one another can be found underneath so many of the challenges we face.

The initial effect of the first sin—Adam and Eve's disobedience in the Garden of Eden—was damaged relationships. Adam and Eve's sin caused brokenness in their relationship with God. But here's the good news: God went looking for Adam and Eve in the Garden because He deeply longed for a relationship with them. And even as He encountered Adam and Eve's painful choices, God announced His plan for restoring relationship.

God was sorrowed because of the loss of relationship with Adam and Eve. He couldn't bear the thought of being separated from the ones He loved, so God devised a plan to reconnect to His children . . . and to you and me. God's plan was to send His Son into our world to become one of us. Jesus came to earth to cancel the brokenness of sin, so you and I could know and experience God's love for us.

The Bible tells us that God is the same, yesterday, today, and forever (Hebrews 13:8). Just as He did with Adam and Eve, God looks for us because He wants a relationship with us. He longs to relate to you. He couldn't bear the thought of being disconnected from Adam and Eve, and He feels the same way about you and me. How does it make you feel to know that God's heart hurts when He thinks about being disconnected from you?

As I reflect on how God hurts when He thinks about being disconnected from me, I feel . . .

How does your heart respond as you consider God's plan for repairing His relationship with you? If you have already received His gift of relationship and have become a follower of Jesus, how might you declare your love to Him?

God, I want to magnify or show how great You are because . . .

I am so glad that You are a God who wants to be with me because . . .
Amen.

Terri Snead, The Great Commandment Network

Week 10, Monday
Perfect Love Drives out Fear!

"There is no fear in love. But perfect love drives out fear, because fear has to do with punishment. The one who fears is not made perfect in love."

1 John 4:18

Let's be honest. We all struggle with fear. What are you afraid of? Maybe it's a fear of heights, fear of the dark, of not being accepted, loosing a loved one, fear of failure, or a fear of not finding that right guy/girl someday. Some things we fear may be small & sound so silly when we say them out loud. Yet, some fears can leave us paralyzed & hinder us from experiencing the abundant life that God desires for us to live.

When my son was a younger, he used to be terrified of the dark. When we would put him to bed every night he would ask for us to leave his closet light on and we always prayed God's armor and protection over him that he would not be afraid. It seems silly, but he feared being alone in a dark room. *"When I am afraid, I will put my trust in You."* -Psalm 56:3 is a verse that we would quote most nights at our house.

We can find so much freedom in our lives when we learn to put our trust in the Lord and in His perfect love. The "perfect love" that 1 John 4:18 speaks of is the love that our God has for us! God is so good to us and we can trust Him! Whatever your fear may be, identify it and lay it down at the foot of the cross! There is FREEDOM found in Christ. He wants to free us and deliver us from the bondage of our fears.

"I sought the Lord, and he answered me; he delivered me from all my fears." Psalm 34:4

Heavenly Father, I thank You that Your love is perfect, and that in You I can find freedom from the fears that the enemy throws my way. Help me to put my trust in You and to turn to You when I am afraid. May I find my security in You and in Your presence in my life. Help me live my life in complete surrender to You that I may have the freedom and abundant life that You desire for me to possess. Amen

Jennifer Mills and Rachel Lovingood, Longhollow Baptist Church

Week 10, Tuesday
We Can Draw Near to Him

"Draw near to God and He will draw near to you. Cleanse your hands, you sinners; and purify your hearts, you double-minded."

James 4:8

As you grow in your personal walk with the Lord you will find out more & more that your spiritual journey comes with its ups and downs. We've all experienced those "spiritual high" moments, maybe at a retreat, a conference, or at a youth camp, when we've experience the Lord so intimately that we just can't get enough of Him. As you look back in His Word, you'll see God's pursuit after his people throughout the Old Testament as they experienced moments like that with Him. There would be times when the Israelites were walking so closely with God, but then they would lose sight of Him. They'd begin to drift away, and their loyalty would be divided between God and the world. The Lord said in Isaiah 29:13, *"These people come near to me with their mouth and honor me with their lips, but their hearts are far from me. Their worship of me is based on merely human rules they have been taught."*

Doesn't this sound like many of us today? We're walking closely with him one moment then wondering off & our hearts far from Him the next. In those times, we must fall on our face before the Lord and confess our sins before Him and pursue that intimacy with our God once again. Our God loves us with a relentless love. He sent His only Son to be the atoning sacrifice for us so that we, as sinful man, can walk in intimacy with Him! Time after time of us failing Him, we find Him right there with us. He is there pursuing us because of His desire that we come near to Him & worship Him wholeheartedly!

So in those times in your personal walk with the Lord, when you may feel distant from Him, you need to stop & examine your heart and ask yourself who moved.

 Heavenly Father, I'm so grateful that You pursue me and that You desire to have an intimate relationship with me. Thank You for Jesus and that through Him; You provided a way to have a relationship with me. Thank You that even when I fail You, You are still there chasing after me. Help me to let go of the things of this world and chase after You. Amen.

Week 10, Wednesday
Holy Is Possible

As obedient children, do not conform to the evil desires you had when you lived in ignorance. But just as he who called you is holy, so be holy in all you do; for it is written: "Be holy, because I am holy.

1 Peter 1:14–16

Do you remember some of the toys you played with when you were younger? You acted a lot different than you do now. As you grow and mature physically, you naturally change and so does the way you act, think and talk. You don't have the same wants and desires that you had years ago and that's the way it is supposed to be.

When you became a Christian you were born again and started out as a spiritual baby. Hopefully you have been doing things like this daily devotion and learning and growing in your faith. That's good and normal. The problem comes when you get stuck in a rut spiritually and your growth gets stunted.

Verse 14 says that you shouldn't give in to the evil desires you had before, when you were ignorant or younger in your faith and yet many believers are confessing the same sin over and over and over. You may be still giving in to the things you did as a spiritual baby and it is stunting your growth.

We are called to be holy like God is holy. That means that we have got to get a handle on the sins that are dominating us. One of the most effective ways to rid yourself of certain sins is to think about them like God does. He hates sin. He loves you but He hates sin. The reason you keep going back to the same sin over and over is because you don't hate it enough. If you did you would avoid it.

Holiness is a pursuit. A process. But it is possible by the power of the Holy Spirit. Keep after it and be intentional about changing your mind about sin. Think like God. It's the first step toward holiness.

God thank You for loving me even though You hate my sin. Help me to think about my sin the same way You do. Take away my desire for anything that is not of You. I want to be holy because You are holy. Show me what that means.

Jennifer Mills and Rachel Lovingood, Longhollow Baptist Church

Week 10, Thursday
There Is Hope

*Therefore, prepare your minds for action; be self-controlled; set your hope fully
on the grace to be given you when Jesus Christ is revealed.*

1 Peter 1:13

If you want to win a contest whether athletic or otherwise, what do you do? You practice and prepare. If you want to win in your spiritual life you do the same thing-practice and prepare with what you know to do. You get back to the basics and really get to know the basics of faith.

These basics are found in Scripture and today's verse has some specific action steps you can take so that you can be a winner spiritually. Look at what 1 Peter says to do.

First you should prepare your mind for action. This is vital and involves things like knowing the Word of God, meditating or thinking about it and how it applies to your life. It also can be the voices you choose to listen to. Are you believing the lies that the world tells you or the Truth?

Secondly you need to be self-controlled. Right. You have to be intentional about denying the urges or desires you have that are not godly. The more that you refuse to give in to sinful desires, the stronger your faith will grow. Sometimes it means that you completely avoid situations that might cause certain temptations.

Thirdly you need to set your hope on grace. Think about what you have set your hope on lately. Grades? Looks? Popularity? Relationships? Possessions? The sad thing about all these is that they can be gone in the blink of an eye. When you choose to set your hope on the grace of God, it will never let you down or disappear on you. It was grace you were saved. That's good stuff and that's good news. Believe it and live it.

*God thank You that there is hope. Thank You that Your Word is practical
and shows me how to live my life. Help me prepare my mind for action and
be self-controlled. I choose to trust and hope in You and the grace You give
me.*

Week 10, Friday
No Waiting Period

But God demonstrates His own love toward us,
in that while we were still sinners, Christ died for us.

Romans 5:8

People in our society are not very good at waiting. Information comes to us at the blink of an eye and we tend to get frustrated when our browser takes more than a few seconds or the line at the drive through is slow.

It's funny that although we hate to wait in so many areas of our lives, many times we choose to wait in our relationship with the Lord. Have you ever found yourself thinking that you will 'wait' until you get your life straightened out or 'wait' until you can shake a certain sin to get serious about your walk with Christ?

Read Romans 5:8 again. There is no waiting period with Jesus. It was while we were sinners that he died for us—for you. There are no conditions that you have to get all cleaned up or straightened out before you start living for Christ or accept Him as your Savior. The truth is that you can't get yourself cleaned up or straightened out—that kind of power comes from the Holy Spirit who lives in you if you know Jesus.

That's good news! You don't have to do the impossible. God will take care of that for you if you are willing to surrender and let Him. Don't wait. Accept what he is offering you today. If you know Him, surrender and let Him do a work in you. If you have been waiting to be 'good enough' to be saved, wait no longer.

Father thank You that I can come to You right now, exactly the way I am. Please help me remember that it's not up to me to get my life all cleaned up first. Thank You Jesus for dying for me even though I am a sinner and help me live my life surrendered to Your Holy Spirit.

Rachel Lovingood, Longhollow Baptist Church

Week 10, Weekend
Possibility and Restoration

Search me, O God, and know my heart; try me, and know my anxieties;
and see if there is any wicked way in me, and lead me in the way everlasting.

Psalm 139:23, 24

Each of us was born with a human nature that goes our own way. We are born separated by our sin from a holy God. Each of us has fallen short of His perfection and that means we are disconnected from God. We become separated from the very One who most loves us and can help us.

Could you take the next few moments and ask God to reveal any areas in which you fall short of His perfection? Pray the Psalmist's prayer: Ask God to search your heart and reveal the things that you need to change. Could it be: anger; pride; selfishness; lying; arrogance; self-centeredness; being rude, disrespectful, or unkind; gossip; lust; unforgiveness; bitterness; sexual sin; insensitivity to others; judgmentalism; betrayal; being critical of others; withholding love; disobedience; coveting; filthy language; an ungrateful attitude; envy; jealousy; unacceptance; deception; a short temper; addiction; or theft? Confess these things to Him as He reveals them.

God, one area in which I fall short of Your standard is . . .

God, I ask for Your forgiveness. I know Jesus gave up His life for this sin in me. I ask You to forgive me and clean up my heart.

Part of why Jesus chose to go to the cross was because of what you and I have just named. He chose to take our sins upon Himself. God is certainly a God who is rich in mercy and He is a holy God. God is so holy that He cannot relate to sin in any form (Ephesians 2:4; Habakkuk 1:13). So rather than lose relationship with us, God restored the possibility of relationship by sacrificing His Son.

How does it make you feel to know that Jesus gave His life in order to lift these burdens and sins from your shoulders?

I feel _____ amazed/grateful/astounded as I think about how Jesus gave His life for my _____ (name one of the struggles you have just identified). I'm especially grateful because . . .

God, I am astounded by Your love for me. I feel unworthy at times, yet I choose to receive Your forgiveness. Amen.

Week 11, Monday
His Child

My son, do not despise the chastening of the LORD, nor detest His correction; for whom the LORD loves He corrects, just as a father the son in whom he delights.

Proverbs 3:11, 12

The idea of discipline and love being in the same sentence is a hard concept to swallow. Love is gushy and warm while discipline stirs up thoughts of losing your cell phone privileges or being grounded.

We think that love should always feel good and that discipline only produces pain, and we wonder how can pain be good for anybody. The truth is, pain can be very good. You see, pain is an indicator that things need to change. For example, if you didn't feel pain, then you might never know that you were critically sick before it was too late. Pain warns us of oncoming doom!

Just as our body uses pain to warn us of trouble, God does as well. The Bible states that God's ways and thoughts are not like ours. He sees things we cannot see and He knows things we cannot know. It is because of this that He disciplines us out of love.

When we were small we ran out into the street only to hear our parents scream for us to get out of it at once. For some of us the scream was enough . . . but for others the curiosity of the street was so strong that it took something more to see our error. It took a harsh scolding . . . It took pain. Without that reminder, the street could have been our destruction. Our parents' discipline was love to us in the form of pain. A warning sign that we were headed for a bad day.

Shouldn't we deal with spiritual and emotional pain the same way we deal with the physical? When hurt, we immediately try to do what it takes to get rid of the cause for pain. When emotionally or spiritually damaged, though, we blame God or say, "Why me!" When God allows pain in our life, He is warning us and wants us to diagnose and work on our problems. In your life right now, what is God saying to you? Are you going to become angry and blame Him or embrace the fact that He loves you and begin to work to fix the issues you are currently dealing with?

 God, reveal to me the things in my life that You want to change. Thank You for love in the form of discipline, and help me learn to embrace it. Amen.

Matt Bartig, First Baptist Church Orlando

Week 11, Tuesday
His Masterpiece

I will praise You, for I am fearfully and wonderfully made.

Psalm 139:14

It's hard to fathom that the God of the world who created us did it with fear. The idea of fear being in the makeup of our Father is a hard concept to swallow. God is strength, not fear, so why is it that when our creation was described in Psalm 139, the writer used the term *fear*? If you look at it in the Greek, you will find that *fear* has many meanings in this context. The first is a feeling of terror, but it goes on with descriptions like respect and honor. Isn't it amazing to think that God so wanted to make us just right that the concept of fear entered the equation? Can you imagine the way He thought about you as He formed your shape, your face, your inner self? He did it with such precision and care.

Sometimes in our life we don't like who we are very much, and it causes us to question the creation of the Maker. We listen to other people as they judge the masterpiece created by God, and we begin to believe that we are one of His flawed attempts.

Can you believe we would have the audacity to tell the God of the universe . . . "Hey, Your creation is ugly"? Yeah, me neither, but we do it every time we question why He made us the way He did.

The Bible states that God made you specifically, that He knows the hairs on your head, and that His plans for you are unique and awesome. He didn't just throw you together! He thought you out and sculpted you with such excellence that the emotion of fear filled His being.

That makes you pretty special, pretty wonderful—and fearfully perfect.

 God, teach me to remember that You made me like I am for a reason. Remind me that I am not a flawed creation, and help me to live in that confidence. Amen.

Matt Bartig, First Baptist Church Orlando

Week 11, Wednesday
His Reflection

"You are the light of the world . . . a city . . . set on a hill [that] cannot be hidden."

Matthew 5:14

In the Bible Jesus referenced the light of the world twice, once to describe Himself and the other time to describe us. If that is the case, then how can there be two lights? Light in this context is of Jesus describing His ability to lead us to eternal life. Obviously He is not giving us the ability to give people eternal life . . . or is He?

In our Earth's atmosphere God created the world with a unique nature. You see, the sun in our atmosphere is what shines to give us the light and the warmth. It is the main source of energy on our planet. If we didn't have the sun, we couldn't have life as we know it! The moon, on the other hand, is another of God's unique creations. It does not give off energy the way the sun does; however, it has been positioned and created to reflect the energy of the sun so that in our darkest times of the night we still have a small light to guide us on our way.

This world is a dark place when it comes to morality and a love for God. Millions of people are lost and wandering and looking for the path. Jesus is the life source for which they are searching, and we are His reflection! He has chosen you to be that small amount of light that will guide those who need a guide to get to Him.

Will you be that reflection? Sometimes in our life we tend to cover the reflection up. We get embarrassed at the fact that God is our Savior and we are His children.

We in essence take the "city lights" that could lead others, and we extinguish them because of our love for this world. Today as you go out, the challenge should be to reflect your Father and guide those who are lost to the only One who can help them be found.

 God, help me as I go out today to reflect You correctly! Please allow me to shine brightly and to not back down in fear, but instead to step forward in boldness! Thank You for making me a light. Amen.

Matt Bartig, First Baptist Church Orlando

Week 11, Thursday
Worth the Sacrifice

"For God so loved the world..."

John 3:16

The number 316 is a number that sports nuts see everywhere. You can't turn on the TV and watch a baseball game, football game, or any other American sporting event and not see some crazed person waving his cardboard thoughts through the air. Why "316," though? Why is that number so precious, important... needed?

The number 316 tells us about who we are in God's heart. It's a number that represents true love, sacrificial love, and a love that shows us we are of great value to God.

You see, 316 comes out of the book of John, where God states that He so loved us He traded the greatness of His Son, and the life of His Son, in order that we might have life.

Can you imagine taking the person you love most in your life right now and trading their life for a group of people? I doubt that any of us would be quick to do that. I imagine that we could find a thousand reasons not to, and a thousand more replacements to take our loved one's place. The reason for that is nothing is worth the sacrifice of the one we love most... nothing!

God, in His incredible wisdom, weighed the option, considered His love for Jesus, looked at the depravity of mankind, and said, "These people are worth the sacrifice."

This world can be pretty lonely and at times we can feel very unloved, unwanted, and unaccepted by our peers, family, and friends.

It's in these times that we must remember in God's heart we were worth the ultimate sacrifice! God released His most prized possession for you, and He did it with great anticipation of the relationship He would have with you!

Take up confidence in who you are! A great price has been given for you! You are worth the sacrifice to Your Father!

God, help me to never forget the price that You paid for me. Allow me to always see clearly the sacrifice You made on my behalf. God, thank You for sending Jesus on my behalf and giving me life! Amen.

Matt Bartig, First Baptist Church Orlando

Week 11, Friday
His Possession

For you were bought at a price.

1 Corinthians 6:20

The idea of slavery leaves a very solemn taste in our mouth. It brings forth ideas of abuse and destroyed lives. It's interesting, then, that God tells us in His Word that we are called to be slaves to Him.

When God paid the ultimate price of His Son for us, we became His possession, and as this verse states, we are not our own anymore. This concept is hard for many of us because we have the idea of having the world and a "little" Jesus too. The idea of Jesus being at the center of everything scares many of us and actually sends some of us running.

Does God really require us to be His slave? The true term is actually *bondservant*. A bondservant in the Bible was a person who had voluntarily (for various reasons of debt) given control of his/her life to another person. The term was usually for seven years and it went as follows:

> The bondservant had a chain around their ankle that attached to a post. In the morning the owner would go out and place the bondservant where he wanted him. The bondservant would then work where the master placed him for that day's entirety. At the end of the day the master would then go to the workplace and retrieve his possession and return the servant back to his living quarters.

This bondservant was the sole possession of the owner and he realized it. He didn't fight the master but instead saw the generosity of the owner and gladly paid his debt.

As a Christian do you really see the generosity of your Master? Are you overcome with gratitude for what God did? Have you become a complacent person who sees the free gift of salvation as something you should expect? If so, that is a dangerous place to find yourself. If you lack gratitude, then nothing holds the bondservant at home and you will tend to wander. How tied to the Master are you right now? Have you given up claim to your life out of a deep desire to serve the One who gave you life to the full?

God, as I go through today, help me to remember that I am Yours. Allow me the ability to walk in such a way that would bring glory to Your great name and be a witness of Your love to those around me. Amen.

Matt Bartig, First Baptist Church Orlando

Week 11, Weekend
It Begins with Love

Taste and see that the Lord is good; blessed is the man who trusts in Him.

Psalm 34:8

Good news can be hard to find. Did you hear the news today? Check out a news site? Hear the latest forecast? There probably wasn't much "good" news to be found. God actually has some great news to share—it's just a matter of whether or not we are listening.

The Good News is the story of God's loving intervention in human history through the person of Jesus. His life, death, and resurrection allowed each of us to enter into an intimate, close relationship with God that will last forever.

Isn't it amazing how this good news—the best news—begins with love. And unlike most human love, God's love is completely unconditional. It's unlike anything in this world. You see, Christ's divine passion to relate to you and enter your world isn't based on anything that you have done or could do in the future. Nothing you do can ever earn God's love. And nothing can disqualify you.

The Good News of God's story is about Christ, who took the initiative and entered our world when we were helpless, unable to even ask for help, and showed us grace. Christ died for you in spite of your sin because He wanted to give you a gift . . . a way back to God! God's offer for relationship is a gift. And like any gift, we must decide whether or not to accept it. Take the next few moments to meditate on His love for you. Quiet your thoughts and imagine God saying to you:

I have great news! My love has no conditions or expectations.
There's nothing you can do to earn My love. And there's nothing you can do to lose My love.
There's no expiration date, no hoops to jump through, and no requirements to fulfill.
I love you. Period.
This Good News is My gift. All you have to do is accept it!

What part of God's good news or unconditional love means the most to you and why?

The part of God's good news/unconditional love that means the most to me is . . .

 God, thank You for offering Your love to me with no strings attached. I am especially grateful to You because of the good news that . . . Amen.

Week 12, Monday
Give It a Break

"But you shall destroy their altars, break their sacred pillars...."

Exodus 34:13

We are in God's heart. Truthfully, we've always been there. Sadly, we don't experience this soul-stirring truth as real, because we have a distorted image of God, which needs to be smashed.

Christianity is a steady process of *growing beyond* seeing God as an uncaring, indifferent, overly judgmental, score-keeping, constantly angry God who makes up rules that we can't possibly keep. It's a journey of tearing down an image of God that is ticked off at a certain sin—a God who is always looking to cut us off from Him at even the slightest presence of a mistake.

A false image of God was the struggle of many people of the Old Testament. They were constantly trying to reduce God to their own image and attempt to control Him while resisting the real image of God. Even when God revealed Himself, they did not recognize or hear Him.

This is precisely why Jesus stepped into human history—to show us the true image of God. Through His miracles, message, and ministry, Jesus reveals God to be extravagantly generous, excessively loving, a canceller of debt, a seeker of stray hearts, and a listener to prayers. Jesus gives us the true image of a God who forgives rather than condemns, fulfills rather than coerces, and frees rather than constrains.

Breaking up with our false images of God may be painful, but it has to be done.

We must smash our illusions of God. Slam them to the ground. Shatter them to pieces. When our untrue image of God dies, our untrue images of ourselves die with it.

 Lord, I admit I want to make my own decisions and run my own life. I have had a tendency to reinvent God into someone I can live with, to create an image of God who can coexist with my pride and my preferences. In this quiet moment, show me who You really are. I need the help of the Holy Spirit to confront and destroy every false image I've held of God. Give me courage. Lead me into experiencing the truth of who You really are. Amen.

David Edwards, David Edwards Productions

Week 12, Tuesday
Develop a Holy Hunger

O God, you are my God; early will I seek You; my soul thirsts for You; my flesh longs for You; in a dry and thirsty land where there is no water.

Psalm 63:1

Developing a hungry heart after God is an intentional pursuit. The journey is tough. The competition for our heart is fierce: phone, Internet, television, classes, projects, friends, money, things, work, and fun. When we crave everything, we end up with nothing. The noise and confusion of a crowded heart can block our access to Him.

Hungering for the presence of God begins by realizing that our whole destiny depends on our friendship with Jesus. What will we do to maintain contact? To what extent will we go to nurture this relationship? Will we overcome personal habits that threaten our connection with Jesus? Will we deal with that which might displease Him?

We must come to Him in total honesty. Hungering speaks of longing, yearning, waiting for His presence to fill our souls, turning to His Word and hearing Him speak life into our dry and weary places.

The quality test of our hunger is: Does it impact our choices, beliefs, perspective of our culture, and response to adversity? Do we crave what God craves? Has a holy hunger profoundly shaped us? As each day passes, do we find ourselves less distracted by the competition of our lives? This holy hunger forces us to see that it is God alone who must occupy our hearts. False hungers and shallow cravings do not feed our soul. On the contrary, they starve it.

Do we know the passionate thrill of loving the crucified Christ?

Today, isolate a competing hunger. Give it up for a week. See if a holy hunger for His presence in your soul begins to increase.

Lord, I have wanted so many things. My appetite for the things of this world has taken me to a place where I have reached for things that were not that important, while disregarding the things that matter to You. Create in me a thirst to seek You like a desperate person looking for water in the desert. Amen.

Week 12, Wednesday
Stop Trying and Start Trusting

The grace of our Lord was exceedingly abundant, with faith and love which are in Christ Jesus.

1 Timothy 1:14

There comes a time in a believer's life when we are awakened to the reality that the Christian walk isn't dependent upon us, but only on Jesus. Great is the moment when we truly understand that success in our relationship with Jesus has nothing to do with our best efforts. Were it not for Jesus we would have no hope. All we can do is trust.

One of the greatest examples of strong trust is the thief who hung next to Jesus on the cross. Tradition says that his name was Dismas. He was known as a villain, rogue, and outlaw. Having done the acts that come with such titles, he had been found guilty in all courts. But in a moment of incredible, unrestrained trust, he cried out, "Lord, remember me when You come into Your Kingdom," to which Jesus replied, "This day you will be with Me in paradise."

Think of it. One act of trust canceled out a lifetime of crime. Once a thief, he was delivered into the Kingdom in a single moment of trust.

Look at the cross. See that Jesus' love is not like our love. We are full of revenge and selfishness. We love only those who love us. Jesus' death on the cross was not a shining, pristine moment like our jewelry portrays. He was broken, ripped, cut, covered in blood, and spat upon, yet the cross was the pinnacle of the affection, acceptance, and love God has for us.

Trust increases through our personal effort. It is given to us. He is our trust. We are told only to look to Him. God's love for us is always there. We need only to turn to Him. Trust comes when we realize He is fully pleased with us. The disturbing message of trust is that it is not about us. It is about Him.

 Dear Lord, today I push my trust to the brink. I know I cannot generate my own trust, so I look to You. I lean the full weight of my life onto You, and I receive the love You have for me.

David Edwards, David Edwards Productions

Week 12, Thursday
Know His Kindness

But when the kindness and love of God our Savior toward man appeared....

Titus 3:4

Kindness is both simple and profound. On the surface, although kindness appears to make God out as a pushover, He is not to be looked upon as a heavenly grandfather that can be used and manipulated. Kindness is not at the outer edge of God. It is at the core of His identity.

Through the dark corridor, into the drab convent cells of San Marco at Florence, Friar Angelicose painted the sweet angelic faces of heaven on barren walls to calm the spirits of those who looked upon them. The frescoes were intended to help monks know that God dwelt with them. The holy inspiration of this artistic genius produced a work of the kindness of God. The friar painted, not in the sanctuary, but in dark places where we might least anticipate it.

It is within the cells of our souls where we expect to find God's cold, hard judgment and condemnation. Yet, instead we find the kindness of God, unexpected and undeserved. This is the very definition of the kindness of God. A King of all creation has stooped into the darkened prison of our pride to paint us with His favor and love.

Forgiveness is bound tightly to kindness. Without forgiveness, kindness cannot exist. It is through God's forgiveness that we are reunited, accepted, and received as we are by God. In our private struggles, we find God is unflinchingly faithful to us. Only when we are sure of His relentless kindness, can we live confidently.

Lord, I welcome You now into this place to fill it with Your presence. Awaken every part of me so I will know that You are closer than I ever thought. The prayer of my heart speaks, "Only You, Jesus. Only You, Jesus." You are here every moment. When I feel condemned, You make me righteous. When I am lonely, You increase Your presence. When I fail, You help me to return. When I am tempted, You strengthen me. When I fall, I fall toward You. When I despair, You give me grace. Regardless of what I feel, no matter what I am going through, I know You are here and I will be alright. Amen.

Week 12, Friday
So Be Happy

I know whom I have believed and am persuaded that He is able....

2 Timothy 1:12

Our culture defines happiness as a euphoric feeling from problems solved, needs met, and hopes and dreams fulfilled. When everything goes the way we want, we have been led to believe that happiness means that life has to go according to our liking. If it doesn't, we feel rejected, defeated, and ripped off. Then we spend our time complaining about how unfair life is. We have forgotten that because we are in God's heart, we find happiness from a source greater than people and possessions.

The living presence of Jesus is at work in our lives. He is building us through all things good and bad. We can believe it. God wants our lives to work. We can be convinced that He is at work. Happiness means that we can look at our circumstances and not lose faith, because our happiness is based on God's ability.

So be happy, not in the petty, fleeting moments offered to you by the world, but by focusing your head and your heart on the things Jesus has done for you.

He changed you: Christ abolished death and established life. In fact, the worst day of being alive is much better than the best day of being dead. You're not dead. He brought His life to you and changed you. You now belong to God and nothing can change that. How could you not be happy?

He called you: There is meaning in your life. Coursing through your body is the purpose and the promise of God. If you are unsure of this, read the call of Jeremiah (Jeremiah 1.) God knows why you are here and so should you.

He cares for you: It is God who watches over every part of your life, and it is He who empowers you to accomplish that which is in front of you. Our happiness comes from knowing that God is God and believing that He is able.

Dear Jesus, today I choose to believe that You have not only changed me, but called me and continue to care for me. And I believe You are positively responding with Your ability to the details of my life. My happiness is in You. Amen.

David Edwards, David Edwards Productions

Week 12, Weekend
He Moved First!

I will remember the works of the LORD.

Psalm 77:11

Can you think of a time when someone else's actions caused discomfort or trouble for you, even though you did nothing to deserve it? Or can you recall a time when someone else's actions resulted in good things for you and you did nothing to deserve their kindness?

God's good news story is very much like that. In the Garden of Eden, Adam's one act of disobedience brought sin into the world and caused all of humanity to be separated from God. In beautiful contrast, Jesus' one act of obedience allowed each of us to enter into a loving relationship with God.

Imagine that God watched with grief and sadness when you and I were born . . . because we were born into this world where He and Adam once shared a fantastic friendship. The world was perfect then—their relationship was perfect. But because of Adam's sin, the world became different.

God longed to relate to us, just as intimately as He once did with Adam. He wanted to enjoy hanging out with us, but that wasn't possible. This close, intimate relationship with God wasn't possible because from the very first moments of our life, we have chosen to live a life apart from God.

Because God loved us even in our sinfulness, and because He knew that we were powerless to find our way back into a right relationship with Him, He took the initiative by sending Jesus to earth so that we all might receive life through Him. He wanted to enjoy a deep closeness with us, so God took the initiative. He made the first move to show us His love! How does it make you feel to consider what God has done for you? Is your heart moved that He has:

- Noticed your need?
- Took action because of His love for you?
- Been so moved with compassion that He died for you?
- Gone first to meet your need?
- Wanted so badly to relate to you?

Remember some of the things the Lord has done for you. Be sure to tell Him how you feel.

God, You are great because You took the initiative to give to us. You are great because You didn't wait until I noticed You; You gave first. I am amazed because You gave up Your Son so that I could relate with You. Amen.

Week 13, Monday
Perfectly Imperfect

Simon Peter, a bondservant and apostle of Jesus Christ . . .

2 Peter 1:1a

Talk about a turn-around story. A young, unpredictable fisherman named Simon one day met Jesus and his life was changed. This part of the story is obvious, but do we realize everything that went on through Simon's journey?

Think about this in your own life. You may have not had the best beginning, or you may be thinking that you want God to use you, but you are the wrong person! Look at Simon's life for encouragement. Simon was unstable—in his speech (he was always talking during the most inappropriate times), in his life (remember, he denied Jesus three times), and in his commitment (he deserted Jesus during His trial). However, Jesus changed his name from Simon to Peter (*Petros*). *Petros* means "rock." Jesus gave an unstable man a name of stability.

After Jesus' resurrection Peter would be the one who addressed the crowd at Pentecost (Acts 2). Peter would be the one to carry the message of Christ to Cornelius (Acts 10). Now, we read that this rock has two letters included in the Bible! The point of this is to realize that if you think you are the wrong person, God is searching for you. Throughout Scripture there are illustrations of this. Moses, who could not speak, was called to be a spokesperson. David, who was overlooked by his own father as a potential king, was victorious over Goliath. Mary, an unwed teenage girl, was chosen to be the mother of the Messiah!

As you begin this week, thank God for placing you in the perfect position to be the most unlikely person to make an impact for His Kingdom. Do not look at today in drudgery, but in expectation of God setting you off on an incredible journey!

Father, I thank You for Your sovereignty. I do not understand all that is going on, but I trust in You. Thank You for my circumstances, my opportunities, and my future. You will not leave me how I am, but You are constantly changing me into Your image. As Your Word says, I will fear no evil but trust in You. Amen.

Scott Dawson, Scott Dawson Evangelistic Association

Week 13, Tuesday
Precious Faith

To those who have obtained like precious faith with us by the righteousness
of our God and Savior Jesus Christ: grace and peace be multiplied
to you in the knowledge of God and of Jesus our Lord.

2 Peter 1:1b, 2

What is your most valuable possession? Older people would sometimes think of a home, a car, or even a memento, but there is something much more valuable than temporal items. In this chapter of Scripture, Peter puts a great amount of emotion in his writing. Notice the term *precious* as he addresses his faith. Do you consider your faith "precious"?

This term indicates the placement of a significant amount of worth in an item. Our greatest asset in this world is not something that can be easily taken away from us. Wealth comes and goes very quickly in this world, as does the stuff we buy with our wealth. Even reputations can be tarnished very quickly if built upon public opinions. So, what is the most valuable asset you possess? To me it is my faith. Just like Peter's, it is "precious" in that nothing can replace it nor can anything compare with it.

Peter addresses where his faith comes from: not from personal opinion or merit, but through the righteousness of Christ. A "precious" faith is built on a personal relationship with Jesus. Not hanging out with people who know Him, or even by hearing about Him, but knowing Him personally. If there has not been a life change taking place in your life, receive Christ today. Right now. There is no better time to receive this "precious faith" than right now.

When you do know Him, He gives you "grace and peace." Peter uses a Greek participle, *dia*, which means "through the means of." It is through a relationship with Christ that grace and peace will be multiplied to you. When you have grace, you will always have peace. Even during the turbulent times of life, God grants us peace "through" our relationship with Christ.

Father, today I commit my life to You. I know You love me; help me to love You. Thank You for the grace and peace that comes to me by knowing You personally. Thank You for the life change that is found in Jesus. Help me to share You today. Amen.

Scott Dawson, Scott Dawson Evangelistic Association

Week 13, Wednesday
Stay on Course

As His divine power has given to us all things that pertain to life and godliness, through the knowledge of Him who called us by glory and virtue, by which have been given to us exceedingly great and precious promises, that through these you may be partakers of the divine nature, having escaped the corruption that is in the world through lust.

2 Peter 1:3, 4

Recently I found myself in a new city with a deadline to be at a certain location. When the plane touched down and the rental car was chosen, I was en route to this important meeting. It was here that I was thankful for a little-known device called GPS. I am not the smartest person in the world, but I am smart enough to know when I need help. After typing the address into the system, I was taken directly to the building for the appointment.

Wouldn't life be so much easier if we had a GPS system for all the important decisions in life? It seems that if I could find a navigation system, I would even take a map to help make the most important decisions in life. It would be so much easier. Well, according to Scripture, we have such an asset. Notice what Peter is saying in this letter: "having escaped the corruption . . ." The term *escaped* is used as a navigational opportunity. Through the power of the Holy Spirit, He actually guides you to safety through life.

I want you to look at these verses carefully today. He has given us "all things that pertain to life and godliness . . ." This means you lack nothing. There is no power on earth that can move you from the destination that He has set you on. Stay on course. Just like with the GPS system, I could have made a detour and gone my own way. However, I needed to stay on course.

Second, He has given us "great and precious promises." This refers to our confidence during the journey. He will not send you where He does not want you to go! Finally, you will "escape the corruption." Firmly fix your faith on Him and let Him guide you today!

Father, thank You for the mighty power of Your Spirit. Guide me today through the journey and help me trust Your path for my life. Amen.

Week 13, Thursday
Eight Keys

But also for this very reason, giving all diligence, add to your faith virtue, to virtue knowledge, to knowledge self-control, to self-control perseverance, to perseverance godliness, to godliness brotherly kindness, and to brotherly kindness love.

2 Peter 1:5–7

Eight keys to maturity. You would think it would be much harder, but Peter addresses the vital steps in his letter. However, in order to be mature you must have all eight. Four, five, or even seven are not enough. Let me give you an example. Suppose you were waiting on an operation and the surgeon explained that he had six of the eight needed aspects of the procedure, but he was going to perform it anyway. As crazy as that sounds, many believers are walking around trying to get by with as little as they can instead of experiencing the fullness of the Christian life.

Here are the eight keys: faith, virtue, knowledge, self-control, perseverance, godliness, brotherly kindness, and love. We spend a lifetime discovering these keys, but today allow me to introduce them to you. It all begins with the faith that is given through Christ. In your relationship with Him, He gives you the sustaining faith for the journey. Virtue is built upon your faith. Virtue is considered "moral excellence" in Scripture. As a follower of Christ, we do not accept the standard; we set a standard according to Him.

Then upon virtue we have knowledge. Knowledge is more than the accumulation of facts; it is having the wisdom to act upon those facts. It is more than a straight-A report card; it is being the type of person who knows how to place this in living out your faith. Then comes self-control and perseverance. Both of these refer to not taking shortcuts in daily disciplines, to being the type of person who finishes the race of faith. Godliness—that means what it says. Be more like Jesus tomorrow than you are today.

Finally, brotherly kindness and love. Be the type of person who looks at people as souls instead of flesh and bone. We do not use people to get what we want, but we love them as Christ does. Eight keys to maturity—go for it!

    Father, I am on a journey of faith. Please develop in me all eight of these characteristics. I want You to be my standard and not the world. Amen.

Week 13, Friday
These Things

For if these things are yours and abound, you will be neither barren nor unfruitful in the knowledge of our Lord Jesus Christ. For he who lacks these things is shortsighted, even to blindness, and has forgotten that he was cleansed from his old sins. Therefore, brethren, be even more diligent to make your call and election sure, for if you do these things you will never stumble. . . .

2 Peter 1:8–10

The Christian life is not boring. Anyone who thinks it is probably has not experienced the eight characteristics we looked at yesterday. Think about it. Peter says in this passage that "If these things are yours . . . you will be neither barren. . . ." The word *barren* refers to being idle. If you are busy about building your life upon "these things," which are those eight characteristics, you will not have time to be bored in the Christian life.

The second myth Peter debunks is when Christians say they just don't get what life is all about. He quickly states that if "these things" are not present in your life, you will be shortsighted or even blind. When sight is impaired there is no focus. My wife almost lost her sight in 2008, and I remember the trials we faced. I can only imagine how a believer must feel when they are blinded to the things of God. Build on these things to have a clear sight during foggy times of life.

The final myth Peter hits is when a Christian says that he or she simply cannot live for Christ. Look at the last words, "For if you do these things you will never stumble." These things are those eight key aspects that are necessary for a mature believer. When you are focused on the task at hand, you will not be swayed to follow after stupid things. Instead of thinking you can't live the Christian life, why don't you focus on allowing Christ to live through you by building on "these things"?

Father, today I do not want excuses to control my life. I want to be complete in You. Develop me into a mature follower. Please allow these things to take prominence in my life. I ask that You focus me in to You and Your work so I can be productive for Your use. Amen.

Scott Dawson, Scott Dawson Evangelistic Association

Week 13, Weekend
Anytime, Anywhere

*Now hope does not disappoint, because the love of God has
been poured out in our hearts by the Holy Spirit who was given to us.*

Romans 5:5

God increased the closeness of His relationship with us by coming to earth in the person of Jesus. Jesus lived among other men and women, talking with them one-on-one, sharing meals with them, doing life together, and revealing His feelings to them. But God's plan for increasing the closeness of His relationship with us did not end there.

When Jesus died on the cross and raised from the dead three days later, these miraculous events restored the possibility of a close relationship with God by dealing with our sinfulness. They also enabled a deeper closeness and intimacy with God because He was able to send the Holy Spirit to dwell within us.

This means that God doesn't just relate to us as a Father who looks down on us from heaven, nor even as a gentle friend who walks among us as Jesus did. Rather, if we have accepted God's gift of salvation, God lives within us as part of our very being. By the Holy Spirit, He is not only with us; He is in us and is thus available to love, comfort, encourage, correct, and guide us anywhere at any time.

Here are just some of the blessings that are available to you because of God's Spirit. If His Spirit lives inside you, because you have received God's gift of salvation:

- He will never leave you alone (Matthew 28:20).
- He will be your Helper and your Counselor (John 14:16; 16:7).
- He will strengthen you (Philippians 4:13).
- The Spirit can help you in your weaknesses (Romans 8:26).
- The Spirit intercedes for you—He prays for you! (Romans 8:26).

Stop and consider these amazing blessings that are available to you through God's Holy Spirit. Which of the blessings give you the most hope?

As I consider the blessings that are available through the Holy Spirit, I am most glad to know that . . .

*God, thank You for the gift of Your Son and the gift of the Holy Spirit. It's
these gifts that give me hope for . . . Amen.*

Week 14, Monday
Love on a Plate

*And being found in appearance as a man, He humbled Himself and
became obedient to the point of death, even the death of the cross.*

Philippians 2:8

Have you ever eaten dinner off a plate that is considered fine china? If not, that's okay because most people haven't. Eating dinner off expensive dishes requires a very special occasion and the company to be very special people. You won't see fine china at a backyard cookout or a picnic in the park. However, what you will see being used at all of these functions are paper plates. Paper plates are an easy cleanup and easily disposed of. Paper plates are cheap. In the same way, many people feel like their worth is the same as a paper plate. They are cheap and easily tossed away when they get dirty. It seems like no one cares to help when you make a mess of your life. But there is hope. There was a special occasion that took place over 2,000 years ago where God invited very special guests to be served on His finest china.

According to Romans 5:8, God shows His love for us in that while we were still sinners, Christ died for us.

Can you believe that? God's special guests are sinners like you and me. God, even though we rejected Him, allowed His finest piece of china to be broken for you and me. He chose to serve up His Son to the cross of Calvary and go on record as to how much He loves you.

Isaiah 53:5 tells us, "But He was wounded for our transgressions, He was bruised for our iniquities; the chastisement of our peace was upon Him and by His stripes we are healed."

When you are in the presence of God, you are in very special company. His love toward you is not paper thin. His value on your life is worth more than a paper plate.

*Dear Lord, I know that I am a sinner and my life feels like it is worth
nothing. I know You would never throw me away. Please forgive me for all
my sin and disobedience. I surrender my heart and life to You. You are my
Lord, and I belong to You now. Take me and use me for Your glory. Amen.*

If this is your first time to ever pray a prayer like that, tell someone!

Joey Hill, Scott Dawson Evangelistic Association

Week 14, Tuesday
All Access

Then Jesus said to them again, "Most assuredly, I say to you, I am the door of the sheep."

John 10:7

It is amazing how many doors we walk through every day, isn't it? Some walk through front doors, car doors, back doors, and side doors. We even have pet doors for our pets. Our culture is a culture of doors. We like our doors. We like having access to things. One thing we hate are closed doors. We can't stand to be locked out and we certainly don't take to kindly to a door being slammed in front of us.

Adam and Eve in the Garden of Eden had the most amazing door open. They had an ALL-ACCESS door to God and nirvana, a perfect peace and place to live. But something happened in the Garden.

Genesis 3:1 says, "Now the serpent was more cunning than any beast of the field which the Lord God had made. And he said to the woman, 'Has God indeed said, "You shall not eat of every tree of the garden"?'"

On this day, Adam and Eve spoke for all of mankind. They took the door of ALL ACCESS to God and slammed it in His face. They turned their back on this door, on this relationship, and they tried to find their own door because they thought that would lead to an even better life. So they did their own thing. And the Bible tags this behavior as sin. That's what it's called: sin. We slammed the door in God's face, and we deserve the wrath of God.

So the question here is: What value does your life have in the heart of God? Simple. When we said no, He put a big yes on our no! He didn't give up on us. Jesus on the cross ripped open a door that had been slammed in the Garden of Eden, and it is now open again with all access for anyone who would come through it.

Like a shepherd who would literally lie down in the doorway to protect his sheep, Jesus laid down His life and is now our all-access door to God. That is how much value that is tagged to you. We are worth an emphatic yes even when we say no.

 Enter that door today and pray for God to open up doors that need to be opened in your life and in your heart.

Week 14, Wednesday
God Is Hoooge!

"To whom then will you liken Me, or to whom shall I be equal?" says the
Holy One. Lift up your eyes on high, and see who has created these things, who
brings out their host by number; He calls them all by name, by the greatness of
His might and the strength of His power; not one is missing.

Isaiah 40:25

A three-year-old girl came in from Vacation Bible School smiling from ear to ear. She looked up at her dad and just kept smiling. He asked her what was she smiling about, but she didn't say a word. Finally he asked her to give it up. What was she so giddy about? The little girl finally broke the silence and said, "Daddy, guess what?" "What?" he asked. She said, "God is HOOOGE!" He said, "What?" She said, with passion, "God is HOOOGE!" The father, not understanding her undeveloped language, asked her if she was trying to say "God is huge," to which she replied with an emphatic "YES!" The father was so convicted how he had known this truth about God for most of his life and yet never shared in the wonderment he just saw in his own daughter's eyes.

To whom will we compare God? Who is His equal? When you begin to think about such things as what we read in Isaiah, it becomes kind of crazy to think we could actually dodge or fake out God. Who are we that He would even be thinking about us? He doesn't even need us, yet we read where we are on His mind.

Psalm 8:3–4 tells us: "When I consider Your heavens, the work of Your fingers, the moon and the stars, which You have ordained, what is man that You are mindful of him, and the son of man that You visit him?"

Ask yourself this question: *Do I really show up on God's radar?* We are talking about a God who knitted together your DNA. A God who knows your thoughts before you think them. Rest in this comfort today: a God from whom nothing is hidden is also a God who desires an intimate relationship with you on a personal level.

Take some time today to pray and thank God for how hoooge He is.
Thank Him for what He knows about you and the fact that He still loves
you. Don't let this world tell you different!

Joey Hill, Scott Dawson Evangelistic Association

Week 14, Thursday
Reflections

What then shall we say to these things? If God is for us, who can be against us?

Romans 8:31

If you had to describe God in one word, what would it be? What word would the Bible use? When you consider every scripture that pertains to describing who God is and how He feels about us, there is only one word that will do. *Generosity!*

When you read John 3:16 you are looking deep into the heart of God. When you read Romans 8:31 you can't help but get an obvious picture of how He feels toward you. Think about it. God is for you. God is for all of us. A lot of times we have a difficult time accepting that and swallowing that fact. God is for us. He wants us to have a life of excitement, adventure, vitality, and fun. Living the Christian life is the best way to live.

God is a God who wants us, who desperately desires us to live for His glory. We, as followers of Christ, need to be God-hearted. We need to reflect the majesty of who God is. If we know God personally, we should mirror who He is. We should have His character qualities; we should reflect the stuff that God is about. We should understand the fact that everything we have comes from God—our gifts, our aptitudes, our abilities, even the material stuff that we have. And because God has given it to us, we should reflect that.

Romans 8:32 says, "He who did not spare His own Son, but delivered Him up for us all, how shall He not with Him also freely give us all things?"

Our God is a God who is generous. He spared not even His own Son for us. How much more does He intend to bless us if we just trust Him? Since we are the recipients of His generosity, we should reflect what we have received. One of the greatest values that could ever be given to you as a person is for God to entrust His name to your care. Do you reflect His name? Do you reflect to others the heart of God?

 Take some time today and pray. Ask God to help you reflect the same generosity He has shown to you. Take how God has blessed you and become a blessing to someone else.

Week 14, Friday

Carry the Name

*Jesus answered and said to him, "Most assuredly, I say to you,
unless one is born again, he cannot see the kingdom of God."*

John 3:3

Vietnam is one of the world's few remaining Communist nations. Though Vietnam's constitution provides for freedom of worship, the government continues to restrict organized activities of many religious groups. Unregistered churches and ethnic minority Christians suffer outright persecution. In spite of all this, a recent returning missionary from Vietnam shared something very special. He said that in spite of the persecution, the church in Vietnam is growing by leaps and bounds. The Vietnamese people, knowing they are putting their lives in danger, are still coming to Christ. But here is what is so amazing. He said that when a Vietnamese comes to Christ, they will actually change their name to signify they have been born again. Wow!

Second Corinthians 5:17 tells us: "Therefore, if anyone is in Christ, he is a new creation; old things have passed away; behold, all things have become new."

If you have been born again in Christ, you were given a new name to carry with you the rest of your life. This is not saying you should change your actual name to be Jesus' disciple, but if you have surrendered your life to Christ, you answer to a different name that is above every other name. How valuable we must be when we not only get the honor of bearing His name, but we get the privilege of carrying His name to the ends of the earth.

In Acts 9:15–16, the Lord said to him, "Go, for he is a chosen vessel of Mine to bear My name before Gentiles, kings, and the children of Israel. For I will show him how many things he must suffer for My name's sake."

Just like Saul of Tarsus, who would later become the apostle Paul, we are a chosen instrument to carry the name of God to the ends of the world. We are very important couriers carrying a very important name, and we have been chosen for such a mission. God has singled you out for such a great task. You are something special when you carry the holy name of God.

Pray today that God will remind you of the name you carry, and no matter where you go, no matter how dark the darkness, that you would carry the name of Jesus with you.

Joey Hill, Scott Dawson Evangelistic Association

Week 14, Weekend
Incredible Value

For You [God] meet him [us] with the blessings of goodness.

Psalm 21:3

Jesus' sacrifice on the cross served as a declaration of our immense value and worth in God's eyes. Because God created you and you bear His image, He has the right to declare your value—just as the government has the right to declare the value of currency that it produces and marks with its unique images. By sending Jesus to earth to die for you, God declared that you are worth the life of His only Son. Imagine that these words are coming straight from Jesus as He talks with you:

- You are especially valuable to Me. You represent My thoughts, My personality, and what's important to Me. You are important to Me. I gave My life for you.
- You are especially valuable to Me because I cherish our relationship. I see how much you love others, and I smile when I think about how that's only a fraction of the love I have for you. After all, I gave My life for you.
- I would risk My life to save you. In fact, I did. I gave My life for you. I saw that you were in danger of being separated from Me forever, so I chose to die for you.
- You've been through so much. I want you to know that I love you and I'm here for you. You're not alone.

God's declaration of your worth is mighty, awesome, and powerful! It's personal—just for you. It's the best news we could ever hear!

Since God has declared your worth at Calvary and sent His Son to die in your place, how do you respond to Him? Could you give your life to the One who has distinctively placed His mark on you that reads: "Worth the gift of My Son"? Could you follow a God like that? Could you declare that you belong to Jesus?

Talk to an adult, pastor, or older student who loves Jesus and can be excited with you about these things. Ask any questions that come to your mind and heart. Talk to them about your response to God's goodness!

God, I am humbled by Your declaration of my worth. Thank You for sending Your Son to pay my debt. I am in awe of Your goodness to me. Amen.

Terri Snead, The Great Commandment Network

Week 15, Monday
The Gift of Influence

But you are a chosen generation, a royal priesthood, a holy nation, His own special people,
that you may proclaim the praises of Him who called you out of darkness into His marvelous light.

1 Peter 2:9

Everyone loves getting a gift. Whether it's for a birthday or Christmas, we are all filled with excitement when we see a wrapped gift with our name attached to it. It's hard to keep from tearing through the paper in anticipation of seeing what's inside. What's inside could be that special something that is going to make life better.

You have a gift inside of you. This gift was intended to help make your life and the lives of those around you better. This isn't a gift for you to keep; it's a gift for you to share. This gift is called *influence,* which leads to impact and life change.

Influence is the ability to have an effect on the character, development, or behavior of someone or something. Jesus came and "dwelt among us" (John 1:14). He was 100 percent God and 100 percent man. He lived a sinless life. Then He willingly gave up His life for us on the cross. But it didn't stop there; three days later He wasn't dead anymore. This perfect life allowed Jesus to have an everlasting influence on people He came in contact with: Peter and Andrew (John 1:40–42), the Samaritan woman (John 4), the adulterous woman (John 8), and a man born blind (John 9). That same influence Jesus had on people over 2,000 years ago is the same eternal gift of influence He desires to have with you.

Jesus has called us out of darkness and into His marvelous light. The influence He has in our lives empowers us to influence the lives of others. He has chosen us to be His hands, to be His feet, to be His mouth, and to be His eternal influence.

Thank You, God, for the eternal gift of life change You have given me. Thank You that You have blessed me with a gift that I not only get to receive but that I get to give away. Help me have eternal godly impact and influence on those around me the way You have had life-changing impact in and through me. Allow me to show others an eternal gift that they can't wait to open. Amen.

Shaun Blakeney, Christ Fellowship

Week 15, Tuesday
The Gift of Service

As each one has received a gift, minister it to one another, as good stewards of the manifold grace of God. If anyone speaks, let him speak as the oracles of God. If anyone ministers, let him do it as with the ability which God supplies, that in all things God may be glorified through Jesus Christ, to whom belong the glory and the dominion forever and ever. Amen.

1 Peter 4:10, 11

You are never more like Jesus than when you serve. Serving others is a gift. It's a gift to those who are receiving the service, and it's also a gift to the one who is doing the serving.

The Bible says that when you surrender your heart to Jesus and put Him in complete control of your life, He gives you a spiritual gift. This spiritual gift isn't to be used by you for selfish gain, but it's a gift for others to experience to draw them closer to God. In this way, serving others is sometimes difficult because it goes against our selfish nature. It's countercultural to everything we are taught in our world today: "Have it your way." "You deserve a break today." Everything communicated today tells us to look out for ourselves and focus on getting our own way.

Jesus taught us by His example to serve others (John 13). Jesus didn't come to be served, but to serve. He didn't ask all of humanity to do something He wasn't willing to do (Matthew 20:28).

Serving others is something you have to work at every day (1 Corinthians 9:19). You don't just wake up one morning and have an attitude of service. The more you pray about serving others, the more opportunities you will have to serve and use the gifts God has blessed you with—and the more willing you will be to enthusiastically accept these opportunities. The question is, What will you do with those opportunities?

Lord, please give me a willing and enthusiastic heart. Help me see the needs around me and respond by serving and giving my best. I love You and surrender my wants and my desires today, so that I can serve You. Amen.

Shaun Blakeney, Christ Fellowship

Week 15, Wednesday
The Gift of Encouragement

*But no man can tame the tongue. It is an unruly evil, full of deadly poison. With it we bless our
God and Father, and with it we curse men, who have been made in the similitude of God. Out of
the same mouth proceed blessing and cursing. My brethren, these things ought not to be so.*

James 3:8–10

There is power in words. There is also power in the way that we use those words. Negative words can
be devastating, but positive words can bring life. One of the things we all have in common is that we
love encouragement. No one woke up this morning and said, "Please stop encouraging me. If one more
person says an encouraging comment to me, I'm going to scream." The Bible tells us in James 3 that the
tongue is a small part of the body, but it has the ability to either do great things or cause great damage.
People are craving encouragement, and encouragement can be a powerful tool.

Giving encouragement is a choice; it is a gift. Encouragement is something we all crave, but it's also
something we all have the ability to give. Encouragement is a constant "For Sure" in a world that says
"No Way."

Just stop and think about the messages coming from the world every day. What are some of the
messages they're sending? "You're not intelligent enough." "You're not good enough." "You're not rich
enough." "You're not skinny enough." No Way. No Way. No Way. We are products of that culture. We hear
this all day, every day, and then we wonder why we feel discouraged. Encouragement is the constant "For
Sure" in a world that says "No Way."

Help others see themselves as God sees them by sharing an encouraging word. Learn to give the gift
of encouragement and watch others around you begin to live a life that says, "I'm loved. For sure."

*Lord, help me to be encouraging to others. I want to have a heart like
Your heart. Give me a heart that sees the best in others. Give me a heart that
speaks words of love and life. Give me eyes to see those who need encouragement. Give me lips to speak words that uplift and not tear down. Amen.*

Shaun Blakeney, Christ Fellowship

Week 15, Thursday
The Gift of Sacrifice

"This is My commandment, that you love one another as I have loved you. Greater love has no one than this, than to lay down one's life for his friends. You are My friends if you do whatever I command you."

John 15:12–14

Sacrifice means you are willing to give up something of value or worth for someone else.

The gift of sacrifice can manifest itself in two distinct ways: selfishly and selflessly. Selfish sacrifice says, "I'm going to sacrifice to get something in return." You don't really want to sacrifice, but you know that if you do, you will benefit from it. Selfless sacrifice says, "I am willing to sacrifice even though I know I will get NOTHING in return." Selfless sacrifice is real sacrifice.

The gift of selfless sacrifice requires being willing to sacrifice something and focusing on the true example of sacrifice.

Be willing to sacrifice something. You have to look in your heart and ask, "Am I willing to give something up in my life so someone else can benefit?" This is hard and usually easier said than done. It takes a change of heart and a change of mind. We live in a selfish world, and because of that you may have to do some soul searching and ask yourself if you are willing and prepared to make a sacrifice, not just putting someone before yourself but understanding that it requires a sacrifice to do so.

Focus on the true example of sacrifice. Jesus was the ultimate sacrifice. He is the example of what it means to give up willingly. He didn't give Himself up because He would get something in return. He gave Himself up to give you a hope and a future with Him. He gave us the opportunity to see Him as our Savior and Friend—hoping for it but not demanding it as repayment. Jesus was the ultimate gift of sacrifice, and He wants you to respond in the same way. If you are focused on keeping Jesus at the center of your life, then sacrifice shouldn't be a problem for you and you should love doing it.

Lord, sacrifice is hard. Sacrifice requires trust. You gave us the ultimate example of sacrifice by giving Your life. Thank You for modeling what true, selfless sacrifice should look like. Help me learn to give the gift of sacrifice and put others first. I want to love others the same way that You love me. Amen.

Shaun Blakeney, Christ Fellowship

Week 15, Friday
The Gift of Honesty

Therefore, putting away lying, "Let each one of you speak truth with his neighbor," for we are members of one another.

Ephesians 4:25

Not telling the truth has become just another part of our culture.

- Advertisements tell us that if we do sit-ups for ten seconds a day we will have abs of steel.
- *American Idol* contestants hire voice coaches, and the voice coaches tell them how great they are when they really stink.
- When someone is trying to set you up with their friend and you ask if the person is good-looking, what do they say? "They have a great personality." In other words, "No."

Honesty is a gift. When it comes to honesty, it doesn't matter who you are or where you are on this spiritual journey of life, everyone benefits from the truth. You may not always want to hear it, but if you want to grow and develop into the likeness of Jesus, then you will welcome it. When someone shares honestly with you, you become a better person because of it. It will help develop your character, relationships, work, and life.

Honesty is a gift because it brings depth. When you realize that people around you deserve the truth and you share it with them, depth will develop. It will bring depth to your friendships, because speaking truth identifies weaknesses that they can begin working on. It will in turn bring depth to you because you took a hard step in integrity to be open with your friend. It will bring depth to your relationships with others because now you are growing together and you have gone to a whole different level in your spiritual journey and in your relationships with others.

Realize that being honest is difficult. Honesty needs to be shared, but it needs to be shared in love. If you want to be a better person, then be accepting of the truth and realize that truth brings depth and depth makes you better.

 God, thank You for honesty. Thank You for truth. Thank You for giving me the opportunity to speak truth into the life of my friends. Let me be open when others share honestly with me. Help me to recognize that honesty is a gift that will bring depth to my life and make me a better follower of You. Amen.

Shaun Blakeney, Christ Fellowship

Week 15, Weekend
God's Welcome Mat

"Freely you have received, freely give."

Matthew 10:8

We all have a need for acceptance. God meets our need for acceptance in spite of our differences, faults, and failures. He then calls us to meet others' need for acceptance in turn. Accepting another person usually includes making someone feel welcome, helping them sense that they belong without any experience of rejection. We can see Jesus making someone feel welcome without any experience of rejection during Christ's encounter with Zacchaeus in Luke 19:1–10. In spite of Zacchaeus's behavior, Jesus still welcomed him and showed a great willingness to accept him. Jesus relates to you in the same manner. In spite of our behavior, Jesus still welcomes us and accepts us. There is no rejection, only accepting love.

Accepting another person includes being willing to love someone unconditionally, in spite of any of their faults. It means not withholding forgiveness. The stories of Christ's encounters with the woman caught in adultery and the thief on the cross, remind us that Jesus loves us without condition (John 8:1–11 and Luke 23:39–43). There is nothing that we can do to stop or limit His love or forgiveness. There is no sin too big and no choice too painful. Jesus loves you with accepting love.

Finally, accepting another person means being willing to care for someone in spite of any ways in which they might be different from us. It means not trying to fix or change another person. We can see Jesus' willingness to care for someone who might be different and the absence of trying to fix another person during His encounter with the woman at the well (John 4:1–26). The story shows that Jesus deeply loves and cares for you, even if others don't.

Reflect on these ideas for giving to others in the same way that Jesus has given to you.

- Go out of your way to welcome people who may look, believe, live, or act differently.
- Try to notice anyone who may feel uneasy or alone and initiate a conversation.
- Look beyond someone's faults and meet their need for acceptance.
- When someone makes a mistake or offends you, be quick to forgive.

God, thank You for accepting me unconditionally. Please make me more accepting of my family, friends, and those around me. Help me to be more accepting by . . . Amen.

Week 16, Monday
Giving Makes a Difference

One of His disciples, Andrew, Simon Peter's brother, said to Him, "There is a lad here who has five barley loaves and two small fish, but what are they among so many?" Then Jesus said, "Make the people sit down." Now there was much grass in the place. So the men sat down, in number about five thousand. And Jesus took the loaves, and when He had given thanks He distributed them to the disciples, and the disciples to those sitting down; and likewise of the fish, as much as they wanted.

John 6:8–11

It's easy for us to believe that the gifts and resources God has given us are too small to make a difference. One of the most famous miracles Jesus performed involved feeding over 5,000 people with only two small fish and five loaves of bread. What is easily overlooked is the role of a little boy who simply gave Jesus what he had. It would have been easy for that little boy to believe that the paltry amount of food he possessed would not make any difference when attempting to feed so many. But his small donation of food was the starting line for a miracle. The meaning of this passage is clear. Our giving opens the door to the miraculous. Jesus will multiply what we give so that it makes a tremendous impact.

As a student, perhaps you've thought about the crisis in Darfur, or the tragedy of human trafficking. You're deeply concerned about the AIDS epidemic in Africa and the thousands of orphans who are hurting. Immediately you think, *I'm broke, I'm just a student, and I can't travel to Africa! What can I do?*

You could be the start of a miracle! Maybe you could start an Aids Awareness Club at your school, or sponsor an orphaned child with a group of other financially challenged students. Remember, Jesus takes the little that we have to offer and multiplies it so that it can make a powerful impact!

Lord Jesus, help me today to understand that an incredible difference can be made when I choose to give what I have to You. Though I may not have much to give, I trust in Your ability to multiply its impact. Help me see new opportunities to make an impact on others. Lord, I surrender all that I have to You. Use it in whatever way You see fit. Let my giving be an opportunity for You to do a miracle today. Amen.

Dennis Steeger, Grace Outreach

Week 16, Tuesday
Giving as a Relationship

So let each one give as he purposes in his heart, not grudgingly or of necessity; for God loves a cheerful giver.

2 Corinthians 9:7

Everything in life is relational. I have a relationship with my family and friends that I am very thankful for. I also have relationships with my car, my money, and even my computer. Some would even say I have a deep relationship with my iPhone! Because everything in life is relational, we need to take inventory of our attitudes. In every relationship the right attitude is necessary.

When I truly value my family and friends, I will reap the benefits in those good relationships. If I neglect them, ignore them, or take them for granted, then my relationships suffer and breakdowns will occur. If I neglect to change the oil in my car for too long or fail to properly care for it, eventually it will break down. If I fail to handle my relationship with money wisely, I might experience the adverse affects of greed and debt.

Our attitude toward giving is particularly important. Nothing reveals our attitude quite like giving. Giving is more than a transaction of us distributing what we have to someone who has a need. It is a revelation of the condition of our soul. Our attitude in giving will reflect the generosity or selfishness hidden in our hearts. At its best, giving can be a vivid demonstration of God's care and concern for others. Nothing nourishes our heart as profoundly as authentic giving does. Authentic giving communicates love and value to those you are giving to. It is important to note that the purpose of God's blessing of Abraham was so that he in turn could be a blessing!

What is your relationship with giving? Is it flourishing to the point that giving is second nature to you, or has your relationship been so neglected that giving anything is a challenge?

Jesus, help me today to appropriately communicate Your love to others through my giving. Help me to be a blessing to others just like Abraham. Lord, I never want to give to be seen, I want to give because I care. Lord, help me to live unselfishly today! Lord, help me be aware of the needs around me so that I can be a light that shines Your goodness. Help me to always have the right attitude toward giving so that our Father may be glorified by the care and concern that is shown. Amen.

Dennis Steeger, Grace Outreach

Week 16, Wednesday
What Motivates Our Giving

*Though I bestow all my goods to feed the poor, and though I give my body
to be burned, but have not love, it profits me nothing.*

1 Corinthians 13:3

We see the commercials of a starving child in a third world country. We watch the multitudes of people whose communities have been decimated by famine or the unfortunate families whose lives have been ravaged by civil war or natural disaster. Our hearts feel an uneasy tug when they ask for help. We know they need help. We know we should help. But for some reason, we don't ... we just change the channel.

What is it about ourselves that so easily allows us to ignore the suffering that is all around us? Could it be that we simply lack compassion because of our selfish and sinful nature? Jesus warned us that the last days would be marked by a deficit of demonstrated love (Matthew 24:12).

There is only one motivation for giving that matters. Love. That's it. Period. The motivation of God's most precious gift to humanity was love. Think about the words of John 3:16 for a moment: "For God so loved the world that He gave ..." God wrapped the single greatest demonstration of His love for you in the context of giving His Son. We need to allow God's presence and His Word to fill our hearts so greatly that love is produced in our life.

When our hearts are appropriately filled with God's love, giving becomes part of our DNA. It becomes as normal as breathing. Our capacity for receiving is directly proportional to our willingness to give. Our ability to inhale is tied directly to the amount that we exhale. Just try inhaling a few times without exhaling and you'll see what I mean. When God's love is present in our hearts, giving becomes as easy and effortless as breathing.

Dear Jesus, today I offer my heart to You, to shape and mold it into a loving, giving heart. I never want to be considered selfish or greedy. Help me to be sensitive to the needs of those who are around me, and those who are far away. I pray that my heart never becomes callous to the hurt and suffering of those who are less fortunate than I. Lord, fill my heart with love, so that compassion flows naturally out of my life. Amen.

Dennis Steeger, Grace Outreach

Week 16, Thursday
Giving Good Words = Encouragement

Then Moses called Joshua and said to him in the sight of all Israel, "Be strong and of good courage, for you must go with this people to the land which the Lord has sworn to their fathers to give them, and you shall cause them to inherit it."

Deuteronomy 31:7

Great friends give each other great words. Words are powerful; they can encourage our souls and restore our hope. Great leaders such as Moses understand that their good words can be powerful weapons to combat the fear and doubt that many of us face.

On the day Joshua was chosen to be Moses' successor, he found himself fearful of the many challenges that awaited him. Eight times in scripture Joshua was encouraged to be "strong and courageous." The task was overwhelming, and Joshua's confidence was shaken.

Moses would be the man to encourage Joshua. Moses was aware of the fear and trepidation Joshua must have been feeling. He had experienced those same emotions as a young man when he encountered God in the form of a burning bush.

Then at Joshua's most fearful moment, Moses presented him in front of the entire nation and told him to "... be strong and courageous for *you will* take Israel into the Promised Land and *you will cause* them to inherit it." Moses spoke to Joshua: "I believe in you!" "You can do it." Courage and faith began to flood into Joshua's heart. He was ready to lead.

In classrooms, football fields, and band halls just like the ones at your school, there will be many moments similar to the one Moses and Joshua experienced. Perhaps you will encounter someone who is fearful or timid, a person who needs to hear a word of encouragement from someone who believes in them. Moses was that man for Joshua. Will you be that person for someone else?

Dear Jesus, help me to speak words of encouragement to those around me today whenever I have the opportunity. Lord, give me the courage to speak good words over my friends even when I may want to keep those words to myself. Help me to understand that the power of my words can inspire the hope and confidence that others may lack. Help me to speak the words that will bring life and blessing to all those who hear. Amen.

Week 16, Friday
Inconvenient Giving

He [Jesus] left Judea and departed again to Galilee. But He needed to go through Samaria. So He came to a city of Samaria which is called Sychar, near the plot of ground that Jacob gave to his son Joseph. Now Jacob's well was there. Jesus therefore, being wearied from His journey, sat thus by the well. It was about the sixth hour. A woman of Samaria came to draw water. Jesus said to her, "Give Me a drink."

John 4:3–7

Giving will force us out of our comfort zones. Inconvenient giving will require us to go places we don't want to go and reach out to people whom we typically would not. Jesus demonstrated that He was willing to travel outside His comfort zone to help one person.

If you look at any map of Israel, Samaria was on the way. Follow a straight line down through Samaria and you will run right into Judea. However, the Jews made it a point to *never* pass through Samaria; they traveled around it. It's not that Samaria was a bad place; it's just that the Jews and Samaritans didn't see eye-to-eye on the subject of religion.

So why did Jesus "need to go" there? What was so pressing that Jesus had to break with the time-honored tradition of avoiding Samaria? Jesus had an appointment to meet a woman who was desperate for "living water."

The world around us is thirsty. Our friends at school are thirsty. The guys on the football team and the girls on the drill team are all thirsty. I believe that Jesus Christ is the only Person who can quench our spiritual thirst. We have the same living water to offer those who are thirsty spiritually. How far are you willing to go to give someone who is thirsty a drink of living water? Jesus went to Samaria; where will you go?

Lord, help me to see all the thirsty people around me. Help me to have an open heart to also see those who are far away. Let me give a drink to all who are thirsty. Lord, let me be a willing servant today, ready to go wherever You need me to go so that I can do what You need me to do to glorify Your name. Amen.

Dennis Steeger, Grace Outreach

Week 16, Weekend
The Power of Gratitude

Freely you have received, freely give.

Matthew 10:8

Do you sometimes have trouble giving? I do. There are times when it's hard for me to muster up the courage, the motivation or the "want to." That's when I apply the truth of this Scripture. I remember how I've received, how Jesus has given to me. Our gratitude for how we have received is what empowers us to give.

• Are you being asked to give your time or energy?

• Are you being called upon to give your compassion, patience, encouragement or attention to others?

• Do you need to share more of your support or joy with those around you?

I know that I need to do a better job of giving _____ to _____.

Now, spend the next few moments reflecting on how Christ has given to you … in the same ways. Read each passage of Scripture and let His Spirit lead you into a greater experience of His gifts for you.

Jesus makes Himself available to you 24/7. His time is abundant and in plentiful supply. You can call on Him every moment of every day. Jesus gives you His time and attention any time that you need it (Psalm 34:17).

• Jesus offers compassion for you. Just like His response to Mary, Jesus' heart is moved with compassion any time that He sees you hurt (John 11:35).

• Jesus is patient with you. His love is renewed for you every morning (Lamentations 3:23).

• Jesus gives encouragement to you. He knows there's trouble in this world, but offers hope that He has overcome (John 16:33).

• Jesus offers you His support. Just as He did with David, the Lord can be your rock of strength and your ever-present help (2 Samuel 22:19).

• Jesus' joy is available to you. He longs for you to experience it and hopes that His joy will remain in you for all eternity (John 15:11).

God, thank You for giving to me. I am especially grateful for how You …
I want to experience more gratitude for the gifts that I've received. Let me
be reminded of how much I have received from You and then be empowered
to give to others.

Week 17, Monday
Wilderness of Aloneness

*Then God opened her eyes, and she saw a well of water. And she went
and filled the skin with water, and gave the lad a drink.*

Genesis 21:19

God promised Abraham a child, but in his old age his wife, Sarah, began to doubt. Sarah took matters in her own hands and gave Hagar, her servant, to Abraham to father a child. Before long Hagar was with child, and soon after was despised by Sarah and banished to the wilderness.

We can imagine her fear as she finds herself alone in the wilderness. Intimacy in a relationship with God and other persons is the antidote for aloneness. He created the desire within us because He longs to be intimate with His creation. This is experienced in every dimension of our being—spirit, soul, and body—in a genuine, continual way. We should never be willing to settle for imposters, such as sexual intimacy or emotional, conditional bonding.

But many people do not know of God's provision, and they seek to be fulfilled in other ways. We are called to put an end to their loneliness by sharing God's unconditional love through our actions and the sharing of Scripture.

Notice that God found Hagar in the wilderness and asked, "Where have you come from and where are you going?" He knows the answers, but He wants her to stop and think about where her reactions will take her. Often we are called to ask people that question and to listen, really listen, to what they are feeling.

In her case, she *sat down,* meaning she completely gave up and waited to die. After all, no water in the desert means certain death. But God opened her eyes and told her to look *up.* When she did, she saw that God had provided not just a skin of water, but a whole well!

We can point out God's provision and care in the Scriptures and tell our own stories of His provision in our lives. By doing so we have the privilege of rescuing people from the wilderness of aloneness, just as He does for us. What a grand life He plans for us if only we *open our eyes*!

*My Jesus, thank You for living within. I am never alone because of Your
care. Teach me to love others in the same way and to rescue them from the
wilderness of aloneness. Amen.*

Dr. Jay Strack, Student Leadership University

Week 17, Tuesday
Personal Faith, Personal Peace

Martha said to Jesus, "Lord, if You had been here, my brother would not have died. But even n ow I know that whatever You ask of God, God will give You." Jesus said to her, "Your brother will rise again." Martha said to Him, "I know that he will rise again in the resurrection at the last day." Jesus said to her, "I am the resurrection and the life. He who believes in Me, though he may die, he shall live. And whoever lives and believes in Me shall never die. Do you believe this?" She said to Him, "Yes, Lord, I believe that You are the Christ, the Son of God, who is to come into the world."

John 11:21–27

This is an intimate look at a humble friendship. In despair and anger, Martha spit out to the Lord Jesus, "It's Your fault my brother died!" Jesus did not join in the reaction, but instead responded to the situation with understanding. He could see that she was overwhelmed, and He did not judge her for it.

A genuine relationship seeks to comprehend the pain behind the accusation and looks to offer comfort and love in response. How many relationships have ended because a person is unwilling to look beyond ill-spoken words and into the heart? Our first reaction should be to try to understand why the words were said, not how we are personally offended. Sometimes an irrational emotional response is really the symptom of a spiritual or emotional need. Responding thoughtfully to irrational conversation instead of reacting to my own hurt allows me to communicate clearly, find resolution for conflict, strengthen and maintain relationships, and display the character of Christ.

In this situation, what Martha proclaimed as an emotional need of grief for her brother, Jesus rightly judged as a spiritual need. Martha said the right words, but it wasn't until Jesus led her patiently to a personal faith that she experienced peace.

If we are to help people through tough times in life, we have to be sure that we ourselves have a genuine faith. Ask yourself, "Do I believe that Jesus holds the key to all the needs in life: emotional, relational, physical, spiritual? Can I confidently lead others to trust Him?"

Lord, may I display Your character of genuine love instead of judgment or hurt. Make me an example of godly, unconditional relationships and confidence in You. Amen.

Week 17, Wednesday
The Power of Forgiveness

*Jesus said to them, "Come and eat breakfast." Yet none of the disciples dared
ask Him, "Who are You?"—knowing that it was the Lord. Jesus then came
and took the bread and gave it to them, and likewise the fish.*

John 21:12, 13

Does Jesus truly understand what it feels like to be betrayed? Yes, He does. Peter, His partner in ministry, walked with Jesus in a privileged relationship as genuine friends. Jesus sweat drops of blood in the Garden and asked Peter to "watch and pray," but Peter slept instead. Jesus warned Peter that he would deny Him, but he replied, "Never!" But that night, on the way to the cross, he denied Him three times.

Afterward, we find Peter depressed and lazy (they often go together), and back to doing what he knew best, fishing. He wasn't having much luck until Jesus came along. Soon his net was full and close to breaking, and Jesus said, "Come and eat breakfast."

The depth of such a personal love is astounding here. Not only was Jesus willing to forgive Peter, but He came looking for him. He then humbled Himself to be Peter's servant as He provided bread and fish, and then cooked it for him. Peter was no doubt embarrassed, yet grateful for the unconditional love as he sat at the fire.

Certainly forgiveness is grace, unearned and undeserved. Jesus made a choice to forgive His offenders. On the cross, with His last breaths, He first forgave the thief, and then the others as He said, "Father, forgive them, for they do not know what they do" (Luke 23:34). Certainly, Judas, the soldiers who beat Him, and the Jews who hated Him were part of His prayer. As He hung bleeding and beaten, Jesus most certainly did not rely on *feelings* to enable His choice to forgive. No, it was a pure act of the will, the canceling of a debt, a choice reflecting the unsurpassed love of God.

In the end, the love of Christ brought Peter to full repentance, and he endured persecution as he preached the Gospel of Christ. He penned the books of 1 and 2 Peter before dying as a martyr for the faith, proving the power of personal forgiveness.

*Lord, may I humble myself to fully and unconditionally forgive those
who betray me, praying for their good and the furtherance of the Gospel
through this act. Amen.*

Dr. Jay Strack, Student Leadership University

Week 17, Thursday
An Offer of Hope

*When the woman saw that she was not hidden, she came trembling; and falling
down before Him, she declared to Him in the presence of all the people the reason
she had touched Him and how she was healed immediately. And He said to her,
"Daughter, be of good cheer, your faith has made you well. Go in peace."*

Luke 8:47, 48

Jesus had just healed a man possessed of demons, and people were spreading the news everywhere. One man was at His feet crying and begging for his daughter to be healed while throngs of people surrounded Him, pressing in on Jesus from every angle.

In the midst of this craziness, Jesus stopped and said, "Who touched Me?" Peter reminded Him that there were huge crowds pressing in on Him, but He insisted, "Power has gone out from Me; someone touched Me." A woman stepped forward, shaking, falling on her face, and said, "I did it, and I was healed immediately." For twelve years, she had gone to doctors without success, but in one moment, she was healed by the Savior. This woman suffered from an issue of blood and would have been considered ceremoniously unclean according to the book of Leviticus, meaning she would be shunned by the people. She hid in the midst of the crowd in shame, sneaking a touch of His garment, but was known openly by Jesus. In front of everyone, He called her "daughter," a very personal name that immediately changed her from rejected to accepted and beloved. We learn in this passage:

- Jesus values everyone, regardless of reputation or past circumstance;
- In the midst of every crowd, there is one person waiting for your touch;
- Shame can be erased with one genuine word of acceptance;
- We should learn people's names and speak to them with respect;
- We should listen to their stories with interest and do what we can to help; and
- God uses the humble to proclaim His story of love and power.

There are many things Jesus did that we cannot do: we could not heal the demoniac or raise the dead, but we can show love to one lonely, rejected person, and offer hope and healing of the heart.

 My Lord Jesus, make my heart one of acceptance; to think first of caring and accepting instead of judging. Show me what I can do in Your name. Amen.

Week 17, Friday
Hearing His Call

*Let this mind be in you which was also in Christ Jesus, who, being in
the form of God, did not consider it robbery to be equal with God, but
made Himself of no reputation, taking the form of a bondservant, and coming
in the likeness of men. And being found in appearance as a man, He humbled
Himself and became obedient to the point of death, even the death of the cross.*

Philippians 2:5–8

As soon as you wake in the morning, your mind begins receiving messages through your phone, technology and media, your music, your parents and friends, and on and on it goes.

The first choice you make is whether you will choose to focus on the mind of Christ or whether you will simply go with the flow of messages coming your way. When we do not make a conscious effort to fill our mind with the character of Christ, then we must make separate choices throughout the day, and hope that we make the right ones each time. Life becomes more like a video game, where we play along toward the prize, hoping to avoid traps and enemy attacks.

This is not God's intention. A life submitted in humility to the will of God and the way of God is a life of adventure, inspiration, and purpose, one constantly looking for the best use of time and energy, specifically meeting needs and encouraging those in our circle of influence.

Pride has to be resisted because it comes naturally, but one can only be humble on purpose. The definition of humility is not thinking less of yourself; it is thinking about yourself less.

We see the example of Christ, who humbled Himself on purpose in order to serve man and fulfill the will of God. To "let this mind be in you," you must choose to give Christ the first influence of your day and the first priority in your planning. This mind-set is essential if we are ever going to truly see people the way He did, feel the way He felt, and be willing to be an imitator of Christ.

*Lord, I let go of the pressures of messages calling to me throughout the
day and humble myself to receive Your character of humility. May I arise
tomorrow a servant, ready to hear Your call. Amen.*

Dr. Jay Strack, Student Leadership University

Week 17, Weekend
Craving Attention

"A new commandment I give to you, that you love one another; as I have loved you."

John 13:34

We all have a need for attention. God created each of us with a need to sense that others care and demonstrate concern for us. We need other people to express genuine interest in the things that matter to us. Just like we need air, food, and water, we need other people to "enter our world" and meet our need for attention.

Jesus confirmed our need for attention in many ways. First, Jesus often ministered to large crowds of people, but He also frequently took the time to show attention to specific individuals, including Nicodemus (John 3:1–21), the lame man at the pool (John 5:15), the woman with the issue of blood (Mark 5:25–34), and Bartimaeus (Mark 10:46–52). God continues to demonstrate His care and concern for each of us by giving us His undivided and unlimited attention when we speak to Him in prayer.

Scripture also tells us that God knew each of us in the womb (Psalm 139:13) and knows our innermost thoughts (Psalm 139:2). Philippians 2:6–8 confirms that God wants to spend time with us. God thought it was important to know what it's like to be in our world because Jesus left His incredible mansion in heaven to enter our world and live here on earth. He wanted us to know that being a part of our world is a priority to Him.

Think about the people who are in your life right now. Who might benefit from receiving your attention? Meeting someone's need for attention might look like:

- Spending time with a person so that you find out about their struggles, joys, and dreams.
- Entering another person's world—being involved in their interests and activities.
- Being a listener who gives good eye contact, shares appropriate feedback, and hears a person before responding.

How might you meet another person's need for attention this week? How could you give first?

I think _____ (a specific name) could benefit from my attention this week. I plan to give him/her attention by . . .

 God, thank You for entering my world. Help me to do the same for others. Amen.

Week 18, Monday
Secondhand Comfort

Blessed be the God and Father of our Lord Jesus Christ, the Father of mercies and God of all comfort, who comforts us in all our tribulation, that we may be able to comfort those who are in any trouble, with the comfort with which we ourselves are comforted by God.

2 Corinthians 1:3, 4

Our God is a God of many things. He is a God of power, love, wisdom, strength, and compassion. He is also a God of comfort. Jesus says, "Come to Me, all you who labor and are heavy laden, and I will give you rest. Take My yoke upon you and learn from Me, for I am gentle and lowly in heart, and you will find rest for your souls. For My yoke is easy and My burden is light" (Matthew 11:28–30). Jesus gives us the green light to be open and honest with Him about our struggles and problems, and He says that we can find rest in doing this because He has the power to give us that rest. He desires to comfort us and for us to comfort each other.

From a young age, we learn the power of a comforting touch or word. I'm sure you can think back to a time of struggle in your life when someone loved you enough to sit beside you and comfort you with a hug or a kind word. In that moment, you felt comforted because they selflessly gave of themselves to comfort you. They didn't lecture you about what you could have done differently or give you a wordy Christian answer for why bad things were happening. They simply sat with you and let you know that you weren't alone. They took it upon themselves to show you love that day. God longs to do the same thing with you when you hurt, and then He expects us to do that for others when they hurt. Because He comforts us in our times of pain, we can then pass that comfort on to others when they are in pain.

 Dear God, thank You for being there to comfort me. Thank You for loving me so much that You want to hear about my pain and help me through it. Help me to see others and love them the way You do so that I can comfort them as You do. Amen.

Chad Moore, First Baptist Church Oviedo

Week 18, Tuesday
Aliens and Allies

"A new commandment I give to you, that you love one another; as I have loved you, that you also love one another. By this all will know that you are My disciples, if you have love for one another."

John 13:34, 35

A little while back, my wife and I drove down to Miami for a football game between the New England Patriots and the Miami Dolphins. As Patriot fans, we were in enemy territory and the Dolphin fans were kind enough to remind us of that fact. Therefore, we felt very alone and uneasy, but whenever we saw another Patriot fan it was comforting, even though the person was a complete stranger. These were people whom I had never seen before and probably never would again, and yet I found myself celebrating with them through high-fives and chest bumps during the night as we celebrated touchdowns and other great plays. We acted like family with these strangers, because we had one clear thing in common. We might have nothing else in common but that one thing, being a follower of the Patriots, united us together in the midst of enemy territory. We were allies and friends without even knowing each other's names.

We as Christians have a huge thing in common. We have surrendered our lives to follow Jesus. The same God is the ruler of my life and yours. This binds us together as a family. We should be allies and friends, especially in enemy territory as "aliens and strangers in the world" (1 Peter 2:11, NIV). So after being beaten down by this world, the Church must be a place of comfort where we support each other like family even though we might not have anything in common other than Christ. We should have the same feeling when we see other believers as I did at that football game. In fact, our love for and treatment of each other should be so striking that it screams to others that we are Christians.

Dear God, please help me to be a source of comfort to other Christians. Help me to not focus solely on my own needs but learn to love others like You love me. I know we may not have lots in common, but they are my family and need my support. Please give me the strength to love. Amen.

Chad Moore, First Baptist Church Oviedo

Week 18, Wednesday
Powerful Words

Look also at ships: although they are so large and are driven by fierce winds,
they are turned by a very small rudder wherever the pilot desires. Even so the tongue is
a little member and boasts great things. See how great a forest a little fire kindles!

James 3:4, 5

History shows us that words have tremendous power and potential. Inspiring words start revolutions. A kind word in a time of pain can make a tremendous difference in someone's life. A nation can start a war by the uttering of a word. God spoke the universe into existence by saying, "Let there be . . ." and there was (Genesis 1:3).

We, too, have great power in the words that we say. Our words are like that small rudder on a ship that can control the course of our lives and those around us. A few careless words can be like a lit match in the middle of a forest that ignites a devastating fire, ruining homes and lives. The potential for destruction is always there and we are left to choose what to do. We can use our words to burn other people or we can use them to heal those who have been burned. Paul writes, "Let no corrupt word proceed out of your mouth, but what is good for necessary edification, that it may impart grace to the hearers" (Ephesians 4:29). How much of what you say benefits those around you? It may not be that you intend to harm others with your words, but even careless words can do damage. Remember, God says that someday we will have to explain every careless word that we have spoken in our lives (Matthew 12:36).

We must decide to use our words to help and heal others, not to harm them or make ourselves feel better by burning them. Commit today to take control of every word and use it to glorify God and comfort His people. By being obedient in this, we bring glory to God and His name.

Dear God, I know that what I say matters to You, and I want to show that I love You through what I say. Please help me to control my words and not use them to hurt other people, but to use my words to comfort others and build them up. Amen.

Chad Moore, First Baptist Church Oviedo

Week 18, Thursday
Testing My Motives

So, affectionately longing for you, we were well pleased to impart to you not only the gospel of God, but also our own lives, because you had become dear to us.

1 Thessalonians 2:8

As mentioned earlier in this week's reading, comfort ultimately comes from God (2 Corinthians 1:3–4). Jesus told His disciples that He was not going to leave them as orphans, but that He was going to send the Comforter to dwell within them (John 14:16–18). Today, we're united as Christians through the power of the Holy Spirit (Ephesians 4:1–4), and we're even called the body of Christ (1 Corinthians 12:27). In yesterday's reading, we saw that our words have the power to both harm and heal people. Today's reading takes this idea of bringing comfort to others one step further by challenging our motives toward how and why we live the way we do.

Did Jesus assure His disciples with His words? Definitely. He often comforted them with sayings such as "Let not your heart be troubled . . ." (John 14:1). While this truth is important, Christ displayed His greatest love for the disciples by laying down His life (John 15:13; 1 John 3:16). Christ did not have a hidden agenda. He came to this earth to bring glory to God and salvation to men. His ways were pure in both word and deed. We can trust that God cares for us because His Son died so that we can live with Him forever.

In the same way, Paul did not have a hidden agenda when he presented the Gospel to the Thessalonians. He didn't use words of flattery or speak for his own glory (1 Thessalonians 2:5–6), but rather, his genuine and deep love for them motivated his actions. Jesus reminds us that the greatest commandments in all of Scripture are to love God and to love others (Matthew 22:37–40). In 1 Peter 3:15, we're challenged to always be prepared to give an answer for the hope that is found within us. However, before we can give an answer, we must first be asked the question. So with this idea in mind, what in my life begs the question?

Lord, thank You for loving me. Thank You for bringing comfort through Your words, but also through Your sacrifice. Help me to have pure motives as I both share Christ with my words and show Christ with my actions. Amen.

Jonathan Kragel, First Baptist Church Oviedo

Week 18, Friday
Changing Perspectives

His divine power has given to us all things that pertain to life and godliness, through the knowledge of Him who called us by glory and virtue, by which have been given to us exceedingly great and precious promises, that through these you may be partakers of the divine nature, having escaped the corruption that is in the world through lust.

2 Peter 1:3, 4

It's amazing to read all of the powerful truths packed into these two short verses! The same power that spoke this world into existence (Genesis 1:1) has given us all that we need to succeed in life. God has given us everything because we have a living God (1 Timothy 4:10), a living Savior (John 14:6), a living Spirit (John 7:38–39), and the Living Word (Hebrews 4:12). The better we know Christ, the better we can live for Him. Notice that God called us before we ever called Him. Romans 5:8 reminds us that while we were still sinners, Christ died for us.

God's gifts and promises to us are out of this world (see Romans 6:23). And God has given us these promises not so He could experience us, but so that we could experience Him. Not only are we given eternal life, but we have been saved from the corruption of this world. For those who believe in Christ, this world is the closest thing to hell that we'll ever experience (that's comfort). However, for those who reject Christ, this earth is the closest thing they'll see of heaven (that's urgency).

We can bring comfort to others by recognizing that God did not come to this earth to experience us, but so that we could experience Him. When comforting others, we must remember that the trials and tribulations of this world are temporary when compared to the future glory we'll experience with God in heaven (2 Corinthians 4:16–18). We can take courage that His ways are higher than ours (Isaiah 55:9), and no matter what our circumstances, God has a plan for our lives.

Lord, thank You for Your great and precious promises. Thank You for eternal life in the future and abundant life in the present. As I face the trials in my life, help me remember that I am here to experience You. Help me bring comfort to others by reminding them that we're here to be a part of Your greater story. Amen.

Jonathan Kragel, First Baptist Church Oviedo

Week 18, Weekend
Can You Hurt for Him?

That I may know Him and the power of His resurrection, and the fellowship of His sufferings.

Philippians 3:10

Scripture tells us to respond to the hurt that others carry by offering comfort (Matthew 5:4, Romans 12:15). Yet, all too frequently, Christians view sadness or expressing comfort as a signs of weakness. The truth is: God cares about what we are feeling. He is not responding to our hurt by saying, "Keep a stiff upper lip." God actually tells us to get His grace into circulation by offering some of His comfort to others who are hurting (2 Corinthians 1:3-4).

It may sound weird, but sometimes, in order to express compassion for people around us, we must fellowship in the sufferings of Jesus. Simply put, if we can hurt for Jesus, we can hurt for others. Reflect for a few moments on some of the ways that Jesus suffered. What does it do to your heart to know that Jesus experienced these things?

- Our Savior was betrayed by His closest friends. Peter (one of the closest disciples) denied even knowing Jesus. Christ overheard this denial as He was lead to the cross.
- Jesus' own family and closest friends rejected Him and ridiculed Him. They didn't believe a common man should warrant such honor and respect.
- Jesus' disciples were often preoccupied with their own selfish agendas. Even during the one of their last meals together, the disciples were preoccupied with who would be greatest in His kingdom.
- Jesus, the Great Physician healed ten lepers – restoring their health, their lives and their ability to live with their families. Only one of these men returned to give Him thanks.
- In His darkest hour, Christ asked His disciples to pray with Him, support Him and demonstrate care for Him. The ones who were supposedly closest to Him didn't care enough to stay awake. Jesus experienced excruciating agony and his friends fell asleep.

Take the next few moments and express your heart to Jesus. How does it make you feel to know that our Savior went through these painful circumstances? Can you fellowship with Him and feel for Jesus?

Jesus, when I consider that You (of all people) had to go through _____.
My heart is moved with compassion because _____. I am saddened when
I remember that You experienced _____.
Please know that my heart hurts for You.

Terri Snead, The Great Commandment Network

Week 19, Monday
Giving Encouragement

"Be strong and of good courage, for to this people you shall divide as an inheritance the land which I swore to their fathers to give them. Only be strong and very courageous, that you may observe to do according to all the law which Moses My servant commanded you; do not turn from it to the right hand or to the left, that you may prosper wherever you go. This Book of the Law shall not depart from your mouth, but you shall meditate in it day and night, that you may observe to do according to all that is written in it. For then you will make your way prosperous, and then you will have good success. Have I not commanded you? Be strong and of good courage; do not be afraid, nor be dismayed, for the LORD your God is with you wherever you go."

Joshua 1:6–9

The pressure was intense. The stakes were high. After escaping Egypt's enslavement, the people of Israel had spent the last forty years wandering the desert. They had just suffered the loss of their leader, Moses. How was Joshua going to fill the leadership sandals of Moses and lead this ragtag bunch of untrained Israelites into battle to take hold of the land that God had promised them? In short, Joshua trusted God. God stated three times to "be strong and of good courage," and He followed each statement with a practical application. Notice the paraphrased flow below:

Be strong and courageous –>	Remember God's Promises.
Be strong and very courageous –>	Obey God's Precepts.
Be strong and courageous –>	Acknowledge God's Presence.

How did Joshua respond to God's commission? He rallied the people of Israel to begin their conquest of the Promised Land (1:10)! Just as Joshua was commissioned in this passage, we have been commissioned to "go and make disciples of all nations" (Matthew 28:20). How can we encourage others to take hold of this charge? We remember God's promises, obey His precepts, and acknowledge His presence in our lives!

Lord, help me remember Your promises regularly. Help me think upon Your Word daily. Help me know that You're always with me and that the Holy Spirit dwells in my heart. May the courage I receive from You lead me to encourage others to live for You. Amen.

Jonathan Kragel, First Baptist Church Oviedo

Week 19, Tuesday
Answer God's Call

*Then the L*ORD *put forth His hand and touched my mouth, and the L*ORD *said to me:*
"Behold, I have put My words in your mouth. See, I have this day set you over the nations and
over the kingdoms, to root and to pull down, to destroy and to throw down, to build and to plant."

Jeremiah 1:9, 10

Jeremiah finds himself living in a time when God's people are distant from Him and have been for a while. They abandoned God and worshiped other gods (Jeremiah 2:13). No one was genuinely seeking God (Jeremiah 5:1–2). They were sin-happy (Jeremiah 9:2–3). They wronged each other (Jeremiah 9:5) and rejected God's Word (Jeremiah 11:10). If Jeremiah were alive today and living in America, he would find himself in a very similar context!

It was in this context that God called Jeremiah to be a difference-maker while impacting his culture. Let's look at Jeremiah's calling.

First, God communicated to Jeremiah that he was known by God, set apart by God, and appointed by God before he was even born (Jeremiah 1:4)! God had a specific mission for Jeremiah to accomplish.

Second, Jeremiah faced obstacles that provided an opportunity for him to avoid God's calling on his life. It is understandable to see why he was nervous (Jeremiah 1:7): he was young, the content of God's message to be spoken through him was very difficult (Jeremiah 1:10), and he didn't have prior experience to lean on as this was all new territory. We find later that God would prove to be bigger than all of these obstacles.

Third, God encouraged Jeremiah that not only was He bigger than all of the obstacles, but He would be with him every step of the way until the mission was completed (Jeremiah 1:8).

Jeremiah took these three elements to heart as he answered God's calling on his life, and he became a major difference-maker in his day. America is desperate for modern-day Jeremiahs. Be encouraged to answer God's call today!

God, thank You for giving me a life mission, for setting me apart, for be-
ing bigger than my obstacles, and for being with me. Help me to answer Your
call and make an impact on this world in a way that honors You. Amen.

Jonathan Kragel, First Baptist Church Oviedo

Week 19, Wednesday
Execute God's Game Plan

"And as you go, preach, saying, 'The kingdom of heaven is at hand.' Heal the sick, cleanse the lepers, raise the dead, cast out demons. Freely you have received, freely give. Provide neither gold nor silver nor copper in your money belts, nor bag for your journey, nor two tunics, nor sandals, nor staffs; for a worker is worthy of his food."

Matthew 10:7–10

Can you picture the coach of a football team giving his pre-game pep talk? He huddles the team up close enough to hear his voice, he gives the team some instruction on what to expect during the highs and lows of the game, he reminds them of their game plan, and then he inspires the team to win a victory!

In this passage, you can picture Jesus as the coach giving a pep talk to His team, the disciples. He's giving them the game plan that will lead to spiritual victory. In this segment of the motivational talk, Jesus instructs His team with three essential elements to remember for their mission to be a success.

First, we need to remember that not only did God bless His followers with a specific mission to accomplish (we see this in biblical characters throughout the Bible), but He has given all of His followers a general calling as well. This general calling, or mission, is to make disciples (Matthew 28:18–20). As followers of Christ, we should be reproducing ourselves in others as we follow the Head Coach and add more players to the team.

Second, Jesus tells His team to have faith to do the impossible. Matthew 10:8 cannot be accomplished unless the Spirit of God is working through us. The Jesus journey requires us to take risks that have a prerequisite of walking in the Spirit (not possible with human strength).

Third, Jesus tells His team not to pack their uniforms or equipment for the game. He tells them that He will be all that they need. Christ followers need to move to a position of total dependence on Jesus and trust that He will be enough.

God, help me to view this world through Your Kingdom lens. Give me the courage to take risks for You as You move me to a place of total dependence on You. Amen.

Jonathan Kragel, First Baptist Church Oviedo

Week 19, Thursday
Live Loud

"Whatever I tell you in the dark, speak in the light; and what you hear in the ear, preach on the housetops. And do not fear those who kill the body but cannot kill the soul. But rather fear Him who is able to destroy both soul and body in hell. Are not two sparrows sold for a copper coin? And not one of them falls to the ground apart from your Father's will. But the very hairs of your head are all numbered. Do not fear therefore; you are of more value than many sparrows."

Matthew 10:27–31

As Jesus' pep talk is continued in Matthew 10, He is telling His team that they are being sent out to live LOUD as they broadcast the things of God, both verbally and with their actions. In the crazy media-driven world that we live in today, a quiet generation who whispers the name of Jesus will not be heard. It seems that our loud shouts have become quiet whispers as we have attempted to be sensitive to the culture around us. As Jesus told His disciples, it's time to get on the rooftops of our spiritual houses and shout for the cause of Christ! As Team Jesus was told to live LOUD and bring attention to the cross, Jesus knew that they were going to stick out of the crowd. They were going to be made fun of, made to look like they were crazy, etc.

It's during these difficult times that they would need to remember to only fear God. Why would we be scared of what people think about us? Why would we be scared of what people can do to us? God is the only One deserving of our fear since He is the only One powerful enough to be in control of all things, including eternity! No matter the circumstances you face, remember that God is in complete control. As we live LOUD, we need to rest in His sovereignty. We need to feel secure that the Rock can never crumble. As the old saying goes, we need to live LOUD with "NO FEAR!"

 God, give me the boldness that it is going to take to live LOUD in a culture that is telling me to be quiet. Help me to fear no one but You. Amen.

Week 19, Friday
Be All In

"And he who does not take his cross and follow after Me is not worthy of Me.
He who finds his life will lose it, and he who loses his life for My sake will find it."

Matthew 10:38

We have reached the end of Jesus' pre-game speech. Jesus speaks in black and white: You're either a follower of Jesus or you're not. You're either all in or all out. You either love Him or you don't. He knows that clarity of the mission is of utmost importance for the success of the mission. There is no room for self-promotion, self-ambition, self-gratification, or selfish motives. Jesus makes it clear that we must deny self, crucify self, and resist self in order to be a devoted follower of Him. We are His extension, His representatives, His hands and feet. As self creeps in and tempts us to dishonor God's Kingdom by running our own way, we must not forget that it is an honor and a privilege to be aligned with Jesus and pursuing His cause. This is "High Risk, High Reward." The risk is denying and losing ourselves. Will God really be there on the other side? So many never take this faith step and end up trying to get all they can while they can here on earth. These people come up empty every time and never find the true meaning to life in Christ. The reward is that when we finally can totally lose ourselves, our desires, our wants, our motives, our plans, our security, our satisfaction . . . we find Him. We find Him and realize that He is enough. Be encouraged that He's enough for His calling on our lives. He's enough for the abundant life. He's enough for true satisfaction, peace, and joy. He's enough for access to the Father, both now and for eternity.

God, help me to remember the very words that You told Your original team over 2,000 years ago. Help me to live life with You at the center instead of me. Help me to put Your ways ahead of my ways. I want Your thoughts to be my thoughts. Help me to proactively eliminate my selfishness. Help me to lower myself so I can lift You high. Amen.

Jonathan Kragel, First Baptist Church Oviedo

Week 19, Weekend
I Got This

"Freely you have received, freely give."

Matthew 10:8

One of our critical needs is a need for encouragement. We all have a need for someone to cheer us on. God meets this need for us and then calls us to encourage others. Giving encouragement involves speaking positive words to others, giving others reason to hope, and urging others to persevere in the pursuit of goals and dreams. Here are some of the ways that God wants to encourage you. As you read these thoughts, reflect on some of God's words that are especially meaningful to you right now.

• You might say, "This is impossible."
God says, "Nothing is impossible with Me" (Luke 18:27).
• You might say, "I'm too tired. I give up."
God says, "I will give you rest" (Matthew 11:28–30).
• You might say, "I can't go on."
God says, "My grace is enough. You can do it" (2 Corinthians 12:9).
• You might say, "I can't make it. There's no way."
God says, "I've got what you need" (Isaiah 40:28–29).
• You might say, "I'm not able."
God says, "I AM able. I've got this" (2 Corinthians 9:8).
• You might say, "No one gets it. No one understands."
God says, "I have heard you and I will be with you" (Psalm 10:17; 91:15).

I am especially thankful for God's encouragement, when He says _____ because . . .

Now because God has encouraged you, consider how you might share words of encouragement with others around you. How could you give first and meet their need? Your encouragement might sound like:

• *I have a lot of confidence in you because . . .*
• *I believe you can handle this situation because . . .*
• *I know you can do this because . . .*

   God, thank You for being a God who sees the times when I am discouraged and need more of Your hope. Thank You for Your encouraging words. Please help me to be an encourager to others. Amen.

Week 20, Monday
Giving First: Love

*We love Him because He first loved us. . . . And this commandment
we have from Him: that he who loves God must love his brother also.*

1 John 4:19, 21

Have you ever noticed how many ways we use the word *love*? Just for fun, try walking through the mall and eavesdrop on different conversations that are taking place around you. A couple holding hands might talk of their "love" for each other. Someone in the food court might talk about dining at a restaurant they "love." At the music store someone may talk about how much they "love" a certain band. The word has been used so often, its meaning has become diluted.

We can get a distorted view of love if we have the wrong definition of love. We may think that love is based on feelings and emotions or that it comes with certain expectations. Love, when understood with the wrong definition, always has strings attached: "I will love you if . . ." or "As long as you do this . . . I will love you." Is this love?

The true definition of love is found in Scripture. God is love (1 John 4:16). His love has no strings attached. We could not earn it if we tried. Take a moment to think about that. There is nothing we can do to earn God's love, and there is nothing we can do to lose His love. Those thoughts are both humbling and freeing.

Why does God pour out His love on us? The answer: so that we will love Him and love the people whom He places in our path. Remember what the passage said: "He who loves God must love his brother also." Our ability to love others is found in our desire to love God. The closer we are to Him, the more we allow His love to flow through us and into the lives of those around us.

The more we love God, the more we will love others.

*Father, thank You for the amazing love that You have poured out on me.
I recognize that the more I experience Your love, the more I am able to love
those around me. Help me to understand that true love is unconditional
and undeserved. But because of Your love for me, I can show true love to
others. Amen.*

Jay Hackett, Peachtree Corners Baptist Church

Week 20, Tuesday

Giving First: Acceptance

Therefore receive one another, just as Christ also received us, to the glory of God.

Romans 15:7

We live in a world that daily asks us to accept different things. When we upgrade our iPhone or computer, we are asked to read an agreement and accept it. If we are honest, we have come to the point that we no longer read the agreement; we just scroll down and click ACCEPT! We accept people on social media, even though we have no clue who they are. We accept the transaction fee to withdraw our own money from an ATM machine. We punch the button to accept the fee and pay an extra five bucks to get twenty dollars. In the midst of this "blind" acceptance, one can't help but wonder if we are blindly rejecting the people that God has placed in our paths?

We pass by people every day at school, practice, work, and even church who are longing to be accepted. We don't notice them because we enter the room looking for people with whom we already have a relationship. We join them and block out everyone else.

If a new person was pointed out to us, we say, "I already have a good group of friends," or "I'm not sure that's the kind of person I need to be associated with." Read those two statements out loud. Now, go back and read Romans 15:7. We should be glad that Jesus didn't say that about reaching out to us! He willingly accepted us, regardless of our past!

We sometimes forget where we came from and think that we are better than we really are. Remember that Jesus reached out to us and accepted us. He told us to do the same for others. The next time someone is sitting alone in the cafeteria, in class, or even at church, remember this verse and step out to make a new friend.

Jesus, where I would be if You had not reached out and accepted me? Thank You for seeing past my faults and failures and taking me in. Help me to see people the way You see them. Help me move past my fear of rejection and the opinions of others so that I can take the first step and reach out in Your name. Amen.

Week 20, Wednesday
Giving First: Comfort

*Blessed be the God and Father of our Lord Jesus Christ, the Father of mercies and God
of all comfort, who comforts us in all our tribulation, that we may be able to comfort those
who are in any trouble, with the comfort with which we ourselves are comforted by God.*

2 Corinthians 1:3, 4

What is the difference between a major problem and a minor problem? The answer depends who is asked. If the problem is happening to us, it's usually major, but if it's happening to someone else, it's usually minor. This may seem funny at first, but in reality it is major because we face it on a daily basis.

We all encounter difficulties in life: the loss of a friend or relative, the pain of a relationship ending, the hurt of not making the team. These are just some of the bumps we encounter along the way. With each trial come the questions: "Why is this happening to me?" and "What can I learn through this experience?"

It is completely normal for us to ask the first question. After all, it is human nature to want to know why we are experiencing pain. But in order to grow, we need to move from ourselves to the bigger picture. According to the Scripture passage, there are two things that happen when we experience pain. The first is that we will experience the comfort of the Father. What an amazing promise that the Father of mercies and the God of comfort is with us in every struggle! We never have to walk through pain alone. The second thing is the ability to comfort others. God allows us to experience pain so that we can be a blessing to someone else further down the road.

In the midst of your next major struggle, allow your heavenly Father to be your greatest source of comfort. Let His words bring healing to your heart. As time with the Father strengthens you, look for an opportunity to share that same comfort with someone who really needs it.

 Heavenly Father, thank You for being the Father of mercies and the God of comfort. There is no way to make it through this life without You! Help me grow through my pain and look for opportunities to be a blessing to someone else. Amen.

Jay Hackett, Peachtree Corners Baptist Church

Week 20, Thursday
Giving First: Forgiveness

Therefore, as the elect of God, holy and beloved, put on tender mercies, kindness, humility, meekness, longsuffering; bearing with one another, and forgiving one another, if anyone has a complaint against another; even as Christ forgave you, so you also must do.

Colossians 3:12, 13

As you get dressed each day, you choose slacks that look sharp, your favorite shirt, comfortable shoes, and the right accessories to define your style. In your spiritual closet, you choose to put on kindness, meekness, and mercy, but you may hesitate when it comes to putting on forgiveness. After all, that really doesn't fit you very well.

In order to wear forgiveness, you must go back to the time in your life when you were deeply hurt. Recall the specifics of that situation. See the face of the one who hurt you. It may seem like it took place yesterday, even though the event was years in the past. Pain tends to find a home in your heart. You may hold on to it and *burn in* anger toward that person.

Examining the hurt in your heart, you find that there may be shame, embarrassment, and pride—layer upon layer of negative feelings, each one feeding on the one before and growing the unforgiving spirit inside of you. You begin to believe you have a right to be angry, a right to be bitter and resentful. Forgive? No way!

Why is it so hard to forgive? It is very easy to accept the forgiveness that Jesus offers (1 John 1:9), but it is not so easy to show forgiveness to others. What change needs to take place to be able to forgive? The answer is found in the passage. You must understand how much you have been forgiven in order to forgive others.

If we put on our tender mercies of God, with kindness, humility, meekness, and patience, recognize our sin, and receive His forgiveness, then we cannot do anything but forgive others. The more we see how great is the forgiveness we have received, the more we are able to forgive others and the closer we are to Christ.

 Jesus, thank You for forgiving me. I fall every single day. You forgive me and accept me back into Your presence. Lord, let me never take You for granted. Please give me the willingness to forgive as You have forgiven me. Amen.

Jay Hackett, Peachtree Corners Baptist Church

Week 20, Friday
Giving First: Ourselves

One of His disciples, Andrew, Simon Peter's brother, said to Him, "There is a lad here who has five barley loaves and two small fish, but what are they among so many?"

John 6:8, 9

You probably know the story. It is in all four of the Gospels, and every time I read it I get excited. There is a huge crowd that has been listening to Jesus all day and dinnertime is getting close. The disciples try to get Jesus to send everyone away, but Jesus says, "*You* give them something to eat." Their response is exactly what ours would be: "What? Where are *we* going to find that much food?" Jesus calmly asks, "What do you have?" This is where it gets awesome! "Well, there is this kid who has some bread and a couple of small fish." You can hear the "not that it will do any good" in Andrew's tone as he looks back at the crowd. Then Jesus does the impossible!

Fast-forward two thousand years. Jesus is still planning to do something impossible. He is asking, "What do you have?" Look at your life. From where you stand, it doesn't seem that impressive. There is nothing on the résumé that says you are qualified. There are faults and failures, nothing that looks very convincing. Embarrassed, you give what you have to Jesus, and He says, "Perfect! That's exactly what I need!" You then stand back and watch as Jesus does the impossible with you.

I gave my heart to Christ when I was eight, but I didn't give Him my life until I was twenty-three. I will never forget the night I said, "What can You do if I give You everything?" Just a few weeks later, I was serving on a church staff and didn't have a clue what I was doing. The past thirteen years have been unbelievable as I have watched God use what I placed in His hands.

Have you given Him the one thing He really wants . . . you?

Lord Jesus, I don't have a lot to offer You, but all I have is Yours. Take my life and use it in any way You choose. I no longer want to do things my way. I surrender everything I am and everything I have to You. Amen.

Jay Hackett, Peachtree Corners Baptist Church

Week 20, Weekend
Good Gifts

Every good gift and every perfect gift is from above, and comes down from the Father of lights.

James 1:17

We all share certain, God-ordained relational needs, and just as God has given to us in order to meet our needs, He calls us to give in order to meet each other's needs. We all have a relational need for acceptance—we all need to experience the feeling of being welcomed by others and sense that we belong. Everyone needs attention—the need for someone to enter our world, be interested in the things that are important to us, and show that they care. Each of us has a need for appreciation—we all have a need to be recognized and thanked for our efforts or accomplishments. We all have a need for encouragement—from time to time, we need someone to cheer us on and keep us going. Finally, each of us has a need for comfort—when we are hurting, we need to sense that others care about our hurt.

Think about these five needs: acceptance, attention, appreciation, encouragement, and comfort.

First, reflect on how terrific it is that we have a God who loves us so much that He meets these needs in our lives. God welcomes you unconditionally and accepts you without demands. God asked His Son to leave the glory of heaven and come to earth so that you would know that He has chosen to enter our world and meet your need for attention. God loves to see you living out His truths and loving others. He appreciates the hearts of those who are truly His. God gives you encouragement through His Word; the Bible is one of your greatest sources of hope. Lastly, God cares deeply about your hurt. His comfort and care can be found in talking with Him, in reading His Word, and through the caring words of other people.

God, I'm especially grateful right now for Your gift of _____ because ...

Because God has given lavishly to you, could you then give to others? How might you give a gift of acceptance, attention, appreciation, encouragement, or comfort to others?

Make a plan and give your gift of God's love this week.

 God, thank You for giving so generously to me. Please make me sensitive to the needs of others around me and empower me to give good gifts, too! Amen.

Week 21, Monday
An Original Fingerprint

I will praise You, for I am fearfully and wonderfully made.

Psalm 139:14

Spend some time and meditate on Psalm 139:14. Do you really understand this verse? At times we all fail to truly grasp and comprehend the love God has for His children—as individuals. What's crazy is that there are no two people with the exact same fingerprints. Just as each snowflake that falls is unique, each fingerprint is unique. God made your fingerprint different from anyone else's, and He did so for a reason. He wanted you to know that you are His original masterpiece. The problem is that you are often not satisfied with what you see in the mirror, and as a result, you find yourself trying to be or wanting to be a carbon copy of someone else. Isaiah 45:9 says, "Woe to him who strives with his Maker! . . . Shall the clay say to him who forms it, 'What are you making?'" In other words, something that is created (clay) has no right to complain to its creator (the potter) about the finished product. You were made the way you are for God's glory. Don't get caught up in wishing you looked a certain way or were more like another person. There is only one YOU.

God has also gifted you unlike anyone else. Your gifts are meant to complement the body of Christ. A car's engine is made up of more than 10,000 moving parts. To the human eye some parts may seem more visible than others; however, without all the parts, even the parts that may seem unimportant, the car doesn't run properly. Likewise with the body of Christ, each person's gift is unique and crucial to the body of believers: "Having then gifts differing according to the grace that is given to us, let us use them . . ." (Romans 12:6).

By not being content with who you are, you are telling God that He as your Creator is not good enough. God is perfect and makes no mistakes, and you have been fearfully and wonderfully made in His image.

Father, first of all I know that contentment is something that I struggle with, and I pray that You will forgive me for not being satisfied in who You've made me to be. Thank You for loving me just the way I am and for putting Your fingerprint on my life. Help me to use the gifts You've given me for Your glory. Amen.

Hutch Kufal, First Baptist Church Bentonville

Week 21, Tuesday
The Apple of God's Eye

For thus says the LORD of hosts: "He sent Me after glory, to the nations which plunder you; for he who touches you touches the apple of His eye."

Zechariah 2:8, 9

Have you ever been bullied or had someone make fun of you? Why is it when something like that happens, or other trials occur in your life, that you allow it to get the best of you? Today, be reminded that the Creator of the Universe knew and cared about you before you were even in your mother's womb (see Jeremiah 1:5). In understanding more about yourself and who you are in Christ, you must also realize that we have a Savior who stands ready to take our burdens and to go to bat for us. Do you recall the story of Stephen, the first martyr, found in scripture? Read the story in Acts 6–7. You will find Stephen being accused for blasphemy and giving his defense before the synagogue leaders. When he finished, the leaders were outraged and began yelling and mocking Stephen, when Stephen, "being full of the Holy Spirit, gazed into heaven and saw the glory of God, and Jesus standing at the right hand of God" (Acts 7:55). Did you know that throughout the New Testament, this is the only time you find Jesus standing at the right hand of God? Every other time, Jesus is sitting (see Colossians 3:1; Romans 8:34; Ephesians 1:20; Luke 22:69). So why is Jesus standing in this instance?

Let's be honest. It feels good when someone stands up for us. Can you imagine the Savior of the world standing up for you? That's exactly what Jesus did for Stephen, and that's exactly what He does for us. He stands up in our defense when no one else will. He stands to show His concern and love. "If God is for us, who can be against us?" (Romans 8:31). So be confident in who you are in Christ, knowing that He has your back and sees you as the apple of His eye.

 Father, forgive me for often allowing others to determine how I view myself. Help me to realize that You created me and formed me just the way I am for Your glory. And thank You for always standing up for me, loving me, and caring for the things I care about. As I go about my day, give me the confidence to be who You've made me to be. Amen.

Hutch Kufal, First Baptist Church Bentonville

Week 21, Wednesday
Sin Does Not Define You

Now if I do what I will not to do, it is no longer I who do it, but sin that dwells in me.

Romans 7:20

Do you ever get upset with yourself because you know there are things that you shouldn't do, but yet you find yourself doing them anyway? Then, on the other hand, there are things that you know you should do, yet you never follow through and actually do them? This is the exact dilemma in which the apostle Paul found himself. (See Romans 7:15.)

However, there is likely a fundamental difference between you and Paul. It is very common for teenagers to identify themselves with their sins. Have you fallen into this trap of defining who you are based on what you've done or haven't done? Listen to how Paul deals with his own identity. In verse 20 Paul separates his identity from his sin. He says it's no longer him doing wrong things, but the "sin that dwells in me." Paul doesn't define himself by the sin he commits, and his theology could not be more correct.

Romans 8:1 says, "There is therefore now no condemnation to those who are in Christ Jesus...." Paul understood this truth and so must you. Are you going to fall in this lifetime? Yes. Are you going to have constant fleshly struggles? Absolutely. However, take confidence in knowing that God does not see us as the mess we may think we are. When God looks at you He does not see your sin, but He sees His Son, Jesus, whose blood paid the penalty of your sin, and you are seen as righteous in His eyes. Not only that, but you are also seen as "joint heirs with Christ" (see Romans 8:17). Let's stop living defeated lives because of our struggles and separate sin from our true identity, which is in Christ. "Yet in all these things we are more than conquerors through Him who loved us" (Romans 8:37).

Father, thank You for sending Your Son to become sin for us on the cross, so that I no longer have to live in sin's bondage, and Father, forgive me for when my flesh gets the best of me. Know that it is not my desire to give in, but my desire is to live for You and Your glory. Thank You that my sin doesn't define me but that the blood of Your Son does. Amen.

Hutch Kufal, First Baptist Church Bentonville

Week 21, Thursday
Your Desires = His Desires

Delight yourself also in the LORD, and He shall give you the desires of your heart.

Psalm 37:4

How often have you heard this verse and thought to yourself, *I desire a relationship with a certain someone,* or *I really desire to be on that team or a part of that group or have that material thing;* and *this verse tells me that the Lord wants to give me my desires, so come on, God—let's do it. I'm ready!* This isn't just an idea or a thought that a teenager could have, but it is often the ideology of adults as well. Here's the problem: we as Christians sometimes take a verse and want to define it on our terms rather than on God's. This scripture actually has nothing to do with us, but everything to do with God. This is crucial in discovering who you are in Christ. The first part of this verse says, "Delight yourself also in the LORD . . ." In verses 3–7 you see key words such as *trust, feed, delight, commit, rest,* and *wait.* The Psalmist is telling us that when we strive to do each of these things to the glory of God, then the Lord will give us the desires of our heart. When you reach this level of spiritual maturity, you will realize that your desires aren't for mere worldly things, but for heavenly things and the things of God.

This spiritual truth is also the key to learning God's will for your life. The Lord's will for your life isn't mysterious. How many times have you talked to a friend or heard someone say that they are struggling to discern God's will, whether it be which college to attend or vocation to pursue? Don't miss this: if you are truly delighting yourself in the Lord and pursuing Him, the personal desires that you may have are ultimately God's desires for you. So go pursue the college, career, or passion of your heart, because in doing what you desire, you are glorifying Christ. Through your delighting in Him first, the desires and passions you may have, in reality, without you even realizing it, are His desires and passions for you.

Father, help me to truly understand what it means to "delight" in You, and through that, God, place within me the desires and passions that You would have for me. Make Your will for my life known through my simple obedience to You. Amen.

Week 21, Friday
Does Satan Know You?

And the evil spirit answered and said, "Jesus I know,
and Paul I know; but who are you?"

Acts 19:15

Check this out! In Acts 19, Paul was in Ephesus, which is a place that had a reputation for the learning and practicing of magical arts. Ephesus was steeped in superstition. In this one instance, some Jewish exorcists and pagan priests took it upon themselves to try to use the name of Christ to cast an evil spirit out of a man. They had heard the name of Jesus had power, so they thought they would give it a try themselves. "We exorcise you by the Jesus whom Paul preaches," reads verse 13. The demon replied, "Jesus I know and Paul I know, but who are you?"

This evil spirit knew the name of Jesus, but it also knew Paul's. Paul knew who he was in Christ. He lived radically for Christ, striving to be all things to all people in order to win more souls. Here's a thought. How cool would it be for the enemy to know your name? Because here's the truth of the matter: we are all sheep, and Jesus is the Great Shepherd. Matthew 10:16 says, "Behold, I send you out as sheep in the midst of wolves. . . ." It does not make sense for a sheep to wander into a wolves' den, nor would a shepherd ever lead his flock of sheep into such peril; but this is exactly where Christ (the Great Shepherd) calls us. As His sheep, He is calling us to go into enemy territory and to make a difference for His Kingdom. So get up and go make an impact on lives for the glory of God. Be confident in who you are in Christ. Be bold, courageous, and intentional—to the point that when you walk into the battle, the enemy knows who's coming.

Father, I praise You because Your name is above all names. I am humbled
and grateful that I have the privilege of carrying that name. Lord, I pray
that today I would be bold and step into the battle for You doing all I can to
make Your name known. I know the enemy is out there, so God, protect me;
let me put on the armor of God and make a difference for Your Kingdom.
Amen.

Hutch Kufal, First Baptist Church Bentonville

Week 21, Weekend
Your Natural Bent

If any of you lacks wisdom, let him ask of God, who gives to all liberally and without reproach, and it will be given to him.

James 1:5

Did you know that you have a "natural bent"—a unique, one-of-a-kind personality and view of the world? God created you that way. He didn't just pour one mold for human beings and call it a day. God uniquely designed you and then broke the mold! There is no one else like you.

Why did God do that? He's a creative God. He loves to express Himself in exceptional ways. God creatively formed your DNA, your personality, your gifts, your talents, and your temperament. Second, God is a Creator who longs to relate to His creation. Therefore, each of us was granted a God-given, one-of-a-kind temperament so that we might uniquely express our love to God and to His people in ways that no one else can. In other words, we have each been created to love God and other people in totally unique ways. No one else can love God in just the way that we can. No one else can love others in the exact way that we've been designed. God created us with individuality and uniqueness because He delights in seeing us express that uniqueness in relationship with Him and others. Isn't that an amazing characteristic of our Creator?

Take time to celebrate this incredible characteristic of our God. How does it make you feel to know that God chose to create you with individual gifts, talents, temperament, and personality? His intention was to create the "rare design" that could only be you!

I'm _____ amazed/grateful/surprised as I imagine that no one else can love God or others just like I can. This truth makes me feel _____ toward God.

Take the next few moments and ask God to show you how He wants to involve you in making a positive contribution to the world. Ask God to show you how your one-of-a-kind personality and talents can make a positive impact on others. Ask for His wisdom, knowing that He promises to give wisdom to anyone who asks (James 1:5).

God, show me how my personality and talents can positively impact the lives of others. Please show me how my personality and talents can positively impact my relationship with You. Amen.

Terri Snead, The Great Commandment Network

Week 22, Monday
Represent

Then God said, "Let Us make man in Our image, according to Our likeness; let them
have dominion over the fish of the sea, over the birds of the air, and over the cattle, over all
the earth and over every creeping thing that creeps on the earth." So God created man in His
own image; in the image of God He created him; male and female He created them.

Genesis 1:26, 27

D o you remember the first time you were trusted to do something really big? Maybe you were trusted to babysit a younger sibling. Maybe it was the first time you were given the keys to the family car. It feels good when others trust us with something, doesn't it?

When we read the creation account in Genesis 1, we notice that God said something very intentional about how He was going to create mankind. As He was talking to the other members of the Trinity, He said, "Let Us make man in Our image." Have you ever given that much thought? You are created in the very image of the most powerful being in the entire universe. God has somehow stamped you with His very essence. That is so profound, but what does it mean?

We read that God said, "Let them have dominion." God placed His trust in humanity to rule and reign over what He created. The fact that you and I are created in the image of God is mysterious, and we probably won't know the full implications of that this side of seeing Jesus face-to-face, but it has a great deal to do with the fact that you and I are trusted with representing the Creator here on this planet. The King of all trusts you. He trusts you with something that is most important: to wear His name and to bear His image.

Creator God, You are my Creator and King and I am blown away by the fact that You have created me in Your image. I know that I have done nothing to earn or deserve this. Thank You. By Your Spirit, will You teach me how to represent You in the way that You deserve? I want to bring honor to You with my attitudes and my actions. Thank You for loving me and for trusting me. Amen.

Matt Crowe, First Baptist Church Black Forest

Week 22, Tuesday
Sojourners and Pilgrims

Beloved, I beg you as sojourners and pilgrims, abstain from fleshly lusts which war against the soul.

1 Peter 2:11

Vacations are a wonderful thing. Recently, my family and I went on a two-week vacation to the beach. It was great. We fished, ate seafood, and played in the sand. We had a lot of fun, and I'll be honest with you; I didn't want to come home. I had gotten so used to being on vacation that I didn't want to come back to the responsibilities of my everyday life. I wanted to continue living as if I were on vacation all of the time. But if we lived our lives as if we were on vacation all the time, that would create some huge problems.

Scripture calls us "sojourners and pilgrims." Quite simply, that means that you and I aren't from here. We've spent our entire lives living somewhere that isn't our home. It's as if we've been on vacation our entire lives. Peter reminds us that our allegiance lies in another place. We are only visiting this world.

So, how do we live our lives recognizing the fact that we belong somewhere else? Peter tells us to "abstain from fleshly lusts which war against the soul." As long as you are placed here on this earth, you need to realize that you are engaged in a battle. Some days this life may feel like a vacation, but don't let your guard down! You are in a war. Look to Jesus. He is the perfect example of a life lived with purpose. Jesus never forgot that this wasn't His home. He lived as a "sojourner and pilgrim." Follow the example of Jesus. Fight against the enemy of your soul; and always remember that you were made for much more than this world.

Lord Jesus, thank You that I was created for more than this world. By Your Spirit, I believe I can live for Your Kingdom. Will You continually remind me that this is not my home? Teach me to live a life of conviction and to abstain from all that wars against my soul, especially when I am tempted. Father, show me how to make every moment of this life count in the way that Jesus did. I want Jesus to be my example today. Thank You for loving and empowering me. Amen.

Matt Crowe, First Baptist Church Black Forest

Week 22, Wednesday
He's Holding You Tight

But now, thus says the LORD, who created you, O Jacob, and He who formed you, O Israel:
"Fear not, for I have redeemed you; I have called you by your name; you are Mine."

Isaiah 43:1

I have a two-year-old little girl. She tells me that I am her boyfriend, and I tell her that she is my princess. There are nights when my little girl will wake up screaming at the top of her lungs. This is not an every-night ordeal, but it does happen on occasion. I know from the tone of her voice exactly what is taking place. My little girl is afraid. She's had a nightmare. I jump out of my bed and run down the hall to her room. I scoop her up and hold her as tight as I can. The effect this has my child is almost immediate. She stops crying and almost melts into my arms. Her fear has evaporated, and all seems right in her world again. It's amazing the effect a father has on his child.

Your heavenly Father wants to have that effect on you. He wants every care you have in the world to evaporate away as you rest in His arms. The God who created you and built you from the ground up commands you to stop being afraid. Read Isaiah 43:2–7. God commands you to give up your fear for a reason. He commands you to give up your fear because you belong to Him. No matter the circumstance in your life, you are not alone. You were created by God and for His glory. He is not going to abandon you, and He is able to hold you tighter and closer than any human Father can hold their child. You belong to your heavenly Father. Live above fear today!

Loving heavenly Father, I am Yours. You are higher and more powerful than any obstacle or enemy I face. Thank You that You did not create me to live in fear. Help me not to focus on my problems, but rather help me to focus on the needs of the people I come in contact with. Teach me to focus on You and the relationship I have with You as Your child. Give me courage as I face temptation and evil. Thank You for being my Father. Amen.

Matt Crowe, First Baptist Church Black Forest

Week 22, Thursday
It Revolves Around Him

And it came to pass, at the time of the offering of the evening sacrifice, that Elijah the prophet came near and said, "Lord God of Abraham, Isaac, and Israel, let it be known this day that You are God in Israel and I am Your servant, and that I have done all these things at Your word."

1 Kings 18:36

There are so many things that stick with us our entire lives that we heard our parents or grandparents say when we were younger. "Well, if all your friends jumped off a bridge…," "I don't care what Jimmy's parents let him do…," "Sticks and stones may break my bones…" There are probably dozens more that wouldn't make any sense to the rest of us, but they resonate with you. It's curious the things we remember. Why do those things stick with us? Maybe it's because they annoyed us so much when we were kids, or maybe, just maybe, it's because some of those statements really do matter.

My parents used to tell me that "the world doesn't revolve around you." At the time this did not make me happy. I knew the world didn't revolve around me, but as a child I wished that it did. I'm glad they instilled that message in me. The world doesn't revolve around me. It doesn't revolve around you, either. Elijah understood this principle. Elijah was facing down 850 angry false prophets when he declared that "You are God in Israel and I am Your servant." Read the rest of the passage. God showed up in power and proved Elijah's claim to be true.

When you know who your God is, then you are free to serve Him with confidence, and it won't matter who or how many are watching. Why? You see, the world doesn't revolve around you. It revolves around Him.

Lord of All, thank You that You have created me to serve. I know that sometimes I act as if the world revolves around me. Thank You that it doesn't. Forgive me for being self-centered, and teach me to follow the example of Jesus, who emptied Himself, took the form of a servant, humbled Himself, and was obedient to death on the cross. Convict me when I act as if life revolves around me. Make me aware of the opportunities You give me to serve You and others. Amen.

Matt Crowe, First Baptist Church Black Forest

Week 22, Friday
You're New

Therefore, if anyone is in Christ, he is a new creation; old things have passed away; behold, all things have become new.

2 Corinthians 5:17

I don't know if you are like me, but I find this verse to be so encouraging. In fact, this may be the most encouraging verse in the entire Bible. Before Christ came to live in me, I was a mess. I was a liar; I was a thief; I was a traitor. According to God's law, I should be in a great deal of trouble. As a matter of fact, I should be and was sentenced to death. However, that was before Christ. I am in Christ now and that makes all the difference.

I don't always live as if I am new. There are times when I forget who I am. I live as if I'm still a liar, a thief, and a traitor. That's why this verse is so encouraging to me. I would imagine that this was a pretty powerful concept to Paul as well.

The only condition in this sentence is the word *if*. The apostle Paul assures us that *if* we are in Christ, then we are, without a doubt, *new*. The facts may be simple, but they don't change. Even when we don't act like it, God stands over us declaring that we are new. His is the only word that matters. That isn't an excuse to live like we aren't in Christ; rather it is our motivation to live for Jesus. It simply doesn't make sense for us to live like we used to. Scripture clearly says that the person that we used to be has passed away. That's just a polite way of saying he or she is dead. You are new. Live like it, and let your actions match reality!

Father, thank You that I am new in Your Son, Jesus. You are the only One who knows all of my junk, and yet You still accept me. You are the only One who could condemn me, yet You choose to give me grace. Thank You for accepting me as Your child. I may not always feel new, but I choose to trust Your Word. By Your Spirit, will You help me to live so that my actions match reality? Thank You for making me new in Jesus. Amen.

Matt Crowe, First Baptist Church Black Forest

Week 22, Weekend
What's God Saying?

As each one has received a gift, minister it to one another,
as good stewards of the manifold grace of God.

1 Peter 4:10

When God created you, it wasn't with some cookie-cutter approach or assembly line procedure. God is a craftsman. And as the Master Craftsman, He carefully shaped each intricate detail of your being. He was like a painter who carefully adds the perfect mix of color with just the right stroke of the brush in order to create an original, beautiful masterpiece. The things that make you unique were intentional. God knew what He was doing. The Master Craftsman created His original masterpiece—in you!

You are God's creation, so you can bet that He knows everything about you. Because He formed you and added every special touch, He knows you deeply and intimately. He is fully aware of all of your thoughts, fears, hopes, dreams, insecurities, joys, sorrows, talents, needs, and quirks. God made you, He knows you, and every day, He steps back to admire His work.

God has lovingly created you as a unique individual because He hopes the two of you can share a great relationship. God has also created you as a one-of-a-kind individual so that He might entrust certain missions and callings to you. He created you with certain gifts and talents so that you will be able to live out your life purposes that serve to bring Him glory. In other words, God handcrafted you with the intention that you would experience His love for you and in turn, love Him back. But we're not supposed to stop there. God deeply desires that you extend His love to others in ways that are uniquely your own. Jeremiah was called to be a prophet to the nations. Moses was called to lead the children of Israel. What do you hear God saying about your life?

Ask God to reveal or confirm your life's calling and mission to you.

Father, You made me. You created me with a special purpose in mind. You created me so that I might enjoy You and that You might enjoy me. You created me to share Your love with others. Open up my ears to hear Your voice calling out to me. Help me to be confident in who You've created me to be. Amen.

Week 23, Monday
God's Masterpiece

Thus says the LORD, your Redeemer, and He who formed you from the womb....

Isaiah 44:24

In the fairy tale *Snow White*, the queen (the stepmother) finds daily disappointment in looking in her mirror only to be told that her beauty doesn't quite measure up to that of Snow White.

While most children want to be Snow White in that story (or the handsome prince ... sorry, guys!), the reality is that most children grow up to find themselves playing the role of the vain stepmother, obsessed with what their mirrors "tell" them each day.

Imagine the amount of time teens spend looking in the mirror. For many, what they see in that mirror is not a reflection of who they really are, but an image that's formed through the lens of what others have told them they are. Good or bad, the labels that are put on teens can distort their true identity. Labels such as "fat," "ugly," or "reject" can lead to a lack of self-worth and an obsession to change one's appearance. Labels such as "hot," "cute," or "popular" can be just as damaging, often acting like a drug to those who become obsessed with maintaining such an others-pleasing image. Imagine what would happen if students looked in the mirror, and instead of first noticing their hair, complexion, or shape, they noticed the amazing realization of Isaiah 44:24 ... that they were formed by the Lord. The Hebrew word for *formed* means "to fashion or mold," much like a potter would create a work with a specific purpose in mind. What an awesome truth!

When God created you, He assigned a value and purpose to you that is priceless. Because your value has been assigned by your Creator, no label, sin, circumstance, or person can ever change that value.

Thank You, God for creating me as a masterpiece. I confess to You the times I've accepted labels others have tried to place on me and how I've allowed them to shape my identity. I pray that I will see the beauty and value You has given me. I celebrate that value with the prayer of Psalm 139:13–14: "For You formed my inward parts; You covered me in my mother's womb. I will praise You, for I am fearfully and wonderfully made." Amen.

Tripp Atkinson, First Baptist Church Columbia

Week 23, Tuesday
An Ambassador of Christ

Now then, we are ambassadors for Christ, as though God were pleading
through us: we implore you on Christ's behalf, be reconciled to God.

2 Corinthians 5:20

This verse has some incredibly good news, and also some incredibly bad news. The good news is that we are ambassadors for Christ. Imagine the significance of that reality. As followers of Christ, we not only receive forgiveness of our sins, have a personal relationship with the Creator of the Universe, and enjoy eternal life that begins at the moment of salvation, but we also have the privilege of representing Christ to this world. What an honor! This isn't about representing your class, school, or even country, but about representing the King of kings and Lord of lords! How amazing that we have such a high commission.

The bad news is that WE are ambassadors for Christ. This same overwhelmingly prestigious honor of being emissaries for Christ becomes sobering bad news when we consider that most who call themselves Christians don't take this responsibility seriously. Think of all the times when "we" Christians grossly *mis*represent our Lord. The very word *Christian* means "little Christ," but how well are we imitating Christ? In fact, instead of drawing this world to Christ, many who claim His name do just the opposite.

Consider Paul's description of his role as an ambassador of Christ, "as though God were pleading through us . . . be reconciled to God." To whom in your life does God want to plead through you?

Do you feel overwhelmed and underqualified to be an ambassador for Christ to this person? The good news is that you do not have to do it in your own strength. (In fact, you can't.) The Holy Spirit will empower you to produce Christlike "fruit" in your life, will give you the words to say, and will fill you with boldness as you yield to His work in your life. Before Jesus ascended to heaven, He left His followers with these words: *"But you shall receive power when the Holy Spirit has come upon you; and you shall be witnesses to Me"* (Acts 1:8).

Lord, help me fully embrace my significance as an ambassador of Christ.
Thank You that I have the power available to be a person of influence for
Your Kingdom. Please grant me boldness as I allow You to work through me
to point others to You. Amen.

Tripp Atkinson, First Baptist Church Columbia

Week 23, Wednesday
An Invaluable Part of the Body

For as we have many members in one body, but all the members do not have the same function,
so we, being many, are one body in Christ, and individually members of one another.

Romans 12:4, 5

Leaders naturally desire more influence. In fact, there are many leaders who begin each day praying a prayer like that of Jabez when he asked God to "enlarge my territory" (1 Chronicles 4:10). While leaders certainly should be driven to increase their influence for the sake of reaching more people with the Gospel, if we are not careful, that desire for more influence can evolve into a desire for someone else's ministry and giftedness. This can lead to a form of "spiritual jealousy" that seems admirable, but can render us ineffective as Christian leaders. It is easy to see the ministry of someone like Billy Graham and desire that for yourself. But don't forget the reality that if God wanted you to be Billy Graham, He would have made you Billy Graham. God doesn't want you to be anyone other than you. In fact, "God has set the members, each one of them, in the body just as He pleased" (1 Corinthians 12:18). And all of these members purposely do not have the same function.

No matter how insignificant or humble you may think your gifts are, the truth is that the rest of the body depends on them. Consider this . . . If you remove your gifts from the body, the whole body of Christ suffers. God has uniquely gifted you to contribute to the body of Christ in ways that Billy Graham never could. There are people you can reach with the Gospel that your pastor never could. God has given you a ministry that is markedly original. Go ahead and be what you were made to be today!

Lord, I confess any "spiritual jealousy" and thank You for uniquely gift-
ing me to do what no one else in the body can. God, help me increasingly
embrace my significance as an invaluable part of the body of Christ.

Tripp Atkinson, First Baptist Church Columbia

Week 23, Thursday
The Delight of God

"The LORD your God in your midst, the Mighty One, will save; He will rejoice over you with gladness, He will quiet you with His love, He will rejoice over you with singing."

Zephaniah 3:17

Have you ever paused to really consider that God rejoices over you? Think about how God. Delights. In. You. As sinful as you may be, you are God's prized creation (Genesis 1:26–27), and He delights in you.

So many student leaders lose sight of this life-changing realization. Instead of humbly celebrating the fact that they are the delight of God, many find themselves exhausted, running on a hamster wheel of religion in an attempt to gain God's favor. This wheel may partially be created by well-intentioned youth pastors and Sunday school teachers who give student leaders "checklists" of spiritual disciplines and Bible studies that will help them draw closer to God. Although such resources can be extremely helpful, it is important not to confuse a list of "do's" with enjoying a relationship with God. This can quickly lead one to feel like a spiritual failure, which is exactly what God does not want.

What God does want is for us to delight in Him. Psalm 37:4 states, "Delight yourself also in the LORD, and He shall give you the desires of your heart." Psalm 70:4 says, "Let all those who seek You rejoice and be glad in You; and let those who love Your salvation say continually, 'Let God be magnified!'" God delights in us as we delight in Him. Just as an earthly father would, God desires for His children to desire and take joy in Him.

Do not forget today the great price that God paid to have this love relationship. While you were still a sinner, Christ died for you (Romans 5:8). Christ's death and resurrection not only offer freedom from sin and death, but they also offer freedom from an exhausting form of religion that seeks acceptance. Accept the fact that you are loved by God with an infinite amount of love. May your acts of service and devotion today be an overflow of your delight in the Lord; not to be checked off a list, but to be given as a spiritual act of worship.

 Lord, as I come to You, may I take time just to delight in You. I pray that I will enjoy Your company as much as You enjoy mine. Amen.

Tripp Atkinson, First Baptist Church Columbia

Week 23, Friday
An Adopted Child of God

For as many as are led by the Spirit of God, these are sons of God. For you did not receive the spirit of bondage again to fear, but you received the Spirit of adoption by whom we cry out, "Abba, Father." The Spirit Himself bears witness with our spirit that we are children of God, and if children, then heirs—heirs of God and joint heirs with Christ, if indeed we suffer with Him, that we may also be glorified together.

Romans 8:14–17

Adoption can be a very tough and costly process for prospective parents as they navigate the necessary channels to acquire the child they so desperately long for. This was certainly true for God, as well, as He gave His very Son to the cross so that we could have the opportunity to be called His children. How amazing it is that God would give so much to choose us! And all we have to do to receive this adoption is choose Him back. That is what being "led by the Spirit" is all about . . . daily choosing to allow God's Spirit to lead your life.

Not only does this passage remind Christ-followers that we are children of God, but it also tells us we are heirs of God. An heir is one who has a right of inheritance. Because of what Christ did on the cross, God has given all Christians the inheritance of eternal life (Titus 3:7; John 3:16). As if that's not enough, Scripture tells us that one day all believers will also inherit all things in God's new creation (Revelation 21:7).

No matter what your earthly family is like, know that as a child of God you are a part of the family of God. You can come before God boldly, knowing that you have full access to your heavenly Father. You can have confidence that no sin, mistake, or anything in all creation can separate you from His love (Romans 8:38–39). Even if you do sin, His discipline is further proof of His Fatherly love. Revelation 3:19 says, "As many as I love, I rebuke and chasten."

Father, today I come to You with confidence. Thank You for giving Your all so that You can call me Your child. Help me to embrace my significance as a child of the King! Amen.

Tripp Atkinson, First Baptist Church Columbia

Week 23, Weekend
God Gives Good Gifts

In everything give thanks; for this is the will of God in Christ Jesus for you.

1 Thessalonians 5:18

Think back to all the Christmas and birthday celebrations of your past. What gifts stand out as your favorites? Do you remember a special bike or a memorable toy? Just as your family and friends have given you special gifts over the years, God has given you amazing gifts and talents. Your totally unique mixture of gifts and talents is just one of the ways that God has demonstrated His ingenuity, creativity, and generosity.

God has given you certain abilities, talents, and passions that are related to your physical or mental abilities, such as athletic skill, artistic ability, academic excellence, or creative problem-solving. Think for a moment about some of the physical and/or mental gifts God has given you.

I'm grateful that God has given me the ability to . . .
(For example: easily understand concepts in science; have some success in cross country; learn Spanish vocabulary quickly; etc.)

Because every aspect of your unique identity is a gift from God, each of these aspects has the potential to help others see God, feel His love, and respond to Him. Be sure to look for ways that might happen!

I feel _____ when I think about how my ability to _____ could help others see God.

God also bestows upon us gifts that are more spiritual in nature. Through the work of the Holy Spirit in our lives, God gives us certain spiritual gifts that reflect His character and His presence in our lives. Has God given you one of these spiritual gifts? What might your role be within the body of Christ?

teaching	exhortation	giving	leadership	mercy
compassion	prophecy	administration	discernment	faith
helping others	knowledge and wisdom			

How does it make you feel to know that our generous God has given you physical, mental, and spiritual gifts? Tell Him about your gratitude.

God, thank You for being so generous to me. You have given me so much.
I'm especially grateful for how You've created me with the gifts of . . . Amen.

Terri Snead, The Great Commandment Network

Week 24, Monday
Significance Lost

So when the woman saw that the tree was good for food, that it was
pleasant to the eyes, and a tree desirable to make one wise, she took of its
fruit and ate. She also gave to her husband with her, and he ate.

Genesis 3:6

Epic is a word used much in youth culture today. It's common to hear phrases like "her clothes are epic" or "his faux-hawk is epic." Did you know the word *epic* actually originated to describe certain works of literature? For example, certain poems were called *epics* because they told powerful stories about great events in history.

The Old Testament records the most epic story ever told. This is our story. It begins in the Garden of Eden where Adam and Eve had a perfect relationship with God. There were no disappointments, unfulfilled expectations, or lack of self-esteem. Adam was strong and capable. Eve was industrious and had purpose. They both found their significance in their connection with their Creator.

This love story goes bad quickly in Genesis 3. Just as if he were cued by a director, Satan enters and tempts the young lovely couple. Eve's lust to be like God leads her to eat the forbidden fruit. Adam is offered the same sweet temptation and blindly follows. This was a monumental moment with epic consequences . . . for us all.

You see, eating the fruit was not the main issue. Adam and Eve's sin was their disobedience. They believed they could meet their *own* need for significance. Truth be known, we are all guilty of this same self-centered sin.

How are you searching for your value in life? Relationships? Athletics? Education? Hobbies? Possessions? These offer only temporary satisfaction. When looking to fulfill the deepest needs of your soul, look no further than Jesus.

Lord Jesus, thank You for loving me enough to passionately pursue a relationship with me. Like Adam and Eve, I, too, have searched for significance in the wrong places. I never found satisfaction. Please forgive me for my selfishness and disobedience. I understand that my ultimate fulfillment comes only in You. I am so grateful that You are in control of my epic story. I declare today my need for You, and I choose to follow You wholeheartedly. Amen.

Scott Sullivan, First Baptist Church Haughton

Week 24, Tuesday
Significance Found

And if you are Christ's, then you are Abraham's seed, and heirs according to the promise.

Galatians 3:29

Congratulations! You have just been named an heir to a fortune with riches beyond your wildest dreams. You didn't earn this grand prize. As a matter of fact, it's not about you. It's really more about the giver than the recipient.

How does that make you feel? Astonished? Excited? Skeptical? This is precisely the feeling many Christians get when they realize their significance in Christ and the inheritance awaiting them. Most are überexcited. Some are cautious, knowing they do not deserve such a gift.

There are several spiritual inheritance principles to remember. First, you must grasp who you are in Christ. Please know that your inheritance as a believer is not related to the things of this world. God never promises big money, popular girl/boyfriends, or a fantastic vehicle. He does offer genuine freedom through your identity in Christ that can be found nowhere else.

Second, you must believe the Bible is God's holy Word. Our heavenly Father actually tells us who we are in His Word. He's not trying to keep our inheritance a secret. God is passionate about us knowing Him and knowing who we are in Him.

Third, accept the responsibility to live your life according to your identity in Christ. A dying, godless world is desperate to see the authentic faith of believers. Do people recognize you as a child of the King (Jesus)? Are you living out who you are in Christ? Allow God to do all He needs to do in you so that He can do all that He wants to do through you.

Lord, I am a blessed child of the King with great responsibility to live well (John 1:12). I am salt and light in this world, affecting everything close to me (Matthew 5:13–14). I am the Holy Spirit's temple and will treat my body with dignity (I Corinthians 3:16). I am a new creation (2 Corinthians 5:17). I'll not be paralyzed by past failures but will focus on future blessings. I find my significance in You, who created me to do good works (Ephesians 2:10). Amen.

Scott Sullivan, First Baptist Church Haughton

Week 24, Wednesday
Satisfied

[I pray] that you, being rooted and grounded in love, may be able to comprehend with all the saints what is the width and length and depth and height [of the] love of Christ.

Ephesians 3:17–19

What drives you to do what you do? Does anything make your heart beat fast and your palms sweat? Is there anything that would cause you to get up early or stay up late? The answer to these questions is critical. At the root of your answer is what you care about most. This can be a life-altering moment for any God-follower willing to be honest.

God desires to meet the greatest need of every human . . . to be loved and accepted. Peace in this life cannot be achieved without grasping this truth. God truly delights when His people find satisfaction in Him.

Satan uses several tools to try to destroy the fulfilling fellowship between God and humans (John 10:10). First, there is the deadly tactic of busyness. It has often been stated that if Satan can't make you bad, he'll make you busy.

A second tool used by the enemy to hurt believers is ignorance. He wants to keep our minds clouded with the cares of this world rather than grounded in truth. God uses the Bible, His love letter, to give us the knowledge we need to stand firm.

A third tool the enemy employs to lead believers to implode is confusion. He regularly tries to trick Christians to believe that God does not care, or that our Creator somehow has too much going on to intervene in our small lives.

Never forget that you have great value because God loves and accepts you. Stand firm against all that the enemy would do to convince you otherwise. There is no greater satisfaction known to man than when we are "rooted and established in [God's] love."

Lord Jesus, I am overwhelmed by how high, long, wide, and deep Your love is for me. I am encouraged that the wellness of my soul is Your passion. Daily I am reminded that my weak efforts just aren't good enough to bring the peace I seek. Thank You for loving and accepting me in spite of my failures. I trust You today to continue to guide, strengthen, and renew me. Amen.

Scott Sullivan, First Baptist Church Haughton

Week 24, Thursday
Created to Connect

...joined and knit together by what every joint supplies, according to the effective working by which every part does its share, causes growth of the body...

Ephesians 4:16

There is no such thing as a self-made man. Our culture teaches students a self-destructive lie that has affected generations: *Get what you can, while you can, before you can't.* This self-serving attitude sends the message that we need only our own strength and wisdom to succeed.

Scripture repeatedly presents the powerful truth that God uses connections to help us realize our true significance and potential. For example, God formed Eve to be a helpmate for Adam because it was not good for Adam to be alone (Genesis 2:18). Barnabas stood with Paul, the former Christian killer now turned preacher, because he could not stand on his own merit.

The Holy Spirit guides Christians to embrace their significance through connections (1 Corinthians 12:13). Believers are led to this realization in several ways. First, they can find great instruction and encouragement through God's Word. If one wants to know the will of God, that person must get to know the Word of God. It is His love letter given to His creation for His glory.

Christians can also learn to grasp their value through intimate conversations with their Creator. We must learn to not only talk to God, but listen for His response. Too many of our prayers sound like Christmas wish lists when they should resemble a beggar's plea for mercy.

Another critical component that offers hope and direction is the local church. Students need a sweet place to belong and be loved. Christian students who are serious about following the Lord should search out authentic, godly mentors who are willing to invest long-term. Many times it is through these quality relationships that we find much needed wisdom.

Lord Jesus, I understand that my future success has little to do with my own skill and everything to do with Your ability. Help me to daily draw strength from intimate time alone in Your Word and in prayer. Please continue to connect me with like-minded believers who are not willing to settle for less than Your best. Thank You in advance for the great works You will do in and through me to make a difference in the world. Amen.

Scott Sullivan, First Baptist Church Haughton

Week 24, Friday
Going Viral

"A new commandment I give to you, that you love one another; as I have loved you, that you also love one another. By this all will know that you are My disciples, if you have love for one another."

John 13:34, 35

The YouTube phenomenon of spreading a video worldwide in minutes is astonishing. Never before could a message or experience be spread so widely and shared so quickly. Some YouTube personalities have made fortunes, changed careers, and even obtained sponsors because of their growing popularity.

Just as YouTube fans are awaiting the next great video, youth culture is awaiting the next great icon. The world is mesmerized by heroes willing to go the extra mile or achieve greatness through extreme commitment. Where are the students willing to live this epic lifestyle that stands against the tide of mediocrity?

While the world waits, comfortable believers lie silent with a virally explosive message that will meet the deepest needs of humanity. We know that the majority of our morally deficient world is lost. Clearly, people are aching to find significance. Who will start the next ministry that spreads across the globe and meets this need for the glory of God?

Once people find salvation and significance in Christ, they should readily share their journey. As recipients of such great love, we must, in return, express this love to others. For this message to go global, we must allow the Holy Spirit of God to fill and use us. The word *filled* in the original language (Ephesians 5:18) means to "be possessed fully by" or "influenced fully by." Maybe there *is* a group within this generation God is calling out to take a stand. Perhaps there *is* a student willing to sacrifice and be the tool through which the Gospel goes viral in our love-deprived world.

Father, may my generation never be content with the desperate conditions of our culture. It is clear that caring for the souls of Your creation is countercultural. I declare today that my heart belongs to You. When people ridicule me I will gladly stand. If I must battle alone, I will stand honorably. No matter what this sacrifice costs me, I will go, so that others might find the love I've experienced in You. Amen.

Scott Sullivan, First Baptist Church Haughton

Week 24, Weekend
Harmony Makes Him Happy

"I do not pray for these alone, but also for those who will believe in Me through their word; that they all may be one, as You, Father, are in Me, and I in You; that they also may be one in Us."

John 17:20, 21

Think about how crucial each of our body parts is to life. Your heart, lungs, and spinal cord have very specific functions. In order for the body to function properly, every part must perform specific tasks in concert. The failure of even one small part can lead to serious illness or even death of the human body.

Just as every body part has a specific function to perform in the human body, you also have a specific function that has been set aside for you within the body of Christ. Your distinctive, God-given identity makes you uniquely suited to serve the body of Christ. Just as an eye is not meant to help us hear and a nose is not meant to hold a tool, we are each called to serve the body of Christ in specific ways, ways in which others may not be suited to serve.

God's desire is that His children would form a single body, united by a shared purpose and driven by a shared commitment to Him. Jesus hopes that you and I will be an expression of His life and His unity with the heavenly Father, and it impacts Him deeply when there is conflict among His body. How do you think it makes Jesus feel to see His followers divided? How do you think Jesus feels when He sees His people being critical of one another, judgmental, harsh, unloving, insensitive, disrespectful, or dishonoring? How does Christ's heart respond to see the body of Christ hurting itself or see His family in conflict?

When Jesus sees His followers divided, it must make Him feel _____.

Pause for a few moments and reflect on the feelings of Jesus. The One who created you and died for you hurts when He sees the conflicts between those He loves. What impact does that have on you?

When I consider how Jesus feels when He sees His followers divided, it impacts me in this way . . .

God, please use me to be an agent of unity and harmony with Your people. Show me one specific person whom I could better love this week. Amen.

Terri Snead, The Great Commandment Network   145

Week 25, Monday
Convince Me!

For I am persuaded that neither death nor life, nor angels nor principalities nor powers, nor things present nor things to come, nor height nor depth, nor any other created thing, shall be able to separate us from the love of God which is in Christ Jesus our Lord.

Romans 8:38, 39

What are you convinced of? Are you convinced that Big Foot exists or that professional wrestling is fake? We tend to be skeptical, so it usually takes a lot to convince us of something. We want evidence. We want to know that what we believe has been confirmed and, therefore, is true—we want to be convinced!

Are you convinced of God's love? If not, let's look at the evidence. God formed you in your mother's womb and knew you even then (Jeremiah 1:5). The word *formed* actually means "to create or shape." Think of an art student working on a final project. They take many hours to create, shape, and mold their masterpiece. To arrive at anything else but art is not an option. They form with their hands what they see in their mind. God has done this with you. He formed you into a work of art, not of your own hands or your own will, but of His.

But God does something that an art student can never really do—He knows His masterpiece! God's plan was never to put you on a shelf for the world to look at and admire. His plan was to create movable art, usable art, art that can change the world. So, He plans your days, your accomplishments, and your journey to coincide with His. He knows you!

Why would He do that? In Leviticus 26:12, God says, "I will walk among you and be your God, and you shall be My people." God's plan was always relationship. Out of His infinite love (it never runs out), He made a plan to form you, know you, and use you for His glory, because of love.

Lord, remind me today of Your love. Help me to know the love that formed me and determined my days. Give me a heart to love You in return. Today, help me to live out Leviticus 26:12—I want You to be my God and I want to be Your child. Thank You for Your love and that my life is significant because of it. Amen.

Doug Biscoff, First Baptist Church Houston

Week 25, Tuesday
How Does God See Me?

And you, who once were alienated and enemies in your mind by wicked works,
yet now He has reconciled in the body of His flesh through death, to present
you holy, and blameless, and above reproach in His sight.

Colossians 1:21, 22

Parents are people who tend to love us, but the don't always like us. Friends can be the same way. In fact, it's human nature to have moments when even the closest of friends or family, whose value you would not question, just get on your very last nerve.

Does Jesus like you? Have you gotten on His nerves lately? It's very easy to take human attributes and attempt to place them on Jesus. Truth is, He *does* like you. He will never remove you from His "friend list." His love for you is unconditional, and His attitude toward you does not change.

That may seem strange to you! But in the passage above we learn that we are reconciled to Him. *Reconciled* is actually an accounting term meaning to bring into balance or to make compatible. You are forever balanced in your account with God. His love or "like" of you will never change.

You have His favor. So, what are you doing with it? Are you living a life of freedom in which pleasing God and making Him happy are distant memories? Or are you striving each day to be the perfect Christian? Make no mistake, God takes sin seriously, and we are to confess our sins to Him each day. But He doesn't hate us when we fail; He doesn't even dislike us.

Lord, thank You for your favor. Help me today to live in the freedom of that favor and to know that my account is settled, my balance is paid, and You look upon me with satisfaction. Let me not ignore my sin, but also don't let it rob me of the joy I have in You each day. Thank You for Your favor and that my life is significant because of it. Amen.

Doug Biscoff, First Baptist Church Houston

Week 25, Wednesday
God in Us

"Nevertheless I tell you the truth. It is to your advantage that I go away; for if I do not go away, the Helper will not come to you; but if I depart, I will send Him to you."

John 16:7

Near the end of His time on earth, Jesus would often sit and explain hard things to His disciples. One of these difficult issues was the fact that soon He would be going away. For those who had followed Him, giving up everything to do so, this must have been terrible news. But in response, He promised them something better. What could be better than Jesus? The answer is, the Holy Spirit. He is better because although Jesus walked with the disciples, He was physical and they needed to be where He was. He is God *with* us. However, the Holy Spirit comes to be God *in* us.

"For God has not given us a spirit of fear, but of power and of love and of a sound mind" (2 Timothy 1:7). Paul, in writing to his young son in the faith, Timothy, encouraged him to remember the nature of this Spirit that God had put inside of him. It is not a Spirit that fears, for God is sovereign and has no need to fear anyone. It is a Spirit of power—God's power. It is a Spirit of love—God's love. And it is a Spirit of a sound mind—the self-controlled balance of the mind of God.

It was important that Timothy understand that he had an immeasurable gift inside of him—a gift given by God at the moment of salvation. As a young pastor, Timothy would need this gift for wisdom and guidance. As Christians today, we have this same Spirit, the Holy Spirit of God. For every difficult decision or problem, the Spirit is within us ready to guide us. We live in the power supplied by God, which is always sufficient for the day.

Lord, I thank You that You gave Your Spirit to me. Help me not to rely upon my own strength, but upon Your Spirit for strength, for wisdom, for guidance, and for truth. Remind me that You are always with me, in fact, actually inside of me. May Your Spirit control my life! Thank You for the guiding of Your Holy Spirit and that my life is significant because of it. Amen.

Doug Biscoff, First Baptist Church Houston

Week 25, Thursday
God Speaks Through You

"You will be brought before governors and kings for My sake, as a testimony to them and to the Gentiles. But when they deliver you up, do not worry about how or what you should speak. For it will be given to you in that hour what you should speak; for it is not you who speak, but the Spirit of your Father who speaks in you. "

Matthew 10:18–20

As God's children, there are times when God gives us the opportunity to speak. Perhaps it's as informal as a conversation in a hallway by a locker or as grand as a speech before your school. Either way, we desperately need the right words to say. But as children of King Jesus, given authority by Him, we have two distinct factors working in our favor.

First, we speak on behalf of the King. As His child, we represent Him to a world that does not know Him. Second, we possess the Holy Spirit of God, which gives us the right words to speak. It is not our own wisdom or logic that works in the hearts of those who hear us. But it is the words of the King, sent through His Spirit and spoken through you.

Has God given you an opportunity to speak? Do you have the ear of friends, classmates, or family members who need a word from the King? Be confident that those words can come through you.

Lord, remind me today of Your ability to speak through me. Even if I stand before governors and kings, You are with me. Give me words for Your glory. Use me today with great courage! Thank You for the words of Your Holy Spirit and that my life is significant because of it. Amen.

Week 25, Friday
God Knows Your Future

For I know the thoughts that I think toward you, says the LORD*, thoughts of peace and not of evil, to give you a future and a hope. Then you will call upon Me and go and pray to Me, and I will listen to you.*

Jeremiah 29:11, 12

Life can be full of difficult decisions—where to attend college, what area of study to major in, when to marry, whom to marry, whether or not to have kids, etc. And the weight of those decisions can be overwhelming. Much is made of making wise choices—no one wants to mess up their life through a wrong decision. Stories of divorce, dead-end jobs, and broken relationships can raise the tension in making the right choices. For many the answer is to give a lot of thought to these types of decisions; some may ask parents, mentors, or other significant people for advice; and some may even pray.

Does it help to know that part of God's love for you is that He has worked out your future? Consider the passage above. He speaks of hope and peace. Does this sound like Someone intent on just telling you what to do? No, God's purposes for you are noble and magnificent.

God has created you for a specific assignment. You are a real and unique part of His plan. You have been given abilities, talents, and gifts made especially to fulfill that plan. All that's left is to rest in His guidance. Each day is a work of great craftsmanship created by a King intent on using you to your fullest for the greatness of His Kingdom!

But God is not an employment agency in the sky. He shares this future with us through a relationship. He requires that we trust Him, love Him, and seek Him. But consider the benefits—what a joy to wake up each morning knowing that you have a purpose and your life is significant because of it.

Lord, thank You for the care and precision with which You planned out my days. Use me fully, King Jesus, for Your glory. Lead me in the path that You have prepared for me and make my life a miracle. Thank You for planning my days and that my life is significant because of it. Amen.

Doug Biscoff, First Baptist Church Houston

Week 25, Weekend
We All Suffer

If one member suffers, all the members suffer with it;
or if one member is honored, all the members rejoice with it.

1 Corinthians 12:26

God has designed you with a distinct identity. You have a one-of-a-kind set of talents, abilities, spiritual gifts, and personality traits. God has lovingly and generously given these gifts to you. As followers of Christ, these gifts are not ours to possess, guard, or even use as we please. They are gifts that we have been given and gifts that we are called to give back to God and others in return. As you come to more fully understand your strengths, abilities, and unique identity as God has created you, let your focus be: How can I utilize all of these God-given gifts to *give* to others?

An important part of being a follower of Jesus is staying aware of what is going on in the lives of others and generously giving of ourselves. In so doing, we are allowing Christ to meet others' significant needs through us. If one person suffers, we can express Christ's love by suffering with them, because we are all members of the same body of Christ.

Who do you know that might be suffering, feeling alone, or in need of support? What are some specific ways in which you can give of yourself and help that person feel Christ's love?

A person who might be suffering is _____. I could share Christ's love with him/her by . . .

A person who might be feeling alone is _____. I could share Christ's love with him/her by . . .

A person who might need support is _____. I could offer my help by . . .

God's Word reminds us many times that when Jesus came across people who were hurting in some way, He was moved with compassion (Matthew 9:36). If Jesus were to see the people you have just named, how might He respond? Jesus would be so moved with compassion for the people you've identified that He couldn't help but respond. He would demonstrate love in action. What emotions well up in you as you reflect on a God who is moved by our suffering, aloneness, and need for support?

  God, when I consider that You are moved with compassion by our struggles, I feel _____. Move my heart with Your compassion and help me demonstrate love in action. Amen.

Week 26, Monday
The Truest Form of Love

No one has seen God at any time. If we love one another, God abides in us,
and His love has been perfected in us.

1 John 4:12

A quick Internet search will reveal dozens, maybe hundreds, of song titles that contain the word *love*. Although there may be many reasons for that, one primary reason that cannot be overlooked is that more people search for love than anything else in all of life. They seek love from their family, from parents, from friends, from dating/marriage relationships, etc.

• *Where have you looked to find love?*

• *What do you think gives people that inner desire to love and be loved?*

As a follower of Jesus, you have been given the privilege of showing others what true love really is! God is love. His very nature is and always will be the truest form of love. When Christians demonstrate love in their relationships with others, the world has the opportunity to see firsthand the authenticity of true love. God chooses to display Himself when we love others. As we love, people see God in and through us. If you choose not to demonstrate love, your actions keep the world from experiencing one of the essential natures of God.

The demonstration of love is one of the most basic, yet essential truths of the life of faith. Contrary to the accepted belief of most people, love is not just being consumed with feeling and emotion for another person. Love is an action. "God demonstrates His own love toward us, in that while we were still sinners, Christ died for us" (Romans 5:8).

How are your relationships with others, especially other followers of Jesus? Do they display love?

Are there any relationships in which you have conflict or frustrations that prevent you from "loving out" the love that you have within?

Continually ask the Lord to abide in your relationships so that others can see love, and through that, see God.

Lord, show Your love to me and help me to show it to others. I want to display Your love in everything I do, every step I take, and every decision I make. Amen.

Matt Lawson, First Baptist Church Woodstock

Week 26, Tuesday
A Unique Calling

"Before I formed you in the womb I knew you; before you were born I sanctified you; I ordained you a prophet to the nations."

Jeremiah 1:5

God called on Jeremiah as a young man to be His servant and a prophet to the nations. Jeremiah questioned God and attempted to give excuses as to why God must have chosen the wrong guy.

• *Have you ever told God that you were not the person He wanted for a specific task?*

• *What excuses did you offer?*

Much like when God called on Moses to be the leader of the Israelites, Jeremiah saw his weaknesses and shortcomings as blocking him from truly being used by God. Yet God would not put up with his excuses. He reaffirmed Jeremiah's identity and reminded him that he was formed and put together intentionally for a purpose. He told him of this unique calling on his life to be a prophet and to speak God's word to the nations.

Just as God had a unique calling on Jeremiah's life, He also has one for your life and mine. He designed you with His purposes in mind, and He desires for you to fulfill His purposes for His glory. He desires for you to realize your gifts and talents and use them in a special way for His Kingdom and to impact the world. Challenge yourself today to use your unique abilities to share God's love with others.

Lord, help me to not give in to believing that my weaknesses and failures will stop me from being used by You. Thank You for creating me uniquely in Your image and giving me a special purpose and calling. Because You have done so, my strength, purpose, and future are completely in Your hands. Help me to believe in You and Your calling on my life. Amen.

Week 26, Wednesday
Our God-Value

Search me, O God, and know my heart; try me, and know my anxieties.

Psalm 139:23

God, in His infinite power, formed every part of you with great intention and design.

- *Do you ever wish you could be someone else just for a day?*
- *What parts of your body do you complain about most that you cannot change?*
- *If you could swap personalities with someone, who would it be and why?*

There is not one personality trait, body part, or talent that God did not give you for a specific purpose and calling. He desires for you to understand whose you are and the way He made you. Recognizing and appreciating who He made you to be allows a believer the freedom to uniquely express His love to those around them.

Do you ever listen closely to song lyrics? Often they reveal the deep feelings, failures, and fears of the writers. The greatest song writer of all time, David, came to recognize and be thankful for the way God had made him. If we will rest in the truth of our "God-value," our lives will best tell the story of the Gospel and of Christ's love. The very fact that God had no need for us and yet created us in His very image is the perfect picture of love and grace. We can display this by living out the unique identities and callings God has given each of us.

Take time to meditate on God's Word in Psalm 139 and discover where your value is found. Then, withholding nothing, be exactly who God has made you to be and give Him all the glory.

 God, help me to discover who You have designed me to be and who You desire for me to be. Then, Lord, I want my life to cause people to want to know my Creator, and theirs, too! Amen.

Matt Lawson, First Baptist Church Woodstock

Week 26, Thursday
A Unique Purpose

Then the children of Israel groaned because of the bondage, and they cried out;
and their cry came up to God because of the bondage.

Exodus 2:23

When the bondage of being led in captivity became so great to the people of God in Egypt, they cried out to God, desperately seeking a resolution to their troubles. The direct answer to the cries of the children of Israel would come through one very unlikely man named Moses. Early in life, Moses survived the river basket, became a foster child, had anger problems, and committed murder. Eventually God called Moses out of the fields as a shepherd in order to lead His people out of bondage in Egypt.

- *Do you know any unlikely heroes who overcame a past to be used greatly by God?*
- *Do you ever feel like an unlikely hero with very little to offer God?*

Even though we live in a world that is sensitive to expressing ourselves uniquely, the reality is that our unique expressions are often simply an imitation of something or someone else. While it is very easy to comparison shop our abilities, looks, or usability against one another, it's also very dangerous.

Why? The reason is because the purpose of your life is specific. You weren't created to be an imitation of someone else's reflection of God and His purposes. You are a unique carrier and purpose fulfiller of God's plans.

Because of that specific purpose of your life, you are uniquely positioned in this world by God to fulfill that purpose. When God had a need, He brought about a solution to accomplish it in the unlikely person of Moses. Throughout Scripture, He uses the unlikely to accomplish the impossible. That is great encouragement! When we feel most useless, God wants to do His greatest works through us!

If you have doubts of your purpose, ability, or usability, trust in God's plans today for you and resist the temptation to see His purpose in someone else. In your praying, waiting, and asking, God will bring to focus the specific call on your life and the need He meant you to fulfill.

God, help me today to live out the imitation of Christ's example and not the identity of someone else. I trust Your plan for my life and desire to be the complete and unique expression of You that I was created to be. Amen.

Matt Lawson, First Baptist Church Woodstock

Week 26, Friday
Love Is Willing

Then the LORD said to me, "Go again...." So I bought her for myself for
fifteen shekels of silver, and one and one-half homers of barley.

Hosea 3:1, 2

It would be appropriate to suggest that a true test of love might include the following two questions:
1. To what extent are you willing to go to demonstrate your love?
2. How much are you willing to give up in order to prove it?

The answers from Jesus' perspective would be: *All the way. Everything.*

Besides Jesus, the story of Hosea and his wife, Gomer, demonstrates a powerful picture of love that is pressed into action. In the midst of adultery on Gomer's part, Hosea was commanded by God to seek out his wife to love her again. The command to "Go again" in verse 1 suggests that this was possibly not even the first time Hosea had to do so. Very few of us could imagine the pain of intentionally seeking out an adulterous spouse in order to restore a marriage.

Verse 2 shows an even deeper love commitment as Hosea has found Gomer in the city square on an auction block. Gomer's adulterous life has marginalized her to the point of being sold as a slave. While many could find satisfaction in Gomer's plight, Hosea shows compassion. At the last moment, Hosea offers everything he has in order to bring Gomer home.

The parallel to Jesus is striking. Even from the Old Testament story of Hosea and Gomer, the extent to which Jesus would be willing to go and to give up for a lost and rebellious world were demonstrated and foreshadowed hundreds of years prior to His arrival on earth. The fact that God commanded Hosea to find his wife again compounds the abiding desire of Christ in pursuing a lost world.

The story of Hosea and Gomer, indeed Jesus' mission as well, could be summarized by the following statements: Love Is Willing to Go. Love Is Willing to Pay. The question for the redeemed of Christ becomes, "What could possibly hinder my love for others as Christ has commanded?"

In John 15:17 Jesus tells us, "These things I command you, that you love one another."

Lord, today help me to be a vessel of love to both the body of Christ as well as a lost world. Amen.

Matt Lawson, First Baptist Church Woodstock

Week 26, Weekend
Special Delivery

"Freely you have received, freely give."

Matthew 10:8

It's no surprise, but none of us can really see God. But the crazy truth is that although people cannot see God with their eyes, when we demonstrate love for others, it's as if people *can* see God. People see God in us when they experience His love lived out through us. In fact, you may be the most important expression of God's love that some people will ever see.

Reflect for a few moments on how you have experienced God's care through the life and love of another friend or family member. Think about those times when God brought someone to help you, listen to you, support you, or encourage you at just the right time. Remember the moments when God sent a friend or family member to pick you up when you were sad, hang out with you when you were lonely, or give you a hug when you were down.

I'm grateful for the time when God sent _____ at just the right time, because . . .

I'm so glad that God brought _____ into my life when . . .

It is our gratitude for receiving God's love through other people that prompts us to show love to others. When we regularly remember how God has brought other people in our lives to love us well, we will be motivated to do the same.

Who are some of the people around you who might especially need to feel some of God's love right now?

_____ (name a specific person) probably needs to experience some of God's love right now because . . .

How can you show love to this person using the unique personality traits, gifts, and abilities that God has given you?

God, thank You for sending people to "deliver" Your love at very important times in my life. Help me to do the same for others. I want people to see the real God in me. Amen.

Week 27, Monday
First Response: Worship

Then some came and told Jehoshaphat, saying, "A great multitude is coming against you from beyond the sea, from Syria...." Jehoshaphat feared and set himself to seek the LORD, and proclaimed a fast throughout all Judah.

2 Chronicles 20:2, 3

The warning sound was given: A "great multitude" of Moab was on its way, and it was not possible to win this battle. King Jehoshaphat's first thought was a healthy dose of fear, and this drove him to his knees. Private worship led to influential leadership as the nation joined him in a time of prayer and worship. His first words were of praise: *"O LORD God of our fathers, are You not God in heaven, and do You not rule over all the kingdoms of the nations, and in Your hand is there not power and might, so that no one is able to withstand You?"* Next, he humbled himself and said, *"For we have no power against this great multitude that is coming against us; nor do we know what to do, but our eyes are upon You."*

The result was influence of the greatest magnitude as all of Judah gathered, bringing their children and wives with them, to stand before the Lord, expecting His protection.

Jehoshaphat's prophet, Jahaziel proclaimed publicly, *"Thus says the LORD to you, 'Do not be afraid nor dismayed because of this great multitude, for the battle is not yours, but God's.'"*

Private worship is essential to public leadership. First, is this your battle to fight or is it God's battle? When it is merely man's battle, fear (absolute fright) and dismay (what might be) dominate our thoughts. When it is God's battle, then we are all in; fear and dismay are replaced by worship and praise for what He most certainly will do.

The people followed the example of their leadership and *"stood to praise the LORD with voices loud and high."* Not in whispers, not to each other, but *loud* enough for the enemy to hear and *high* enough to travel across the land for encouragement.

How did the story end? *"When they began to sing and to praise, the LORD set ambushes against the people ... who had come against Judah; and they were defeated."*

 Lord, I give You praise, for there is none like You. May my heart be focused on Your goodness, mercy, and power, and my praise goes out loud and high to bring others to stand with me in trusting You. Amen.

Dr. Jay Strack, Student Leadership University

Week 27, Tuesday
Choose Wisdom First

That night God appeared to Solomon, and said to him, "Ask! What shall I give you?"

2 Chronicles 1:7

The Lord asked Solomon the big question, "What do you want out of life?" Since God knows our hearts before we do, it is probable that He asked the question so that Solomon could make this important decision as the foundation of his life. He had to examine himself and ask, "What *do* I want? Do I choose wealth, power, popularity, or wisdom?"

Solomon was ready with his answer, and it was the right one: "Give me wisdom and knowledge, that I may go out and come in before this people; for who can judge this great people of Yours?"

Men's character is revealed by their desires, and Solomon was no exception. God answered: "Because this was in your heart, and you have not asked riches or wealth or honor or the life of your enemies, nor have you asked long life—but have asked wisdom and knowledge for yourself, that you may judge My people over whom I have made you king—wisdom and knowledge are granted to you; and I will give you riches and wealth and honor, such as none of the kings have had who were before you, nor shall any after you have the like." So pleased was the Lord with Solomon's choice that He made him the wisest and wealthiest man ever to live.

Wisdom is a gift God loves to give to those who want it. James 1:5 tells us, "If any of you lacks wisdom, let him ask of God, who gives to all liberally . . . and it will be given to him." Is it that simple? Yes, it is. No strings attached.

If God asked you tomorrow, "What is it you want from Me?" what would you answer? In fact, He does ask it, and often. Psalm 37:4 tells us, "Delight yourself also in the LORD, and He shall give you the desires of your heart." Find out what *delights* you, and you will know what you would ask for.

We know that Solomon got his answer, for he concludes his last "wisdom writing" with these words: "Let us hear the conclusion of the whole matter: Fear God and keep His commandments, for this is man's all" (Ecclesiastes 12:13).

Lord, help me to make choices and decisions for a lifetime and not just a day. I ask You for wisdom that I might be a godly leader for Your glory. Amen.

Dr. Jay Strack, Student Leadership University

Week 27, Wednesday
The First Truth

We will not hide them from their children, telling to the generation to come the
praises of the LORD, and His strength and His wonderful works that He has done.
That the generation to come might know them, the children who would be born,
that they may arise and declare them to their children, that they may set their hope
in God, and not forget the works of God, but keep His commandments.

Psalm 78:4, 6, 7

It all begins with knowing the Word of God, not just reading it a few minutes while we multitask, but giving our full attention to the stories of the works of God. The Bible on my phone is a great resource, but having the Word in my heart is a sure strength.

Our mission to become a focused disciple, fully attentive to the words of God and His commandments, must be passed on. Our mandate is to teach the next generation the wonderful works of God so that they will set their hope fully on Him. To do this, I cannot let one word of truth fall to the ground through carelessness.

"Passing it on" has been an ancient tradition since the formation of the Church. Some call it "making disciples"; others use the term "spiritual mentor." The Scripture speaks of infusing the Word into a life by passing it on to the next generation. Can you be both mentored and a mentor? Absolutely.

Ask the Lord to lead you to someone who is biblically sound, emotionally stable, and spiritually empowered. If you expect such a person to carve out time for you, then you must show intentionality in your decisions, priority in your time, a hunger for the Word, and a commitment to being a part of a legacy of faith.

The Scriptures tell us stories of rejection, betrayal, and disappointment to let us know that every person experiences these things. But the news for all generations to pass on is that He still delivers, guides, and fortifies the faithful.

If you are interested in rebooting your mind, your heart, and your life to prepare for the uncertain times ahead, then allow God's Word to penetrate you and leave an imprint.

Lord, help me to be quick to incline my ear to Your Word, to be inten-
tional in my time, and to be a doer of Your Word, not just a hearer. Amen.

Dr. Jay Strack, Student Leadership University

Week 27, Thursday
My First Thought Is "Thank You"

First, I thank my God through Jesus Christ for you all,
that your faith is spoken of throughout the whole world.

Romans 1:8

It doesn't take much to understand how important the relationships of Paul the apostle were to him. Whether it was to the Philippians, Romans, Colossians, Ephesians, or Thessalonians, he began his letters by saying, "I thank God for you."

This was not a mere greeting, but heartfelt gratitude for what they meant to him, and it was important that they know this. He specifically wrote a note of gratitude to:

- The Corinthians because God had *given grace;*
- The Ephesians because they had *faith in the Lord and love God's people;*
- The Philippians because they were *partners in the Gospel;*
- The Colossians because their *faith and love for God's people* was sounded abroad;
- The Thessalonians because of their *work of faith; labor of love; endurance inspired by hope; and because their faith is growing more and more.*

It may be said that you can know a person by the first words out of their mouth on any given day. By these first words you know what is important; what he or she expects from a relationship; what the heart is set upon.

If that is true, then what we know about Paul is that he remains grateful for all that these brothers and sisters in Christ mean to him, not for what they have done *for* him, but because of their godly lives and testimonies. He rejoices in their lives, and, in turn, finds great inspiration for his own.

Paul remained grateful for every opportunity as he wrote to Timothy of his thankfulness to "Christ that He considers me trustworthy and allows me to serve Him." He never "got over" being changed from a bitter, angry tormenter into a passionate messenger of the Gospel, and he takes great joy in being able to say, "I thank *my* God for you."

Lord, I bless Your name for who You are, and for the person You are making me. Give me a heart of unconditional gratitude that can live on as an influence to others. Amen.

Dr. Jay Strack, Student Leadership University

Week 27, Friday
The Right Toolbox

*"For which of you, intending to build a tower, does not sit down
first and count the cost, whether he has enough to finish it—lest, after he
has laid the foundation, and is not able to finish, all who see it begin to mock
him, saying, 'This man began to build and was not able to finish'."*

Luke 14:28–30

The constant explosion of access to technology has made us a people of ideas. We are quick to start projects, explore thoughts, and make friends. Where we fall short is in finishing the project, completing the thought, and sustaining the relationship. As godly leaders, we are called to be strong finishers.

The right toolbox is the key to preparing for the future and attaining well-planned goals. The most basic tool is the ability to build and maintain positive, lasting relationships. In the virtual world of friendship, little effort is needed. Friends are "accepted" without question and just as easily ignored.

If we are not careful, we can dismiss a genuine relationship with the living God because we see Him only in one-dimensional words on pages of Scripture, in ancient stories that don't seem to relate. The truth is that unless I am rightly related to Him, I cannot successfully maintain any earthly relationship.

The Bible teaches that we were created as spiritual beings in the image of God. Our first and most important relationship is with Him.

As a teen, I had not done a very good job making choices, and an emptiness consumed me. I remember saying the words, "God, there has to be more to life than this. I give You my life."

By faith I received Jesus as Lord, and the three greatest needs of my life were met:
- I needed a Father, since mine left when I was six. My heavenly Father met that need.
- I needed a family because mine was fractured. He provided me with thousands of spiritual brothers and sisters around the world.
- I needed a future, and by His grace, His plan for my life has been a grand adventure.

I have learned that once I am rightly related to the Lord, other relationships, no matter how fractured or strained, can begin to heal, be strengthened, and many times, be fully restored.

*Lord, help me do first things first: honor You, care about others, and seek
Your wisdom in my choices. Amen.*

　Dr. Jay Strack, Student Leadership University

Week 27, Weekend
Let Him Make You Strong

Oh, do not remember former iniquities against us! Let Your tender mercies come speedily to meet us.

Psalm 79:8

Everyone wants close relationships. Some of us know we want healthy relationships because we've experienced positive relationships at home or with friends. Many of us, though, know that we want close relationships, but have no idea how to live that out.

God's desire is that His children faithfully love one another and meet each other's needs, and that each of us should take that responsibility very seriously, but He also knows that there will be times when other people disappoint us. Even if this happens, God wants us to know that we can still depend on our loving Father to compassionately care for us. We can trust Him to meet our needs, even if friends or family don't. Our assurance and ability to trust our needs to God is reinforced when we remember that Jesus understands. He, too, has experienced the pain of disappointment.

Matthew 26:36–46 and Luke 22:39–46 helps us remember that Jesus understands. During a critical moment in Christ's life, He vulnerably asked a few of His disciples to help Him. Jesus specifically asked His friends to pray along with Him during some of the most agonizing moments of His life. Jesus was clear about what He needed, but His needs weren't met. In fact, He found the disciples sleeping three different times. Can you imagine what Jesus must have felt?

I can imagine that Jesus must have felt _____ when He found His friends sleeping because . . .

Even though His disciples abandoned Him in His moment of greatest need, God addressed Jesus' needs by sending an angel to comfort Him. In Luke 22:43, Scripture says, "Then an angel appeared to Him from heaven, strengthening Him." Jesus, Himself needed to draw strength from His Father.

My heart is strengthened when I see that Jesus understands how I feel when other people disappoint me. I am especially grateful because . . .

Finally, talk to God about a time when one of your needs was missed, or a time when you were disappointed or let down by others. Tell God about your feelings and allow Him to comfort you. Ask God to strengthen you, just as He did for Jesus.

God, even if others don't meet my needs, I know I can trust You. Please help me to remember that You understand and care. Amen.

Terri Snead, The Great Commandment Network

Week 28, Monday
A Compassionate God

When He saw the multitudes, He was moved with compassion for them, because
they were weary and scattered, like sheep having no shepherd.

Matthew 9:36

Man has never been able to discover words that could fully describe the depth of God's character. There have been attempts to, but we have to settle with words like *awesome, indescribable,* or *overwhelming*. Words cannot scratch the depth of who He is, but throughout the life of Jesus we get to see glimpses into the vast character of God. Jesus was God as a man; He was all-powerful and all-knowing, yet He faced every emotion we experience as humans. In Matthew 9, we find Jesus looking at a crowd of people and the Scriptures say He became nauseated when He saw them. He looked at these people and He saw them as hurting and wounded people who had no one to comfort them. His stomach cringed at the thought that no one could care for their needs or protect them from danger. They needed a leader who could save them in every sense.

We use the word *compassion* to describe the emotion Jesus had toward the crowd that day. It is a part of God's affectionate love toward us as men and women. As Christians, we are to demonstrate that same affection toward the people who live in our city, the students we go to school with, or those who hang out with us. When we are compassionate toward people who are going through tragedy or difficult times, we do not walk by them and just feel sorry them. Being compassionate is feeling the weight of their hurt to the point that we cannot help but be a comforting friend. Jesus would end up giving His life for the people in that crowd—and the students in your school—so they could experience the comfort of a Savior.

It is obvious that Jesus wanted us to see His heart of compassion toward people. We cannot describe the depth of God's love to our friends. But God gives you and me opportunity after opportunity to demonstrate His compassion in their lives. Are you demonstrating the love of God to those around you who are hurting?

God, give me Your heart of compassion so I may see the people in my life
who are hurting. Thank You for Your compassionate love that would die for
me. Help me to live out Your character to those around me. Amen.

Brad Hobbs, Student Leadership University

Week 28, Tuesday
Mourning as the Attitude of Christ

"Blessed are those who mourn, for they shall be comforted."

Matthew 5:4

Mourning is not a hot topic in most of our conversations. We do not like to hang out with people who cry their eyes out and have frowns tattooed across their faces. But in the most famous sermon ever preached by Jesus, He says, "Blessed are those who mourn because they will be comforted." I don't believe Jesus was telling us to dress in all black with a dreadful look painted on our faces, but He was telling His disciples and the crowd that had gathered, "Blessed are those who empathize and befriend the hurt and the unbelieving."

A life that mourns has everything to do with the attitude of one's heart. David wrote that God draws near to those who have a broken, repentant heart (Psalm 51:17). God wants you to live a broken life, a life that is broken over sin, over the hurt and pain others face because of sin, and broken over those who have not placed their faith in Christ. A broken heart is heavy and oftentimes can be burdensome. So Jesus teaches that those who mourn, those whose hearts are broken before God, will find comfort. When you become broken over the devastation caused by sin and the eternal damnation of unbelievers, you will feel the heart of God in the most intimate way.

A broken heart allows you as a believer to be met in the most extraordinary way by the only One who can heal your brokenness, but it also allows you to understand and feel the hurt that others are going through. A broken spirit will be a friend when no one else will; it takes care of the poor and the hurting. A broken spirit is just that; it is broken. Where pride and selfishness often keep us from mourning with others who are devastated by sin, a broken heart is willing to be Jesus to a dying man.

God, teach me to mourn with students who have deep wounds and are in need of a relationship with You. Give me a broken heart that only You can fix and give me the courage to be Jesus to the hurting and the unbelieving. Amen.

Week 28, Wednesday
The God of Comfort

*Now may our Lord Jesus Christ Himself, and our God and Father, who has
loved us and given us everlasting consolation and good hope by grace, comfort
your hearts and establish you in every good word and work.*

2 Thessalonians 2:16, 17

The Christian life is not easy. In fact, it is filled with temptations, emotional pain, hurting relationships, and some times persecution. In all of this, Jesus says we are the light of the world. But in most of our lives our lights tend to become very dim, and some of our lights have even gone out. We get tired, we get hurt by close friends, we suffer through a tragedy, and the last thing we want is to be reminded that we are supposed to be the light of the world.

When our lights grow dim, we become very self-centered and we lose sight of how God has called us to live. We cannot recognize the hurts of others over our own desire to find encouragement and comfort. Instead of serving and helping each other, we want someone to take notice of us and serve us in our pain. But Paul says the God of all comfort comforts us in our afflictions so that we might be able to comfort others who are hurting.

We usually run from hurt and emotional pain, but God, the Creator of comfort, has come to comfort us. We try to avoid difficulty, yet God meets us in the middle of our pain. We have to learn as believers there is no friend, circumstance, or gift that can erase our pain, but God is our comfort through the deepest of hurts. God's comfort is perfect; it is everything you and I need. God's comfort in our lives was not just for our benefit. God comforts us through the pain and hard times, so that we might be a comfort to the people around us. God uses our struggles to show His love to the world. When we run to God for comfort and strength, our lights shine as bright as the sun to the unbelievers around us.

Your pain and suffering are great tools in the hand of God. Make sure you run to Him to find comfort, not a boyfriend/girlfriend, a sport, or success. When you run to God to find comfort, you will find it. And He will use your hurt and pain to encourage someone else who is struggling. Allow God to use your pain so that others might come to know Him.

*Father, open my eyes to areas in my life where I am hurting or wounded but
I have not sought comfort from You. Remove every selfish attitude in my life
and use my hurts and pains to comfort others who do not know you. Amen.*

Brad Hobbs, Student Leadership University

Week 28, Thursday
Mourning for Sin

Oh that my head were waters, and my eyes a fountain of tears, that I might weep day and night. Everyone will deceive his neighbor, and will not speak the truth; they have taught their tongue to speak lies; they weary themselves to commit iniquity.

Jeremiah 9:1, 5

Jeremiah was known as the weeping prophet. Throughout his book we see glimpses into his life, where as a grown man he was overtaken by tears and great sorrow. His tears were not for the hurting or the dying, but the for the people who lived around him. His eyes would fill with tears as he looked at the lives of his friends and neighbors as they were consumed by sin. Jeremiah watched before his eyes people carelessly sinning before a holy God, and he was broken over it. Night and day he would mourn before God because of the sin that existed in the lives of God's people.

Sin is the author of every painful, cruel experience we face as students. Broken relationships, friends who leave deep wounds, and the tragedies of life all happen because of sin. Sin eats away at our lives, causing great pain and sorrow, yet we rarely become broken over the sin that exists in our hearts and in our schools. Sin hardly ever causes us to weep. It is a straight blow to the holiness of God and destroys our lives, yet we live unmoved by what it does to us and those around us. Jeremiah could not apathetically watch sin without being moved to tears because of what it was doing to his city and his friends. Sin was a big deal to Jeremiah, because it was a big deal to God.

When we take God seriously and fall passionately in love with Him, sin will cause us to weep and be sorrowful. When we see it in our life or in our community, it breaks us because we deeply desire for God's holiness to be seen. We want God to transform the lives of our friends and our school. Mourning over sin is learning to cry out to God on behalf of others so He might change their lives. Sadly, most of us are not comfortable talking about sin before God, and it does not move us to tears. Being emotionally broken over sin is often a sign of repentance, because the holiness of God consumes our lives. When we become serious about God changing our school and the lives of our friends, we will become devastated by the way sin destroys our relationship with a holy God.

 Heavenly Father, give me a spirit of brokenness for the sin in my life and in the lives of my friends. Give me a hatred for sin and give me tears of mourning over the devastation of sin. Amen.

Week 28, Friday
A Refreshing Life

For we have great joy and consolation in your love, because the
hearts of the saints have been refreshed by you.

Philemon 1:7

You and I always encounter three different groups of people. There is the group of people we don't remember much about. We remember spending time with them, but that is about it; they have very little influence on our lives. Then there are the people who make us feel like dirt; they talk about others, they have a negative attitude about life, and they never see the good in anything. The last group of people we meet are those who make us fall more in love with Jesus when we spend time with them. We are motivated and deeply encouraged when we are with them.

Paul wrote the book of Philemon to a man he had never met in person. But Paul said his own life had been deeply comforted and refreshed because of this man's love for God and for other believers. Philemon's faith filled Paul's heart with joy even while Paul experienced prison and great difficulty. There was something about the way Philemon lived that when people heard about his faith or they saw it firsthand, it encouraged their own faith and challenged them to love deeper. In his conversations, in the way he treated people in the community, to the way he followed God's Word, it greatly motivated others to live out their faith.

Does the way you pursue God encourage others who might be struggling in their faith? When people see your life and talk to your friends, can they say their lives are comforted because of your deep love and strong faith? Our faith, including how we love those who have hurt us, was designed by God to motivate others and to comfort those who are in tough places. When we focus our lives on passionately following after God and obeying His Word, our school, our parents, and our friends will be greatly influenced by God in us. If you want to live a life that makes others better people and draws your friends closer to Christ, then live out God's Word. It will be a radical encouragement to their lives and make God's glory known in the midst of deep struggles.

God, may my love for You and for others be an encouragement to those around me. Jesus, use my life to draw people to You. Make my life an incredible encouragement to others so that they might fall more in love with You. Amen.

Brad Hobbs, Student Leadership University

Week 28, Weekend
Practice Makes Perfect

*...that I may know Him and the power of His resurrection,
and the fellowship of His sufferings.*

Philippians 3:10

The ability to comfort others during times of hurt and loss is one of the most valuable skills for healthy relationships, but in order to know how to give comfort, we first have to know what comfort is not. Imagine that a friend of yours has just broken up with their girlfriend and is devastated by the loss. Here are the responses that *do not* reveal a skill for giving comfort:

- Advice: "Forget about her. Move on, look for someone else."
- Analysis: "This happened because you're too intense."
- Criticism: "You shouldn't have gone out with her. What were you thinking?"
- Complaint: "I know how you feel. Listen to what happened to me ..."
- Pep Talks: "I'm sure everything will be okay. Get over it."
- Neglect: "Let's go play some ball."

Here's what comfort *does* sound like:

"I am so sad that you guys broke up. I care about you and I'm here for you."

Here's a way to practice the skill of comfort. Imagine this scene in the life of Jesus. See if you can enter into His sufferings and offer words of comfort.

Matthew 26:6–13 tells of a woman who pours very expensive oil on the head of Jesus. She alone understood that Jesus was about to give up His life. Jesus repeatedly tried to explain His approaching death to His disciples, but they never seemed to get it. Not only did they not understand Him or His pain, they rebuked the woman for her act of comfort. What emotions was Jesus feeling?

What does it do to your heart to know that our Savior experienced this pain? What do you feel for Jesus?

Jesus, I feel sad/a sense of sorrow/hurt that the people who loved You didn't show You compassion and offer words of comfort. Please help me to be sensitive to others' needs and practice my skills of comfort and compassion. Amen.

Week 29, Monday
Skills to Relate

"It is more blessed to give than receive."

Acts 20:35

I heard a wise man once say, "You show me someone wrapped up in themselves and I will show you a pretty small package." In Acts 20:35 Paul was concluding his message to the Ephesian elders, after which he would depart for Jerusalem and never see them again. And his final message, or rather the final point in his message, was taken straight from the mouth of the Master. He wanted them to know that the road of blessing is paved with generosity. In one sense he wanted them to guard their hearts against a selfish, me-centered approach to life. While these words of Jesus are not recorded in the Gospels and Paul probably received it by oral tradition, the substance of his testimony screams down through the ages that He came to give Himself "that you through His poverty might become rich" (2 Corinthians 8:9). We give because we have been made rich in Christ Jesus. If grace cannot be tangibly seen, then the act of giving must be recognized as the irrefutable fruit of a life that has experienced grace. The opposite must therefore also be true: if one doesn't give, has that person really been saved? Additionally Paul is not saying that those who receive are not also blessed. Rather, the emphasis is on giving, which makes perfect sense considering his audience is church leaders. It is impossible to have an overemphasized focus on your own needs when you are focused on the needs of others. I hesitate to even say, "give to be blessed," because such a statement seems to reduce grace to something cheap that can be manipulated . . . give God works and He will give you a prize. Instead, let the application of the words of Jesus be understood this way: give because you have been blessed and in so doing you experience the joy and satisfaction of honoring Jesus . . . which is itself an immeasurable blessing.

Lord Jesus, I recognize Your generosity and that You became poor so that I might become rich. Thank You for the richness of Your grace and the blessing to be called a son or daughter of God. Help me to demonstrate Your grace by giving to others who have need. I give because You have given to me. Amen.

Brent Crowe, Student Leadership University

Week 29, Tuesday
Blessings Poured Out

"Give, and it will be given to you."

Luke 6:38

The above verse comes at the tail end of a section of one of Jesus' most important sermons (6:27–38) focused on Christian love and charity. It is interesting that Jesus' standard regarding our disposition and actions toward our enemies, and others, is like His own toward all of us sinners: love your enemies . . . we were enemies of God and He sent Jesus into the world; turn the other cheek . . . Jesus allowed Himself to be beaten repeatedly so that by His stripes we might be healed. The previous verse offers an imperative along with the one in the present verse: forgive (37) and give (38). These are to be continuous actions that should characterize the overall brand of the Christian. What makes this passage particularly fascinating is that it comes with a principle of return: your actions (not judging, not condemning, forgiving, and giving) will be returned to you in the same manner:

- *good measure* —a measurement that is in accordance with God's generosity
- *pressed down*— like grain in a measuring container that is pressed down so that the fullest amount possible fills the container
- *shaken together*—the container is then shaken together to further make room for more grain
- *running over*—the container is filled to the fullest extent so that there is a rounded heap at the top where grain is overflowing the container
- *will be put into your bosom*—picture someone in Bible days wearing a robe or long outer garment. They would oftentimes fold the outer garment from their sandals to their waistline, making it like a big pocket in which they could carry something as large as a lamb or a child.

Dr. Luke concludes by describing how the Christian's behavior toward others directly impacts God's behavior toward them. How is all this to be understood? God wants to pour out His blessing, in a good measure that is pressed, shaken, and running over, right into our laps, but the only thing that can prevent that is the face staring back at you and me every morning in the mirror.

Lord Jesus, thank You that You desire to bless my life. I recognize Your blessing is generous and overflowing. Therefore, I commit to not be judgmental and condemning and to forgive and give generously. I ask You to help my motivation be a desire to imitate You, first understanding that only then will I be living a life worthy of Your blessing. Amen.

Brent Crowe, Student Leadership University

Week 29, Wednesday
Forgive to Be Forgiven

"For if you forgive men their trespasses, your heavenly Father will also forgive you . . . ."

Matthew 6:14

The significance of this verse is directly tied to a portion of the Lord's Prayer (read 6:7–13) when Jesus said, "And forgive us our debts, as we forgive our debtors" (12). Jesus here offers commentary on the forgiveness portion of the prayer as a way of concluding the prayer lesson to the crowds gathered for the Sermon on the Mount. The word "forgive" (*aphiemi*) literally means "to hurl away," and there are two ideas essential to understanding the role forgiveness plays in the Christian's life. First, we cannot know on an experiential level God's forgiveness apart from forgiving others of their mistakes. Second, the only prerequisite for forgiving others is their offense. We need not wait for them to come broken before us to forgive; rather we should liberally offer forgiveness to any and all who owe us any kind of a debt. Because God in Christ Jesus on the cross has hurled our sins away as far as from the east is to the west, so we should offer the forgiving act of hurling away any wrongs directed toward us.

My five-year-old son and I are fishing partners. Our time together at the end of the dock is priceless, and this past weekend he managed to catch the biggest fish of his life! It was so big that at first I thought he had gotten his hook caught on something. It wasn't until his persistence drug this three-pounder up to the edge of the dock that I realized what he had. It was so heavy that I thought his little rod was going to snap in half when I pulled it out of the water. It took two hands to hold and he could hardly contain his excitement as I held it up to show him. Now it was time to take a picture so that the legend could live on for years to come. Then in one moment the fish fought his way free (I think I heard him say in his best *Braveheart* voice: "Freedom!") from my hands as I dropped it back into the water. It was an awkward, shameful moment: how could I drop the biggest fish he had ever caught before even taking a picture of it? I stood there in silence as the fish swam away. Moments later I heard his little voice say, "I forgive you, Daddy. Let's catch another one." Before I could even ask forgiveness, he had taken my mistake and hurled it from his thinking. Forgive and you will be forgiven.

Lord Jesus, thank You that You continue to forgive me of my sins. I commit to forgive this day anyone who has wronged me . . . whether they ask for forgiveness or not. Amen.

Brent Crowe, Student Leadership University

Week 29, Thursday
Types of Love

Beloved, let us love one another, for love is of God;
and everyone who loves is born of God and knows God.

1 John 4:7

There is a kind of love only found in those regenerated by Christ. Because the believer has been saved and therefore knows God, he or she should therefore demonstrate love, and that love points back to a relationship with God. William Barclay, a Scottish theologian, puts it this way: "Love comes from God, and love leads to God." The bottom line is that if you love God, you will love others, but if you don't love others, you probably don't love God (read verse 8). Love is a gift from God that enables us to give love to others. Therefore, how *love* is defined in turn answers how love is to be demonstrated. The term here is the oft-used *agape*. C. S. Lewis said there are four kinds of love, but *agape* is "the best because it is the kind God has for us and is good in all circumstances." This love will many times involve feelings, but it will always involve action. In 1 Corinthians 13, known as the Love Chapter, all fifteen characteristics of love are verbs. Most importantly this love (*agape*):

- Defines God and should thus define our lives (4:8).

- Is demonstrated by God sending Jesus into the world and should be demonstrated as we go into the world sharing Jesus and making disciples (4:9).

- Is given by God sending Jesus to be a sacrifice for our sins, and should given by those saved from their sins as they engage the mission of God (4:10).

The other three types of love come naturally and are as follows: a parental or family love (it is natural for me to love my children); a sexual love that is reserved for husband and wife; and a friendship love. All are good in their place, but none can take the place of God's kind of love that defines, is demonstrated, and is freely given in our lives. It is the greatest evidence that you are a child of God.

Lord Jesus, I confess that I can only love You because You first loved me.
I also realize that Your love for me is what enables me to love others and
allows others to see that I belong to You. Therefore help me to love with Your
kind of love so that others will see You, O Lord, in my life. Amen.

Week 29, Friday
A Need for Encouragement

*I thank God, whom I serve with a pure conscience, as my forefathers did, as without ceasing
I remember you in my prayers night and day, greatly desiring to see you, being mindful of your tears,
that I may be filled with joy, when I call to remembrance the genuine faith that is in you, which dwelt
first in your grandmother Lois and your mother Eunice, and I am persuaded is in you also.*

2 Timothy 1:3–5

This week has focused on the concept of giving from several different perspectives. By way of summary, giving expressed through forgiving and love brands our lives and directly impacts our relationship with Christ. In conclusion, attention will be focused on one more aspect of giving: how Paul used his final words on earth to encourage young Timothy. Paul's final words were penned in a letter to a younger leader whom he had commissioned and entrusted and who would continue his influence way beyond his death. There is no doubt Paul knew his last days were ahead, and knowing this he didn't write a letter to a church or group of churches, but rather to a younger leader. And he began this letter by encouraging Timothy in three ways. First, he remembered Timothy constantly in his prayers (3). Through this use of hyperbole, Paul demonstrates he is unceasingly mindful of young Timothy. Second, he recognized Timothy's emotions and struggles and a joyful anticipation of seeing him (4). Third, Paul reminded him of his faith and spiritual heritage (5), calling it a "genuine" or "un-hypocritical" faith. While this is certainly a recipe for encouragement, young leaders should view themselves through the character of Timothy. Therefore the question becomes not "how do I encourage," but "who is in my life that is encouraging me through prayer, understanding, and reminding me of my faith in Christ?" This may sound self-serving until one understands this important truth: I can never be Paul until I am first willing to be Timothy. In other words, the younger leader must develop him or herself so that they can be an encouragement to others. This many times means having a Paul-like figure in your life (parent, family member, youth pastor, pastor, teacher, etc.).

*Lord Jesus, I recognize my need for encouragement. Thank You for the
encouragement I receive from _____ because they pray
for me, understand my struggles, and point me to You, Jesus (or send me
someone in my life who will do these things). Amen.*

Brent Crowe, Student Leadership University

Week 29, Weekend
God's Crazy Economy

You do not have because you do not ask.

James 4:2

God has a crazy economic system! In God's economy, it is better to give than to receive (Acts 20:35), and when we give it will be given to us (Luke 6:38). Here's the way His economy works. If you give forgiveness, you will receive forgiveness. If you judge others, you will be judged. If you give love, you will receive it. One of the most important skills for healthy relationships is your ability to apply God's mysterious (and sometimes crazy) principles within His economy.

Here's how to apply these principles in your life. There will be inevitable times when friends, family, and other people will let you down and therefore we'll need to receive more of certain needs in our relationships. What needs are missing for you?

At this point in my life, I need more _____ (comfort, support, compassion, friendship, security, acceptance, attention, affection, etc.) because I'm going through . . .

Now in faith, entrust your needs to God and receive assurance of His care, then look for opportunities to give (yes, give) to others the same thing you desire to receive.

- Do you need acceptance? Then look to God, who has accepted you and welcomed you into His family (Romans 15:7), and then look for opportunities to accept others who are feeling excluded.
- Has your need for comfort been neglected? Then call upon God as the "God of all comfort, who comforts us," and then begin to give caring compassion to others who are hurting. (See 2 Corinthians 1:2–4.)
- Are you missing some encouragement? Instead of sulking about it, ask God to remind you of how the Lord will bless the righteous; with favor He will surround you with a shield (Psalm 5:12). Next, begin to encourage others.

Now ask God to be a need-meeting God in your life and look for opportunities to give to others. Wait and watch as God brings blessing to your life.

God, You know I need _____ during this time. I trust You to meet this need in my relationship with You and through others that You desire. Amen.

Terri Snead, The Great Commandment Network

Week 30, Monday
Anger < Forgiveness

He who is slow to anger is better than the mighty,
and he who rules his spirit than he who takes a city.

Proverbs 16:32

Anger is the result of not getting what you want even though you think you deserve it. You show me an angry person and I will show you a hurt person, and that hurt person most likely had something taken away from him. Therefore, usually at the root of anger is the idea that *somebody owes me something*. It is easy to believe that the only remedy for our anger is payback, which is the most common way our society handles anger. The reality is that most people wait, wait, and wait for that moment of retribution, but in the waiting process they have allowed this pent-up anger to fester and spread into other areas of their lives. If you have been deeply wounded in life, technically, you have every reason to be the way that you are! However, in staying there you will miss out on the life that God has called you to live, which is a life of liberation. Anger finds its strength in the realm of secrecy. It is hiding and jading the issue while allowing your feelings to run rampant and out of control, thus hurting other people.

However, the Kryptonite to anger is honesty, transparency, and confession.

I guarantee if you come to the place where you admit that you have anger issues, then you most likely have a story to tell that you have never shared with someone else or maybe only a few people. If you have never shared the story of why you have anger issues, then understand that if you are willing to open up with it, you could be at the doorway of a major breakthrough. *You don't forgive because the person deserves it; you forgive because you have been forgiven yourself.* It may feel like you are rewarding your offender by offering them forgiveness, which doesn't make sense until you are a forgiven person. Therefore, we have to look at things within the story of the cross.

Lord Jesus, I thank You that You were willing to forgive me of my sin. Allow me to demonstrate forgiveness to others in all areas of my life. Deliver me from any bitterness and show me how You desire to use the story of my past to bring hope to those in my future. Amen.

Ed Newton, Evangelist, Memphis TN

Week 30, Tuesday
Generosity > Covetousness

*And He said to them, "Take heed and beware of covetousness,
for one's life does not consist in the abundance of the things he possesses."*

Luke 12:15

Covetousness is an unquenchable thirst for getting more and more of something we think we need in order to be truly satisfied. It may be a thirst for money or the things that money can buy, or even a thirst for position and power.

Jesus talked a lot about money. In fact, sixteen of the thirty-eight parables He told are about money or possessions. Why would Jesus speak more about money almost more than any other subject? Let me answer that in an indirect fashion! Have you noticed the number of storage units being built in your surrounding community? Have you noticed the reality shows that highlight personal addictions of people not being able to let go of their stuff, but instead hoarding it? It is a very clear indicator that we have too much stuff! Jesus wants you and me to value only what is eternal in life, because of its ability to transcend this earth and be taken with us into heaven. Our identity is not found in what we own, but instead in who or what owns us. Therefore, we are called to live generously toward God and other people.

What are the eternal factors of this life that will follow us to heaven? Not an easy answer, but in short, the souls of people and the Word of God will be with us in heaven. The human soul was created to live for all eternity. Therefore, *giving* your life to make Christ known through your resources should be the objective of your life. It has eternal value! You can do this by looking for opportunities to invest in the lives of people by living sacrificially with your time, energy, resources, and most of all your very life. Have you ever seen a hearse with a U-Haul attached to it? Ridiculous, I know, but when we live our lives sacrificially we are pointing to the One who was the greatest sacrifice of all! His name . . . Jesus!

Lord Jesus, help me to live my life with eternity in mind by dedicating all that I have and all that I am to be used by You to make Your name more famous in my life. Allow me to invest in eternity with my resources and my life. Amen.

Ed Newton, Evangelist, Memphis TN

Week 30, Wednesday
Jealousy < Content

But if you have bitter envy and self-seeking in your hearts,
do not boast and lie against the truth.

James 3:14

Jealousy, or envy, desires something that someone has that we personally lack. Oftentimes we look at the people in our lives and we begin to compare and contrast their lives with our own. You don't necessarily mind that God made them cool, smart, athletic, popular, etc. It is the fact that you might lack what someone else has and that upsets you. It is something that you have begun to accuse God of because if *He* had given what you apparently lack, your life would be so much better *now*. It is almost as if we are saying that God has dropped the ball in our lives because in the distribution of good looks, athleticism, intelligence, etc., He failed to meet our expectations. We must understand that the person that we envy has no ability to correct our situation. Therefore, understand that there is nothing that the specific person you are envious of can do for you. They personally cannot change your situation. So, where do you go? You go to the One who can change everything!

This is not to say that we go to God with our personal wish list. Instead, James simply revealed that the source of conflict is deep within our frail, human hearts and that needs to be healed. Therefore, understand the solution to your jealousy is to approach God with the issue and ask Him to give you understanding of His perfect plan in your life. Sounds simple, but James teaches us that we are to bring the very issue to God. (Read James 1:17.)

Aren't you glad that God said no to certain things you have requested in life? God loves you way too much to give you everything you ask for! You might be wondering, *What is the point of asking, knowing He could say no?* It is coming to grips with the fact that God is the giver of all good things and His story lived through you is dependent upon your contentment in Him. Trust Him!

 Lord Jesus, I want to be content in You and You alone! You are my satis-faction, supply, shield, and song! Amen.

Ed Newton, Evangelist, Memphis TN

Week 30, Thursday
Pride < Humility

Pride goes before destruction, and a haughty spirit before a fall.

Proverbs 16:18

Pride is a relational attitude that oftentimes goes unnoticed by you, but is detected often by others. Pride is *dangerous* to us and is *damaging* to God. Pride finds its origination not in the heart of God, but at the root of our adversary, Satan. By reading Isaiah 14:13–14 you will notice approximately five times Satan using the word *I* in his pursuit of being like God. It is not that we would ever say that we "want to be God" in our moments of pride. However, we must know that any moment when we elevate ourselves above someone or any circumstance, we are belittling someone else and what they value.

Did you know that the word *humility* comes from the word *humus*, which means "soil" or "dirt"? God created us out of the dust of the earth. One day we will all return to the dirt once again. Comforting, huh? We are what we are by the grace of God. Therefore, in effort to live a life that is pleasing to God in this specific area of our lives, we must actively pursue the mind of Christ. This description is given in Philippians 2:5–7, which highlights the fact that Jesus made Himself a servant in society by making Himself of no reputation. It seems that most of our lives are spent trying to earn a reputation, but walking in humility is a choice to value others above ourselves. Honestly look at your life and answer the following questions: *Are you critical? Do you take yourself too seriously? Are you easily frustrated? Impatient with delays? Angry when disrespected?* I am convicted even now as I write. So, what should we do about this pride? 1) Recognize it—this is the first step! 2) Repent of it—do something about it before God does! Look for ways to put others before your own needs. Look for ways to give value to someone else and their passions. Put yourself out there and meet someone who is distinctly different from you.

Lord Jesus, I desire to walk in humility by being reminded of Your example of service and sacrifice. Help me to lay down my dreams, desires, and demands by seeking Your face while serving others. Amen.

Ed Newton, Evangelist, Memphis TN

Week 30, Friday
Truth > Slander

He who goes about as a talebearer reveals secrets; therefore do not associate with one who flatters with his lips.

Proverbs 20:19

For Christ-followers, choosing to speak the truth should be as easy as breathing. However, deep in the dark places of our hearts, there is a desire to find comfort in the exaggeration of a story. This verse illuminates a principle that one who slanders or gossips reveals secrets of other people, but most importantly secrets about themselves. This is to say that our words place on public display what is deep down in our hearts. So, when a person chooses to falsify the truth about someone else, it reveals a deeper secret concerning the person sharing the information. Usually, the secret that becomes public is that you as an individual care more about public opinion than God's approval. Why else would we make a story larger than actuality if we were not concerned about whether or not people will like us more?

The feeling of conviction that washes over your soul when truth is not shared bears witness that you belong to God. God is truth and because He, as truth, lives within you, He demands for you to walk in it and speak it. Easier said than done! However, it's not usually that you intentionally set out to live a life of falsehood. It's just that the truth gets bent for the sake of being valued as "cool." Why is this principle so hard for us to admit? Just know that if you can honestly admit the reason why truth is not spoken with consistency in your life is _____ (fill in the blank), then you are on the brink of something big. We cannot address the problem until we get to the source of the issue. The goal of this devotion is not to put a Band-Aid on the issue, but instead to treat the infection at the core. In order for you to grow in discipleship and leadership, truth must be embraced as a value beyond your own value. It has been said that "conviction is not ideas you hold, but ideas that hold you." Truth must be a conviction that holds you. Truthfully deal with the insecurity in your life by admitting your need to be valued and take this to God in prayer.

Lord Jesus, You are the Way and the Truth, and I desire to walk, live, speak, and value truth. Help me to deal with the insecurities in my heart that continue to cause me to value other opinions more than Yours. Amen.

Ed Newton, Evangelist, Memphis TN

Week 30, Weekend
Healers > Hiders or Hurlers

But be doers of the word, and not hearers only.

James 1:22

God's Word reveals the skills for great relationships, but it's up to us to "do" the Word. Ephesians 4:15 reminds us of a simple, but profound truth: Speaking the truth in love promotes the development of healthy, God-honoring relationships. This verse tells us "what" to speak (the truth) and "how" to speak it (in love).

Imagine this scenario and use the following steps to share the truth in love with family and friends.

Your best friend agrees to meet you after school to work on a project. She shows up forty-five minutes after the agreed-upon time. Your friend has arrived late the last several times you've tried to meet.

1. Check in and understand the other person's side.
"Is everything okay? We planned to meet at _____ . Did something happen?"
(If your friend's response lets you know that the situation is/was out of her control, the conversation may end at this time. But if needed, you might also need to share the truth in love.)

2. Briefly explain what happened without judgment or accusation.
"We agreed on four thirty as our meeting time and yet you got here about four forty-five today."

3. Tell how you felt, especially the more vulnerable emotions.
"I was angry and felt really disrespected."

4. Share your need in a loving way. You might start your words with: "Next time, it would mean a lot to me if …"
"Next time, it would mean a lot to me if you would call if you're going to be late and let's make sure to schedule our meeting at a time when you know you can make it."

God, help me to speak the truth in love and to avoid the tendency to hide the truth or speak the truth in hurtful ways. Amen.

Week 31, Monday
In Your Face—Unplugged 1.0

*"Behold, I stand at the door and knock. If anyone hears My voice
and opens the door, I will come in to him and dine with him, and he with Me."*

Revelation 3:20

Consistent face-to-face (FTF) communication builds close relationships. God always uses personal encounters to build lasting relationships. Do you remember His FTF interactions with Adam (Genesis 2:7), Enoch (Genesis 5:24), Noah (Genesis 6:9), Abraham (Genesis 12:7; 17:1; 18:1), Moses (Exodus 33:11), and Elijah (Matthew 17:3)? Jesus also relied upon FTF communication to impact His disciples (John 1:14) and the apostle Paul (Acts 9). Before returning to heaven, Jesus even instructed His followers to receive the indwelling of the Holy Spirit to always remain plugged in to God's presence (John 14:16–18).

Are you plugged into FTF communication God's way, or do you habitually use technology as your main form of communication with others? Christians should take an honest look in the mirror to examine their use of social media like Facebook, Twitter, and texting. Face the fact that your use of social media needs to glorify God. Instead of overusing social media to nurture superficial relationships with lots of people who are merely acquaintances, be intentional about strengthening those relationships the Bible tells us matter the most —God and family. The Ten Commandments provide God's blueprint for investing time in relationships. Focus your time in this order of priority:

1. Your relationship with God (Commandments #1–4, Exodus 20:3–111)
2. Your relationship with family (Commandment #5, Exodus 20:12)
3. Your relationships with others (Commandments #6–10, Exodus 20:13–17)

Follow God's way to build quality relationships successfully with the right people by applying this principle of communication—*the more blood and bread you share with others, the more time you need to spend communicating with them on a FTF basis.*

Jesus, thank You for communicating with me on a personal basis as my dearest of friends. Help me keep my priorities consistent with Scripture. I will plug in to You first since You share the Bread of Life and gave me all Your blood on the cross at Calvary. O Lord, relentlessly impress upon my heart the need to unplug often and engage You and others on a FTF basis, and remind me to give more time to those I share meals with. Amen.

. Michael Roye, Faith Christian School

Week 31, Tuesday
In Your Face—Plugged In 2.0

Let the words of my mouth and the meditation of my heart be acceptable in Your sight, O LORD, my strength and my Redeemer.

Psalm 19:14

*W*eb 2.0 (or version 2) refers to how social networking sites, blogs, and video sharing sites facilitate communication. These technologies allow us to communicate quickly and effectively 24/7, but does *quantity* of communication necessarily equate to *quality*? Misuse of newer forms of communication like social networking negatively affects our relationships. For example, the American Academy of Matrimonial Lawyers reports that over 80 percent of lawyers have seen a rising trend in the number of divorce cases that include evidence retrieved from social networking sites. Over 60 percent of lawyers said Facebook was the primary source of evidence in the divorce proceedings.

Given such eye-opening statistics, Christians must reflect upon how we use technology to communicate. Communicating digitally should never replace the importance of engaging others face-to-face (FTF) because FTF interaction is the best way to communicate on Planet Earth. Since this is true (see 2 John 1:12), we need to make sure all of our online communication mirrors the way we communicate in person. When texting, e-mailing, or blogging, consider the tone of your message. Imagine the actual face of the person you are writing to being on your screen when typing. If that person were really in your presence, how would you talk to them? Remember, even online they deserve the same love and respect you would give to them in person.

Father, as Your child, I know I represent You when I communicate with others. Even though FTF communication is best, I live in a generation when I can converse with others by plugging in to technology. Beloved God, remind me to honor and glorify Your image when I engage others through typing and texting. Please keep me from ever writing evil or slanderous things about anyone by plugging in to my heart the words of Ephesians 4:29. Amen.

Week 31, Wednesday
Silence Is Deadly

Then the man said, "The woman whom You gave to be with me, she gave me of the tree, and I ate."

Genesis 3:12

I awoke to chilling thoughts bouncing around in my head. It was 3 a.m., and my mind simply would not shut down. Rippling through my mind was the effect of Adam's silence in my life. That is right. His silence has a profound effect on my life. My father has Alzheimer's because of Adam's silence. My sister-in-law lost children through miscarriages due to Adam's silence. My pastor suffered moral failure due to Adam's silence. The list, in my mind, continued to grow.

I had read the Genesis 3 passage the night before and was going to share this with a group of students. Silence does have the ability to kill. I have often wondered as to the whereabouts of Adam as Satan was tempting Eve. Why did Adam not step forward and protect his beloved? Why did Adam not stand up and hold up the standard of truth that he had been given by his Creator? Why did he not fulfill his God-given responsibility to protect and provide for, not only his partner, Eve, but all living things? His silence rippled through eternity and was responsible for the need of a Savior dying on a cross, to cover the sin of his silence.

Before I gave this talk, God gently but firmly brought to my heart and mind the fact that WE are all Adam! When have I gone silent, when speaking truth was the right thing to do? When have I not stepped in and stepped up, when injustice was taking place? When did I not protect someone or something that needed protection? When did I not provide for someone because I did not wish to be inconvenienced, or be embarrassed?

Yes, silence can be deadly. Before I judge Adam too harshly, I must come to the realization that my own silence speaks volumes as well. I choose this day not to be silent. How about you?

O God, how quickly I tend to judge others. Search my heart and find any unclean area that would be in need of Your cleansing love. May I then see the injustice and lies of the enemy, clearly. Then I will speak up. Then I will stand up. With Your help, I will not be silent anymore. Amen.

Jon Brooks, Faith Christian School

Week 31, Thursday
A Matter of Life and Death

The mouth of the righteous is a well of life, but violence covers the mouth of the wicked.

Proverbs 10:11

Words matter. In fact, each word spoken is a matter of life and death. When we speak to another human being, we are speaking life or death into that person. This leaves us with a great burden of responsibility when dealing with those we come into contact with. Note that this power is not just limited to our family members. No, the reality is that we speak life or death into all that we come into contact with. When you walk away from a conversation, whether one word or a long dialogue, ask yourself, "Did I just speak life or death?"

This simple but powerful truth was made fresh to me when a dear friend stopped me in my tracks with this statement: "I need to ask you about something you said the other day." He did not even have to finish the conversation for I knew exactly where he was going and what he was going to say. You see, I had been in a meeting two days earlier and I popped off in a way that was not honoring to this man, nor our relationship. God used this confrontation, in which I totally owned up to my poor judgment, to remind me of my responsibility and privilege to speak only life into people who are dying to hear a good word.

We must especially be cautious of the phrase, "I was just joking!" (Proverbs 26:18–19). If we are not careful, we may use this simple statement to cover over the damage done by our tongue. Today, make a powerful decision to be a life giver to all whom you come into contact with.

Father of life, may I be a life-giver today. Guard my heart, my mind, and especially my tongue today. May every word that comes out of my mouth be pleasing and acceptable to You, O Lord. Before I speak a word, may You remind me of this simple yet profound truth. May I understand fully that my every word will bring life or death to all I may encounter. I need Your help. I need Your Spirit to control my every word. Thank You for allowing me the privilege of speaking into others. Amen.

Jon Brooks, Faith Christian School

Week 31, Friday
A Friend Through Thick and Thin

The soul of Jonathan was knit to the soul of David, and Jonathan loved him as his own son.

1 Samuel 18:1

We normally make friends by first making acquaintances. Since we don't know much about the other person, that relationship grows to reach the next level, which is casual friendship. Should that relationship grow, it can become a close relationship. In a few instances, a close relationship can develop into an intimate relationship. Such was the friendship between Jonathan and David.

Their friendship endured although it faced many difficulties. It was very unusual for royalty to be friends with the common person of the day. Jesus taught us, however, to love our neighbor as ourselves, with our neighbor being anyone with whom we are in contact. Jonathan and David did not allow their social standings to keep them from being friends.

Jonathan chose to befriend David though his father, Saul, wanted David killed because of his jealousy (1 Samuel 19:1–2). Danger today comes in many forms; we struggle with the flesh, the world, and the devil. True friends are ever-alert to warn each other of the dangers that lurk about. Jonathan chose this path with David.

Perhaps the most telling evidence of Jonathan's true friendship to David was his willingness to take a lesser role in life (1 Samuel 23:17). We often use the acronym *JOY* to explain Jesus, Others, and You, in that order. That's much easier to say than to do.

To do what Jonathan did to retain his friendship with David took a huge step of faith and went against the protocol of that day. Friends should ask, "Am I willing to reach out to those who are different, defend them, protect them, and be excited for them when they do well?"

Dear God, I am so grateful that You allow each of us to have friends. Thank You so much for the beautiful illustration of true and faithful friendship between Jonathan and David. Help me to be more careful with my friends, to encourage them, caution them, and even rebuke them. Help me to be able to receive the same from them. God, allow me to see each person I meet as a possible divine appointment. May Your Holy Spirit go before me and guide people toward and into the Kingdom. Amen.

Nolan LeBeaux, Faith Christian School

Week 31, Weekend
He Sees Your Hurts

"I have surely seen the oppression of My people . . .
and have heard their cry . . . for I know their sorrows."

Exodus 3:7

Forgiveness is the cure God has given for all forms of anger because God knows how destructive anger is to our lives. Take the next few moments and ask God to bring to your mind any areas of anger that are a struggle for you.

God, show me any ways that I might struggle with:

> *Bitterness*
> *Angry outbursts*
> *Becoming easily frustrated*
> *Talking negatively about someone who has hurt me*
> *Being critical of others*
> *Avoiding or emotionally distancing myself from others who have made me angry*
> *Sarcasm and teasing others who have made me angry*
> *Hurting others with my words, tone of voice, or attitude*

Consider the specific instances and people that God brought to your mind. What vulnerable emotions did you experience in addition to anger? *I felt angry, but I also felt* _____.

One key to forgiving others is experiencing God's care for the hurt you have just identified. Reflect on the hurtful feelings that you've identified above. Now, imagine that Jesus is standing in the room with you. He has these things to say, just for you:

My precious child, I am so sorry that you experienced those things. I care about your anger and I care about your hurt. It saddens My heart to know that you experienced these painful emotions. I noticed your hurt. I heard your cries and I felt your sorrow. Your painful experiences move My heart with compassion. And once you have felt My heart for you, you'll be ready to forgive the offenses of others.

God, help me to sense Your care for my anger and my hurt. Make me ready to forgive because You have forgiven me. Amen.

Terri Snead, The Great Commandment Network

Week 32, Monday
Been There, Done That

For in that He Himself has suffered, being tempted, He is able to aid
those who are tempted. . . . For we do not have a High Priest who cannot sympathize
with our weaknesses, but was in all points tempted as we are, yet without sin.

Hebrews 2:18; 4:15

Have you ever had someone give you advice on something he or she didn't have any experience with? Maybe it was a little brother coaching you on how to properly run a fade route or a little sister explaining how to fix your hair for the homecoming festivities. I remember while playing soccer growing up that it always bothered me when fans who had never actually played soccer before, would shout at us what to do. They would tell us when to pass the ball, where to run on the field, or how to score. However, I never minded getting advice from my coach, a person who has "been there, done that" long before I ever arrived on the scene. I remember my coach practicing drills with us and even breaking a finger when he was acting as a goalkeeper during a shooting drill. We all knew that our coach had our best interests in mind, and from *experience*, he knew what to do.

Why is this important? It's because life is full of temptations and struggles, and it's easy for us to think that no one understands what we are going through. We have a Savior who understands *everything* we go through in life, small or big. When the Bible teaches timeless truths on how to live a pure life or how to be above reproach in our daily decisions, Jesus understands exactly how we feel when going through a tempting situation. Biblical boundaries aren't to stifle us; rather, they are to protect us. Jesus isn't someone on the sideline trying to tell us what to do and how to do it. According to Hebrews, He has "been there, done that," and He coaches us with our best interests in mind.

Jesus, thank You for coming to earth and going through the same hard
things that I am going through, so You can coach me when times are tough.
Please give me strength and courage in moments of temptation to make
the right decision every time, no matter how difficult. In Your holy name I
pray, Amen.

Kory Hicks, Faith Christian School

Week 32, Tuesday
Forgiveness—A Journey

*… bearing with one another, and forgiving one another, if anyone has
a complaint against another; even as Christ forgave you, so you also must do.*

Colossians 3:13

Have you ever had trouble forgiving someone? If so, you're not alone. Forgiveness involves a complex set of emotions often tied to memories—thoughts that seem not to go away as much as we try to erase them. Thus, forgiveness is not an emotional state as much as it is a journey, potentially lasting a long time, but always worth the effort.

Corrie ten Boom, a Nazi holocaust survivor, wrote this about forgiveness: "Forgiveness is to set a prisoner free, and to realize the prisoner was you."

This is confirmed in Scripture, as each time forgiveness is mentioned it is directly related to the life of the *forgiver*, not the forgiven. Those who have trespassed against us are usually unaware of, or uninterested in, the offense. In a sense, we are alone on this journey with God. Yet sometimes the length of the journey discourages us, or convinces us that we truly have not forgiven someone. This need not be the case, *as long as we keep moving forward on the path*. Each time we are reminded of an offense against us and bring it before the Lord as an offering, a sacrifice, and a need, we take a step forward regardless of whether or not we "feel" progress. Even the apostle Peter struggled on this journey, only to be encouraged by Jesus to keep taking steps forward:

Then Peter came to Him and said, "Lord, how often shall my brother sin against me, and I forgive him? Up to seven times?" Jesus said to him, "I do not say to you, up to seven times, but up to seventy times seven" (Matthew 18:21–22).

Stay on the journey of forgiveness!

 Lord, help me to forgive others as You have forgiven me. Help me to see those who have offended me through Your eyes, that they are likely as wounded as I am because of circumstances in their life and therefore also in need of healing. Help me to stay the course, to find peace on the journey of forgiveness, to never be a prisoner of unforgiveness. Amen.

Rick Allen, Faith Christian School

Week 32, Wednesday
Soft on the Edges, Hard in the Center

And when Jesus came to the place, He looked up and saw him,
and said to him, "Zacchaeus, make haste and come down, for today I must stay at your house."

Luke 19:5

The avocado is an interesting fruit. It is high in fiber and nutrients and a staple in many diets, not to mention it is the key ingredient in one of my favorite treats . . . guacamole. Now the physical makeup of the avocado has some characteristics that teach some classic truths found in Scripture. You see, when the avocado is ripe, it has a soft outer shell but its core is extremely hard. When we begin to walk into our God-given potential we will begin to demonstrate the characteristics of an avocado. We will be soft on the edges and hard in the center.

This principle is present throughout all of Scripture, but I believe one of the greatest examples is found in Luke 19. Luke tells the story of Jesus taking time to fellowship with one of the most hated men in the city, Zacchaeus. Zacchaeus was an individual whom many did not want to be around due to his occupation—a tax collector. Yet despite this Jesus went to Zacchaeus's house and ate with him. In that culture, eating with someone was an act of fellowship and friendship. You see, Jesus was first Zacchaeus's friend before He was his Lord. In our world it is easy to be judgmental and require people to "clean up" before they are allowed to be our friend. You see, it is easy to label people until you have to eat with them. Realize that the core of Jesus, His beliefs and purpose, never changed; they remained strong. His exterior, however, was soft. Being soft on the edges says to society, "I have a heart for you right where you are." In life there will be times when we must be soft on the edges in order for others to see the truth that lies in the center of our hearts.

Jesus, help me to soften my edges. Give me opportunities to show friendship to those whom others are quick to dismiss for then will they be able to see the truth that is the core of who I am. Continue to strengthen my core and soften my edges in order to bring love and hope to this world. Amen.

Michael Beeson, Faith Christian School

Week 32, Thursday
Drifting

Therefore we must give the more earnest heed to the things we have heard, lest we drift away.

Hebrews 2:1

One of my favorite things to do while at the beach is body surf. When several of us planned to go out this past summer, we rented the boards, lathered on sunscreen, and walked through the warm sand past lifeguard stand 11. We took a nosedive into the freezing waves, and after hours of thrashing through the waves, it was time to head back for lunch. We exited the water and noticed we weren't quite familiar with our surroundings. Without even noticing it, we were by lifeguard stand 14, about 200 yards away from where we had started. We were so focused on having fun and catching that next big wave that we didn't even realize that we had drifted such a far distance from where we had started.

Drifting away from something does not happen immediately. The author of Hebrews warns us to be careful not to drift away from the truths in God's Word. Have you ever examined your spiritual life and asked, "How did I get here?" We have to constantly be on guard not to allow ourselves to spiritually drift away from God. Many times, we start the drifting process when things are going well, and we feel as if "we've got this." Without even realizing it, becoming lazy in our walk with God is dangerously easy and, like the waves, will gradually carry us further and further away from God. We have to be intentional about putting Him first, and remove anything that may distract us from hearing His voice. Paying careful attention to God's Word requires effort and is difficult to do sometimes. The devil does not entice us with obvious sins that would immediately propel us away from God; these temptations would be easier to recognize and avoid. Instead, he uses tricky tactics that we often fail to identify as traps. If this happens, we need to acknowledge our distance and make every effort to get in right relationship with God.

Dear Jesus, help me to see clearly if there are any distractions in my life right now that would keep me from being in Your will or hearing Your voice. If I have drifted away, give me the insight, encouragement, and strength to do whatever it takes to get back to You. Amen.

Kory Hicks, Faith Christian School

Week 32, Friday
No One Stands Alone

Then He also said to him who invited Him, "When you give a dinner or a supper,
do not ask your friends, your brothers, your relatives, nor rich neighbors, lest they also invite
you back, and you be repaid. But when you give a feast, invite the poor, the maimed, the lame, the blind."

Luke 14:12, 13

After I graduated from college, I embarked on the American dream. I started my career in the financial industry and quickly learned that in order to get ahead I needed to put morals, ethics, and even friendship on the back burner in order to close a deal. I began to believe that in order to find fulfillment I needed to embrace this lifestyle. I viewed individuals as pawns to further my career and wealth. All of my friends shared this same mind-set. Greed and materialism became my sole motivation. Then one night I sat on the edge of my bed in my beautiful house and realized this was not the dream I wanted. I realized I was alone.

I discovered awhile back that aloneness is a reflection of something broken in the world, yet it is interesting that our culture teaches us that in order to get ahead in this world we must position ourselves properly. We serve others only if they can further our career, increase our social status, or increase our portfolios. But when you step back and look at the "friendships" you have formed, you discover that they are not really friends at all. You are alone. We should serve because we love not because we want. In Luke, Jesus told a story of a great feast in which we are to invite the ones who never get invited out. Regardless of social status we are to show love and hospitality to others because that is exactly what God did for us. Why? Because we were never meant to stand alone!

Father, I realize that I struggle with serving others the way You intended. Help me to recognize those who are standing alone. Help me to be a true friend to those in this world who are alone. Help me to give up my desires so that others may have the opportunity to know You. Amen.

Michael Beeson, Faith Christian School

Week 32, Weekend
Confession Sessions Are Good Things

A man's pride will bring him low, but the humble in spirit will retain honor.

Proverbs 29:23

Frequent "confession sessions" are vital for healthy relationships. Humbly admitting we're wrong is not easy to do, but confession brings healing. In fact, confession brings about several kinds of healing—healing our relationship with God, healing our relationships with others, and healing our own hearts as we are released from the burden of guilt.

In order for deep healing to occur, our confessions must be sincere. Here are several guidelines for a meaningful confession.

1. Be specific. Which of these responses would you prefer to hear?
   "If I've offended you in any way, I'm sorry."
   "I was very selfish and insensitive when I . . . That was wrong of me."
2. Use the words, "I was wrong" instead of "I am sorry." To simply say, "I'm sorry" can sometimes mean, "I'm sorry I got caught" or "I'm sorry we can't get along." To say, "I was wrong" is more truthful. Using these words lets the hearer know that you are taking responsibility for your part.
3. Don't offer excuses, explanations, or rationalizations. A good confession has no indication of excuse. Leave out any words like: "I didn't mean to . . ." or "I wouldn't have done that if . . ."
4. Acknowledge how the other person felt. A good confession reassures the other person that you understand why they were hurt. It helps them see that you "get it"!
5. Ask God to forgive you and reflect how your wrong actions have hurt God. Ask for God's forgiveness because God says your choices are wrong and a part of why Christ had to die.
   God, please forgive me for _____. I know that my _____ is a part of why Your Son had to die.
6. Ask specifically for the other person's forgiveness. As a last step of humility, a good confession makes a specific point of asking for the person's forgiveness.

God, please show me any confessions that I need to make. Help me share confessions that I need to make in a way that is humble and brings healing to my relationship with You and others. Amen.

Terri Snead, The Great Commandment Network

Week 33, Monday
Expectancy Is Key

. . . we shall see Him as He is.

1 John 3:2

I remember as a boy there were those special occasions when we would pack the car and travel a great distance to spend time with loved ones and relatives we hadn't seen for quite a while. The expectancy was great! Prior to our arrival there were many things that had to take place. A date was scheduled, money was saved, food was purchased and prepared, bags were packed. Strategizing, mapping the route . . . it all had to be done. The closer it came for the time of our departure, the more conversations we had with one another that consisted of following up on plans and tweaking last-minute arrangements. The anticipation grew and sleepless nights occurred. Once we had arrived, the reunion was sweet. Grandma and Grandpa; aunts and uncles, cousins, nephews and nieces, brothers and sisters, and even people who claimed they were relatives whom I had never met.

Our life is to be lived as an expectant reunion with the Lord as we follow Him from day to day. To follow the Lord without the expectation of seeing Him would be futile indeed! We have a hope and a promise that we will see Him face to face (1 Thessalonians 4:15–18; 1 John 3:2). Many preparations are being made. (See John 14:1–4.) Food is being prepared, and the table is being set (Revelation 19:9). The excitement is building. There is great anticipation. As you follow Him . . . expect a divine reunion at any moment. Expectancy is the key to successfully following Jesus. After all He is the reward of those who diligently seek Him.

My Father in heaven, I long to see You. As I live from day to day, guide my steps so that I follow in Your footsteps. May the Holy Spirit speak to me as I plan and prepare. Redirect me if necessary. I am a vessel in Your hands to do with what You will. Lead me to someone else's life who may need to hear from You through me. Lord, remove anything from me that would enable me from seeing You. My prayer is that You find me to be a true worshiper proclaiming to the world around me that You are Lord of my life. Amen.

Dusty Wilson, Great Commandment Network

Week 33, Tuesday
Following a Sweet Smell

Therefore be imitators of God as dear children. And walk in love, as Christ also has loved us and given Himself for us, an offering and a sacrifice to God for a sweet-smelling aroma.

Ephesians 5:1, 2

Have you ever walked through a department store or a bakery to take in all the aromas and various fragrances? I enjoy smelling fresh baked cinnamon rolls! It's pleasant to walk in the mall and take in the fresh fragrances of perfume when you come close to a particular store. Some companies specialize in the production of various aromas because it is actually therapy to an individual. Some aromas, like ocean water on a beach or a sun-filled day in a meadow, bring about memories that may bring peace to your soul. Some aromas are worth taking the time to purposefully stop and smell. The Scriptures say to follow Him like dear children. Jesus made for us a sacrifice to God—a sweet-smelling savor. People love to follow the things that smell sweet. Second Corinthians 2:15 says that we are a sweet savor to Him. There were times when the psalmist David referred his praise as a sweet savor to God. The world does not issue a pleasant aroma, but they will follow what smells sweet to them. If we are to be Christlike, then shouldn't we display a Christlike aroma? To truly follow Christ should be a sweet experience for us so that others will want to follow, too. The very way that we walk and talk, the things we do, and the places we go should be a reflection of His aroma in our lives. Do not bring anything upon yourself that would cause that fragrance to become polluted or dirty. Walk in love. That's the aroma of heaven on earth.

Dear Jesus, I want to be a living example of Your love in my life as I follow You. Help me to lead others to You by the aroma of love that I produce from within my life. Keep me from the stench of this world so that I may become a sweet-smelling fragrance before You. Let my praise be a special aroma to You. I want to live a life that is pleasing to You, and may it be so pleasing to others that they would want to follow You, too. Amen.

Dusty Wilson, Great Commandment Network

Week 33, Wednesday
Visiting or Dwelling?

"Abide in Me, and I in you."

John 15:4

Not long ago my family and I moved to the beautiful state of sunny Florida. There have been many family vacations to this destination. I have attended conventions, made business trips, and even departed for other destinations through various ports around Florida's coast. I've had friends and family who have lived here in years gone by but never did I think I would have the opportunity to live here myself. Someone once said the phrase, "It's a good place to visit, but I wouldn't want to live here." I remember visiting Florida before but living here is wonderful! It's much better than just taking in a few days of such warmth, white powdery beaches, and tropical beauty just to return from a trip or than to just hear about it from somebody else.

It's not enough to merely visit with Jesus or hear about Him from someone else or read about Him from the pages of someone else's life. I want to live in Him and experience Him for myself! There are a few things the Scriptures say that should encourage us to do more than just visit with Him for a season. We can dwell in the wisdom and richness of His Word (see Colossians 3:16). The love of God is perfected in us as we abide in Him (see 1 John 2:3–6). Like children we can live in Him and not be orphaned in a lost world (see Acts 17:28). As we live in the doctrine of His Word we are never alone (see Matthew 28:20), and we have the fullness of all that He is with us (see 2 John 1:9). It is my desire to dwell in the house of the Lord forever!

Lord, as I seek Your face, it is not my desire to become a stranger in Your house. I choose to abide in You and not to become satisfied with a visit here or there. Occupy the place of my heart so that I may occupy the dwelling place of the Most High. Don't allow me to be so comfortable with the places or things of this life. This world is not my home—I'm just visiting here. May I live each day as a resident of the Lord Jesus Christ. Amen.

Dusty Wilson, Great Commandment Network

Week 33, Thursday
He Can Be Found

Seek the LORD while He may be found, call upon Him while He is near.

Isaiah 55:6

I used to play a game called Hide and Seek when I was younger. It was fun. I taught my children to play that game. My son has a tendency to carry things to the extreme. When he was younger we dropped him off with the sitter. He decided to play that game without her knowledge. He disappeared for hours. She looked frantically for him. After many fearful tears were shed and the family called upon to assist with the search, great discussion was given to calling the authorities for help. To make a long story short, the toddler was hiding in the closet space where no one expected him to be. This is a humorous story, but it was fairly tragic at the time. How miserable this sitter must have been to seek something that seemed lost to her. He was not lost. He was simply lost to her.

In the journey of following Christ, we must not become discouraged in our seeking. All He desires is that we take the initiative to search for Him. He is not lost. There have been occasions when I'm the one who has lost the way. There may be times when we are surprised by a moment when He visits us. Could it be that maybe it was in those times that we might have been seeking other things in life and He showed up? Like a surprise visit from someone you've least expected. I don't like surprises. I like to know what's going on, and I like to have my mind wrapped around what's happening around me. The only way to not be caught by surprise is to be found ready, watching, and waiting. He can be found ... are you looking for Him? (See 1 Chronicles 16:11–12; Psalm 34:1–4; Matthew 24:44.)

O Lord, You are my redeemer, my savior, and my friend. Do not hide Yourself from my presence. I pray that my transgressions be forgiven so that I'm not hidden from You. I want to live my life acceptable and pleasing to You to the point that I am watching and ready to be in Your presence. Allow me to enable others who are seeking to find You through my life. Amen.

Week 33, Friday
Encounter Them ... Encounter Him

Pure and undefiled religion before God and the Father is this: to visit
orphans and widows in their trouble, and to keep oneself unspotted from the world.

James 1:27

As Christians we have a tendency to seek God in all the wrong places. Sometimes even the disciples argued among themselves regarding position and authority in the places of the Kingdom of God. There are even times when we boast and sing about being in the presence of God, which is good. There's nothing wrong with that. However, if the presence of God can only be found while we are in worship or in the comfort of the sanctuary, how then can others find Him? It is our responsibility to obey the command of Christ as He challenged us to go into all the world and preach the Gospel (Matthew 28:19–20). Although we may experience the presence of the Lord in church or a worship atmosphere, we may also encounter Him as we encounter others. Pure religion is that we follow Him to the orphans, the widows, the hungry, the dying, and the hurting of this world.

My son was radically saved from a sinful life to the point that his encounter with God has caused him to live life on the edge. He has traveled into far countries to share the Gospel. He has lived in tents among the homeless. He has carried a cross on the beaches of the east coast of Florida during spring break and led many to the saving grace of Jesus Christ.

It's refreshing to be in God's presence with other worshippers but to encounter God is to also encounter those in their affliction. Scribes and Pharisees questioned Jesus' manner of ministry and Jesus responded to them (see Matthew 9:12–14; Matthew 10:5–10). If you really want to have an extreme encounter with God, try some extraordinary methods you may have not attempted before. Take a mission trip. Feed the hungry. Give to the poor. Volunteer on a humanitarian project or a hospital. Donate time and energy to an orphan. Encounter them ... Encounter Him.

Dear God, I am humbled that You chose me to be here in the twenty-first century. It is my desire to follow You in every way of my life. Open the eyes of my heart to be sensitive to those in need. I seek You among the places of the broken and hurting. Amen.

Dusty Wilson, Great Commandment Network

Week 33, Weekend
He Wants to Talk

The secret of the Lord is with those who fear Him.

Psalm 25:14

Can you remember some times when you were excited to see a family member? Perhaps you were anxiously waiting to see your grandmother because her house was full of fun and special treats? Or maybe you've been excited to visit a friend who lived miles away, but the two of you managed to stay relationally close. Can you remember the anticipation you felt?

Can you recall times when a family member shared some exciting news with you or told you important information in confidence? How did it feel to know that this person trusted you? You undoubtedly felt loved knowing that this person opened their heart with you. Sharing time with people and opening our hearts through vulnerable communication promotes the development of intimate relationships. These two principles are also true in God's relationship with us. He longs to visit with us and to reveal His heart. God can't wait to entrust us with the special parts of His life!

Scripture tells us that God longs to have this same kind of relationship with us (see Genesis 18). He wants to be able to spend time with you and stay relationally close. He can't wait to see you and hear from you! God longs to hear about what's going on in your heart and deeply desires to entrust you with the things that are His.

How do you feel knowing that you can have a relationship like this with God?

I feel _____ when I consider a God who can't wait to see me, hear about what's going on with me, and even tell me what's going on in His heart.

God may not show up at your house and have a chat in your bedroom, but you can expect Him to confide in you. God often entrusts us with the things that are on His heart through:
- His Word—When we read the Bible, God can talk with us.
- His people—By spending time with God's people, we can expect His revelation.
- Times of prayer and worship—By spending time in prayer and worship, God can speak to us.

God, thank You for being the kind of God who can't wait to see me, hear from me, and tell me what's on Your heart. I'm grateful and amazed! Amen.

Terri Snead, Great Commandment Network

Week 34, Monday
Following Jesus' Words of Life

I will delight myself in Your statutes; I will not forget Your word.

Psalm 119:16

After my wife and I had been married for quite some time, she revealed something to me that I had not expected. Oh . . . I see how you are. Now I have your attention because you think I'm getting ready to reveal some big secret or hidden sin. No, that's not it at all. You see, while we were dating I had taken the time to write my thoughts and feelings about her on various types of paper, cards, notes etc. I did not realize it, but she had saved all of those things and placed them in a shoe box. I was surprised. I discovered she had them during one of our many moves from one house to the other. Those words meant something to her. The reason I wrote those words is because she meant something to me. She still means something to me. I continue to write mushy cards and love notes on special occasions and during holiday seasons. I don't do these things so she will love me. She loves me and I do these things.

Such is our relationship with the Lord. To follow someone who loves us enough to lay His life down for us (John 10:15) means that we cling to His every word. I love Him because He first loved me (1 John 4:19), and I would never want to do anything to bring harm to that relationship (Psalm 119:11). His Word is sweetness in a bitter life (Psalm 119:103–105); guidance to my spirit (Hebrews 4:12); cleansing to my soul (John 15:3); faith to my ears (Romans 10:17); truth (John 17:17); and life (Isaiah 40:8). His words were important and powerful enough for Jesus to use the Word against His archenemy, Satan, during forty days of fasting and praying (see Luke 4). His words are life to us. Keep them. Hide them. Cherish them. They will guide you sufficiently through your life.

Dear Lord, let Your Word be a lamp unto my feet and a light unto my path as I follow You each day. Protect me from the temptation of the wicked one as I hide Your Word in my heart. Allow me to hear the voice of Your Spirit as You speak to my circumstances through the power of Your Word. Amen.

Dusty Wilson, Great Commandment Network

Week 34, Tuesday
Accept the Call

But you are a chosen generation, a royal priesthood, a holy nation, His own special people, that you may proclaim the praises of Him who called you out of darkness into His marvelous light.

1 Peter 2:9, 10

The challenge of following Jesus is being courageous enough to travel on an adventure where only He knows the destiny. Although the Word informs us that there is freedom in His words (John 8:31–32), we must learn what it's like to be free. There have been many to testify of leaving prisons where there were more years behind bars than years in the free world. They were more comfortable behind bars, but they were unaccustomed to the ways of living life freely. We understand what it's like to be bound by the things of this world because we were born into this life. When we accept the call of God, He brings us out of the darkness into His light. He makes us new creatures and the old things have passed away (see 2 Corinthians 5:17). To accept the call is to live a new life (Jeremiah 29:11). It's a journey that calls for us to follow Jesus on an adventure that brings about new things each and every day. He has not only called us out of something but He has called us into something, as well. Question: Is the doorway an entrance or an exit? Is the ramp on the highway an entrance or an exit? Is graduation an entrance or an exit? Is college an entrance or an exit? The answer is yes to all of these. To accept the call of God is being willing to move from point A to point B. To obey the Lord in His call is much better than sacrifice (Mark 8:34–37). Following the call means following Jesus. What is He calling to you today?

Lord, as I listen for Your still, small voice, I pray for the courage to be willing to leave the familiar and walk with You into the unfamiliar. Leaving a place of familiarity may require a sacrifice from me, but I must remember that You have paid the ultimate sacrifice in order that I can be free. Thank You for calling me into a hope and a future. My destiny is in Your hands as long as I live my life following the call of my Father. Amen.

Dusty Wilson, Great Commandment Network

Week 34, Wednesday
Drawing Near to God

Then you will call upon Me and go and pray to Me, and I will listen to you.
And you will seek Me and find Me, when you search for Me with all your heart.

Jeremiah 29:12, 13

My daughter is away in college. She has been away from home for a couple of years now. There's definitely an empty place at home, but she is close in our hearts. When she calls, my wife and I stop what we're doing to take time to speak with her. We cherish those times. Technology has enabled us the privilege of having more than just a casual conversation. We can Skype, Facebook, text, e-mail, share face time, video chat, Tweet, etc. We will do whatever it takes to just hear her voice or see her face.

Many of these venues could apply to our communication with God as we endeavor to draw near to Him. He is willing to draw near to us if we draw near to Him (see James 4:7–8). God's Word is His text to us. I haven't met one person yet who ignores a text from a friend. We text in the morning, noon, and night. We text in good times and in bad. We text when we're happy or sad. All occasions, everywhere, anywhere—we text. Drawing near to God involves taking time to read His text to us. First Chronicles 16:11–12 challenges us to seek His face continually. David expressed the vast opportunity we have to draw near to Him (see Psalm 42:1–2, 7–8). He is as close as just mentioning His name (Psalm 145:18). God is not too busy that He would turn us away (John 6:37). Drawing near to God requires a desire from us to long to be with Him. Take time to separate yourself from the obstacles of life. Drop what you're doing to hear from Him. Read His Word. He is there. Listen . . .

 Jesus! Jesus! Hear me, O Lord, I pray. I turn from my ways to draw near to You. I invite You to walk with me throughout my day. Be close by my side. Strengthen me in times of weakness. Encourage me when I feel afraid. Empower me when I am overwhelmed. You are my closest friend. I praise You, Lord, for taking time to hear from me. I love You, Lord. Amen.

Dusty Wilson, Great Commandment Network

Week 34, Thursday
A Formula for Success

Trust in the Lord, and do good; dwell in the land, and feed on His faithfulness. Delight yourself also in the Lord, and He shall give you the desires of your heart. Commit your way to the Lord.... Rest in the Lord, and wait patiently for Him; do not fret because of him who prospers in his way.... Cease from anger.... But those who wait on the Lord, they shall inherit the earth.

Psalm 37:3–9

Have you ever met an athlete who was so naturally gifted that there was no need for them to work out, train, practice, or study the strategy of their opponents? I have met many gifted athletes, but all of them worked hard for the winning prize. All of them had awards and trophies in mind and the goal of being number one. Following Jesus takes a lot of discipline and willingness to lay aside the things that would cause us to be distracted from the prize of life (Hebrews 12:1–2). The Word of God in Psalm 37:3–9 provides for us an ultimate training manual, a list of instructions of sorts, to help us toward a life of success and victory. First, trust in the Lord (Proverbs 3:5) and second, do good (James 4:17). These are the first two components. Then he says to, third, delight in Him (Romans 7:22). Fourth, commit all your ways to Him (Matthew 6:33; James 4:13–15), and fifth, wait patiently for Him (Isaiah 40:31). Sixthe, don't worry (Matthew 6:25), and seventh, don't be angry! (Proverbs 29:22). Now, that doesn't sound too hard, does it? There are many self-help materials on the market today that would like to draw our attention to their product and take our money at the same time, but this portion of Scripture includes a lifetime of learning. If we could apply this passage to our lives, we can follow Jesus, by His Word, to a life filled with overcoming power and victory.

Dear Jesus, each day as I take another step toward the finish line, help me to run the race with the endurance of an athlete. Help me, O Lord, to apply these instructions to my life that I may inherit the earth as the Scripture has said. You are my strength and my portion. As I follow You, Lord, give me the power to overcome by Your Spirit. Amen.

Week 34, Friday
Directionally Challenged? (GPS)

"When He, the Spirit of truth, has come, He will guide you into all truth; for He will not speak on His own authority, but whatever He hears He will speak; and He will tell you things to come."

John 16:13

I have a GPS. This device is wonderful to me because I travel extensively into places I've never been before. Once you enter the address of your destination, the device calculates the fastest route, estimates the time, and determines the best course for your journey. I follow its instructions faithfully. Before I begin the journey, I expect to arrive at my destination. There are various options I can choose in the menu to enhance its performance. I can view the map in satellite or hybrid view. I can listen to a woman's voice or a man's. I can choose the language I want to hear, even complicated with an accent. I can turn it up, down, or off. En route I discover just how much I appreciate this device. There are turns, obstacles, obstructions, traffic, alternate routes, and even distractions that would lure me to leave the beaten path and explore a new route. But I never fear getting lost because I have this little GPS that I've entrusted with all my directional insecurities.

Then it hit me! The Word of God is our GPS (God's Powerful Scriptures)! The more I discover this, the more I'm amazed that we have a tendency to journey throughout our lives without it. There are many turns, detours, dangers, and distractions that may cause harm to us. There are events that could be avoided and blessings to be acquired, but still we don't use His GPS. As ingenious as my travel device is, it is useless to me unless I pick it up and enter the data. The Word of God is powerful, but we must pick it up, open the cover, and enter the data into our heart.

Heavenly Father, I find myself directionally challenged at times in my life. When I'm confused, there are days many voices instruct me where to go and how to get there, and I find myself disillusioned and lost. Lead me into the truth of each day as I apply Your Word to my life. You are my guide. I want to follow You as I listen to Your voice and obey Your instructions to me. Amen.

Week 34, Weekend
A Captivating Read

For whatever things were written before were written for our
learning, that we through the patience and comfort of the Scriptures might have hope.

Romans 15:4

The Bible is great reading! Through divine inspiration of human authors, God has written a Book that is packed with adventure. God's stories tell of His amazing provision and love throughout history. These stories can also provide an incredible source of wisdom for our lives. Spend the next few moments reading several of the passages below. See if there are any truths that you can learn from Scripture. The Bible contains adventures that include: Gigantic fish and man-eating lions (Jonah; Daniel 6); Fire from the sky (Genesis 19; 1 Kings 18); Kings and queens and tales of royalty (1 Samuel 10–11; Esther); Songs, poetry, and love songs (Psalms and Song of Solomon); Bird waiters (1 Kings 17); Bottomless jugs (1 Kings 17; 2 Kings 4); Flying fiery chariots (2 Kings 2); Kidnapping (Genesis 14); Wrestling with angels (Genesis 32); Doing hard time in prison (Acts 21–23); Beheadings and hangings (Matthew 14; Matthew 27); Demons, a dead girl, and a deaf man (Mark 5–8).

As you read, what surprised you? What was new for you? What did you learn from Scripture?

I was surprised to read that the Bible has . . .

I learned some important lessons from Scripture, including. . .

God's Word is also filled with promises that can bring us joy, comfort, and hope. Reading about God's limitless expressions of love can offer relief and security to our lives. Read just a few of God's promises and allow His Word to comfort your heart:

- God always, always keeps His promises (Hebrews 6:18–19).
- God is our protector and our strength (Psalm 46:1, 11).
- God helps us when we're tired and gently guides us when life is hard (Matthew 11:28–30).
- God will meet your needs (Philippians 4:19).
- God forgives, if we do our part to ask Him (1 John 1:9).
- God is both all-powerful and all-loving, all the time (Psalm 89:8; 14).

God, thank You for giving me Your Word. I am especially grateful for
Scripture today because . . . Amen.

Terri Snead, Great Commandment Network

Week 35, Monday
The Priority of Prayer

Now in the morning, having risen a long while before daylight,
He went out and departed to a solitary place; and there He prayed.

Mark 1:35

Mark 1:35 makes it clear that Jesus prayed. There are at least three things that Jesus modeled for us that deserves our attention. First, He shows us the time of prayer. It was early in the morning. Second, the Scripture claims, "He went out . . ." Third, He was alone. As a Divine Teacher, everything Jesus did was a lesson to each of us. While He lived His life among us, He managed to show us various behaviors, habits, and how we should live this life. One of the constants in His life was prayer. There are many different times when prayer is appropriate (Psalm 55:17), yet the Scripture tells us this time was early. Honestly, to pray early in the morning is difficult for me. For others it may not be. The time may not necessarily be as important as the fact that you should simply take time to pray. It is also important to remove yourself from the obstacles of life when you pray. There are so many things that bombard our life today through media, relationships, jobs, and school. These things can often become distractions that limit our ability to clearly hear from God when we pray. Find a secret place as David did (Psalm 91). Remove yourself from the hustle and bustle of life for a while. That place will become your "hiding" place in Him (Matthew 6:5–6). Jesus shows us that He was alone in prayer. Again, we are not to be distracted by the things or people in our daily schedules. Jesus' intent was to talk with His Father. Let that be your constant challenge as you seek to follow Him. I encourage you to not limit your conversation with God to be solely in times of trouble or desperation. I heard a man pray aloud a prayer that went like this; "Lord, don't let me treat You like Tylenol and use You only when I need You."

Dear Lord, thank You for the opportunity and the freedom that I have to call upon You anytime and anywhere. Give me the strength to rise early and the comfort of knowing You are with me even when I feel that I am alone. Grant me the sensitivity to hear when You speak and the courage to obey when You call. I will follow You in the priorities of my life. Amen.

Dusty Wilson, Great Commandment Network

Week 35, Tuesday
Effective Prayer

The effective, fervent prayer of a righteous man avails much.

James 5:16

Volumes of books and literature have been written on the vast subject of prayer. Every religion focuses on some sort of prayer, but not every prayer is focused toward a living God! While I do not confess to be a professor of prayer, I do believe that Jesus practiced principles of effective prayer that should become desires for us as we learn to follow Him in prayer. The disciples asked Him to teach them how to pray (Luke 11:1–4; Matthew 6:5–13), but this desire only grew within as they followed Him (Matthew 5:1). According to Philippians 4:6–7, it is important that we take everything to the Lord in prayer. First Peter 5:7 declares that "He cares for us...." He encourages us to come boldly before Him (Hebrews 4:16), and we must come with faith (Hebrews 11:6). The Holy Spirit provides us with the empowerment to pray (Romans 8:26) and to believe that He hears us when we pray (Psalm 4:3). Lastly, thank Him for answered prayer (Psalm 141:1–2). He is worthy of our praise. Someone once shared with me that prayer is simply talking to God. It's not in the formality, the stature, or the posture we assume. It's not the volume, the quantity, or the event of prayer. Our prayer is an openhearted conversation with the One who cared enough to give His only Son for us. I have listened to the innocent prayers of children, the tearful prayers of the hurting, the exhuberant prayers of warriors, and I have watched the silent prayers of those in mourning. The most important prayer to God today, however, is yours. Will you follow Him in effective prayer?

O Lord, I open up the door of my heart and ask You to enter in. I believe You are listening to me even now. I stand confident in You, believing You are determined to do great things through me. Teach me to pray, O Lord, not as those who would declare to be something that they are not, but see that there be no wicked thing in me and renew a right spirit within me. I praise You in advance for meeting my needs even before I ask them. You are God alone. You are my Savior and I am Your child. Amen.

Week 35, Wednesday
Following Jesus Through the Daily Grind

*"But seek first the kingdom of God and His righteousness,
and all these things shall be added to you."*

Matthew 6:33

Dear Diary, the alarm sounds. When I'm not ready to get up, I don't like that sound. 5:30 a.m. is just too early. A Monster drink and a hot shower sound pretty good, though. "What? No Snow Day?" Grab a burnt piece of toast and out the door. The air is bitterly cold and the wind takes my breath away. The snow is deep. Traffic is slow and almost at a standstill. "I hope I don't run out of gas." I arrived too late to get a good parking spot. Now my feet are not only cold but wet, too. The halls are packed with people going in every direction. My friend isn't here today . . . ugh! Flunked a test. More homework. Forgot my shoes for gym class. Peanut butter 'n' jelly again? They laughed during my class speech. I thought it was good. Finally, on the way home, but not before I stop at the gas station. Two gallons is all I can afford today. Ran into the house—slipped and fell. Went to log on and the Internet is down. No Facebook tonight. After school chores, all the bore. Sitcoms and reruns and if that's not enough, I found a wristband in my backpack that reads; "W.W.J.D."? What would Jesus do? Now, I must confess. I've had somewhat of a bad hair day. But the question remains, Have I followed Him today?

While you may have genuinely, in fact, had a bad hair day, in your opinion, just remember it could get worse. Someone once said that "the only Jesus they see may be the Jesus they see in you." Through all the difficulties, trials, tests, and triumphs, remember to reflect Jesus in all you do. Someone is continually watching.

Dear Lord, this is the day You have made. You made today for me to rejoice and be glad in. Forgive me for grumbling, complaining, and griping when things didn't go my way. I will show others who You are even in the midst of my adverse circumstances, trials, and tests of life. I will follow You in everything that I do so that You may be glorified in my life. Thank You, Lord, for being the center of my life. Amen.

Dusty Wilson, Great Commandment Network

Week 35, Thursday
Following Jesus Totally

They forsook all and followed Him.

Luke 5:11

I love this story about common fishermen who met Jesus on the shoreline one day. Their lives were totally turned upside down after meeting Him. They listened as He taught, and they obeyed as He instructed them to recast their nets after not having caught a single fish all night long. Imagine that a carpenter would come along to teach professional fishermen how to fish! (LOL!) As they followed His instructions, I can almost hear Simon Peter say, "Whatever." Then it happened! The catch of a lifetime! They caught so many fish their boats almost sank as they tried to haul it all in. This would have been equivalent to us making an annual salary in one night. Once they finally filled up their boat, they called for other boats to join them in the catch and assist them with taking it back to shore. Some Bible scholars say that there could have been upwards of 200 boats in the harbor at any given time. The Bible is not specific here, but what if Jesus filled up every boat with a catch like never seen before? Now, once they arrived back to the beach, they didn't cash in their loot. They didn't spread the fame. They didn't run to the market and sell everything. It was never about the fish, the money, the boats, or the "hard day's night" they had spent the night before. The Bible says they forsook all and followed Him. Their hearts were turned toward Him. Following Jesus was more attractive to them than the money, the fame, or the fortune.

What does it mean to forsake all and follow Him? I believe that while Jesus paid the price for us on the cross of Calvary, there cannot be too great a cost for us to follow Him. However, we must follow Him totally, with everything that we are. Typically we speak of the value and the worth of things when it comes to following Jesus. The truth is, the monetary things will all fade away. What Jesus is asking for is who we are as a person: our heart, soul, and mind. If we give ourselves to Him totally, He will provide everything else.

O God, You are my God. You are my Father in heaven. I yield myself to You and submit all that I am to You. Amen.

Week 35, Friday
Truthful Followers

"But the hour is coming, and now is, when the true worshipers will worship the Father in spirit and truth; for the Father is seeking such to worship Him."

John 4:23

In the biblical narrative of Jesus' meeting the woman at the well, she was obviously in search of something or someone who would satisfy her present way of life. She was certainly living under adverse circumstances, and mostly dysfunctional, even according to our present-day standards. She had some knowledge of religion and spiritual heritage, as we discover in her conversation with Jesus. As the story indicates, Jesus told her that the Father was seeking true worshipers. In so doing He also lived out the life of a follower of God while He Himself submitted to the will of the Father in His everyday journey. His travel plans were to be in another area, but He followed the will of the Father. Had He continued on with His plans and stuck with the disciples, He would not have met the Samaritan woman at the well.

Following Jesus may require that we change a few plans, give up a few habits, confess some extra baggage that is cluttering our heavenly relationship, and allow Him to change us. The proof of His touch was evident as she left what she had to tell others about what He had done in her life (John 4:28–29). Ask yourself a few questions as you begin your journey today. *Is there anything in my life keeping me from being a true worshiper? Have I included the Lord in my schedule today? Do others know about my relationship with the Father above? Can they witness something different about me today?* You can make a difference!

Dear heavenly Father, help me to truthfully follow You. It's not about my traditions, my heritage, my namesake, or even what I've done. It's about living my life in truth before others so that they may see who it is that lives in me. Transform me. Change me into what You want me to be. I pray that the experience the woman at the well had with You would be a living experience for me. Remove the baggage in my life that prohibits me from following You in worship freely so that I may tell others. It's because of whose I am. Amen.

Dusty Wilson, Great Commandment Network

Week 35, Weekend
Jesus' Prayer List

He always lives to make intercession for them.

Hebrews 7:25

Prayer isn't an obligation. It's an incredible privilege. We actually get to talk to our Creator! But here's another amazing truth: Jesus is praying for us! Scripture tells us that Jesus is in heaven praying for you! That's how He spends His day. The book of Hebrews says that Christ "always lives to make intercession for us" (Hebrews 7:25). Romans 8:34 explains that Jesus is at the right hand of God interceding and praying on our behalf.

Imagine that when you awoke this morning, the house was quiet, and no one else was awake. You walked toward the living room and only a small lamp illuminated the darkness. When your eyes adjusted, you couldn't quite believe what you were seeing, but there He was. Jesus was on His knees in your living room! And as you walked into the room, you could tell His lips were moving . . . you realized He must be praying. You were careful not to disturb the Savior, so you sat down softly beside Him. In the stillness of the morning, you were able to make out more of Jesus' words. Jesus was praying for you! He was praying for the concerns of your heart. He was praying to God on your behalf. It was as if Jesus was sitting beside His heavenly Father and He was carefully reviewing all the important parts of your day. He was rejoicing in the good parts and praying for you in the hard moments.

Father, did You see the way that Your precious child has grown over the last few months? Did You see how he has become more and more like You? Isn't that terrific? Did You see how hard he worked this week at school, at the new job, and at home? What a diligent young person!

Father, please remember this child of Yours today. See the way his heart is anxious and fearful. I know You've seen the hurtful times and the pain-filled moments. I am hurting for him and I know You are, too. Please comfort him and bring someone into his life to care for him. Let him know that We are here and We love him deeply.

Take the next few moments and join Jesus in prayer. He's praying for you. Could you meet Him there?

 Jesus, I am grateful and amazed that You spend Your day praying for me. Thank You that . . . Amen.

Week 36, Monday
The One Thing

And she had a sister called Mary, who also sat at Jesus' feet and heard His word.

Luke 10:39

The lesson of Luke 10 is so important for those who really want to follow Jesus. It is so important because we live in a society that is constantly demanding our time, attention, and best efforts. If we aren't careful, we can easily find ourselves feeling more pressure by the end of the day instead of relieved we have made it through another day.

Martha was the sister of Mary, and she opened her home to Jesus and the disciples. Scripture gives us an up-close-and-personal view of Martha's priorities for this visit from Jesus. While Mary was found in an intimate, humble posture, ready to hear and learn from the ultimate Teacher, Martha was "distracted with preparations" missing what was most important. Jesus addressed Martha's attitude as "worried and upset" and taught her that "few things are needed—indeed, only one."

Reflect upon what Christ was really saying to Martha. What had become most important to Martha didn't matter at all to Christ because it had nothing to do with His Kingdom. The one thing Christ desires from us most is an intimate and personal relationship. He is near and wants to share life with us. However, when we are hit with the pressuring demands from coaches, teachers, parents, friends, and sometimes even enemies, we can lose sight of the one thing that should matter most.

A priority is something that is important and usually comes first in our life. What comes first in your life? Are the important things in your life Kingdom-connected? Consider reprioritizing what matters most.

Reflect upon 1 Corinthians 2:16 and Psalm 27:11 and pray this prayer.

Lord, I thank You that as You help me learn to have the mind of Christ, I will not lose sight of what matters most to You and Your Kingdom. Give me strength each day to keep first things first, and as I do this, I believe I will be a more effective vessel for Your Kingdom and a better follower of You. May Your ways become my ways and Your thoughts, my thoughts. Amen.

Mario and Meagan Hood, Great Commandment Network

Week 36, Tuesday
Tiny Moments, Great Followers

"If you keep My commandments, you will abide in My love,
just as I have kept My Father's commandments and abide in His love."

John 15:10

Each of our lives is made up of billions of moments that can appear too tiny to be significant. These moments may seem to disappear as quickly as they appear. Moments, though short-lived and seemingly insignificant, carry great advantageous opportunities for our walk with Christ. When you look back over the life of someone who has died, you can probably observe some dominant themes of their life that now boldly represent the person's character, beliefs, and priorities. The truth is, people don't become people of great character without taking advantage of small, opportune moments. The tiny moments that build great, influential followers of Christ have one thing in common: they give a person the chance to be obedient and the person does not resist.

Recently, I was able to spend time with a dear friend who is relocating from Tennessee to Cambodia to do mission work. This friend has a great job, a beautiful house, two degrees, and she is surrounded by friends and family who love and support her. What would make such a talented and beautiful young woman leave such success behind, to live among the uneducated and poor? Why would someone so stable and independent leave a salary position only to live at the generous expense of others? It is simple; obedience.

What a testimony to our generation! Not all of us are called to move across the world and relocate to such drastic measures, but we are all called to be obedient. As followers of Christ, we must understand when we walk in obedience to God's Word it will look rather different from another's answer to obedience. I know that I am in the center of God's will right here in Orlando, Florida, caring for my two children in the comfort of our nice and cozy apartment. I know that every time I stand alongside my husband in ministry and go out on my own to minister, I am answering the call of Christ. As we follow Christ, we must redefine *success*. Success is not the results we achieve from the act of obedience, but rather the act of obedience itself.

Meditate for a moment on the personal calling Christ has for you. Are you walking in obedience daily to better fulfill this personal calling? See these verses: Luke 9:23, Romans 8:28, and 2 Timothy 1:9.

Mario and Meagan Hood, Great Commandment Network

Week 36, Wednesday
Learning to Deny

"No one can serve two masters; for he will either hate the one and love the other, or else he will be loyal to the one and despise the other."

Matthew 16:24

It isn't wrong to want things for ourselves. We all have dreams and desires we hope will one day come to pass. You may even have a bucket list or a dreaming board of things you want to accomplish or own before your time on earth is over. God isn't against His people having things, but when *things* take over us, we have a problem.

When things become more desirable than a closer walk with Christ, we must learn to deny ourselves (see Luke 9:23). Denying ourselves means that when we begin to desire something that could possibly drive a wedge between us and our Lord, we will sacrifice that certain thing for the sake of our relationship with God. There is only room for one Master in our lives. When we begin to desire things more than Him, we have allowed something else to take the place of honor that once belonged to Christ.

Most of us have probably heard of idolatry. You may even get a hazy picture in your mind of a statue or god that you have seen being worshiped by others or on television. While those can be accurate depictions of what idolatry is, idolatry is really anything that is receiving more love and commitment than Christ. Idolatry can be money, clothes, relationships with significant others, or other gods. It is important to define these idols in our lives.

There isn't room for God and any other god. What areas of your life do you see that need purging? Do you care more about yourself, material goods, or money more than God? If so, are you willing to surrender these areas to Christ? (See Exodus 20:3.)

 Lord, forgive me for placing other things before You. As I receive Your forgiveness, help me to turn from these things unselfishly. May You have full reign in my heart and life. Amen.

Mario and Meagan Hood, Great Commandment Network

Week 36, Thursday
Follow the Leader

"For even the Son of Man did not come to be served, but to serve."

Mark 10:45

When you speak of following, you can't get very far without observing leading. When speaking of our Christian walk, we know Jesus is the ultimate Leader. Everything we desire to do and be in life should be based on His model of leadership. He led without leading anyone astray, and everything He did led His followers back to one thing: His Father's business.

We know through Scripture that Jesus is a King and the Son of God. He was the Chosen One, who left heaven and invaded the earth with the purpose to fulfill the will of the Father so that we might one day reign with Him (see John 3:16). In knowing these things, we must not forget that though Jesus was a king, He never saw Himself so lofty that He was exempt from serving. In fact, Jesus came for the exact opposite purpose: to serve others.

It is important that we always know that no matter how long we have been saved or what titles or positions we possess, none of us are exempt from serving. Reflect upon this: if Christ's ultimate reason for coming to the earth was to serve, can we really follow Him without also serving others?

In what ways do you serve others? In what areas could you serve better? How important has serving been in your Christian walk?

An easy way to hold yourself accountable to serving and staying about the Father's business is to ask yourself, *Is what I'm spending the most time on today the thing that will matter most tomorrow?* Jesus was always about serving now so that someone's future could be secure in Him tomorrow.

Quietly reflect upon what matters most today. What are you devoting the most time to?

    Lord, thank You for the being the perfect model of a leader and servant. You show us that through leading and serving, no one can be led astray, because it was and is Your ultimate purpose. Show me opportunities to serve others, as I serve You. Amen.

Week 36, Friday
The Great Reward

He is a rewarder of those who diligently seek Him.

Hebrews 11:6

When I was sixteen, I heard the gentle voice of the Spirit calling me, all of me, for His ministry. I wasn't exactly sure how my future would turn out or what exactly the plan would look like, but I remember saying, "Yes!" Over ten years later, I feel as though I have the best job in the world. Although you won't find my name on anyone's payroll, I have the honor of serving alongside my husband as we minister to the youth and young adults of our local church.

I get a front-row seat to God's goodness and provision unfolding in the hearts of so many young people. Another reason I feel I have the best job in the world is because, while following Christ is challenging and costs us everything, I get the honor of seeing the rewards of those who really desire to follow Jesus. I see the fear and anxiety in the lives of young people all of the time. They fear what they will have to give up and lose if they follow Christ. The truth is, when we make our life about Him, He makes His blessings about us.

Consider how blessed we are as followers of Christ that because we have given up our life to serve Him, we can lay our hands on the sick and they can recover! How amazing it is to know that in every battle we face, we can experience victory through Jesus? Be encouraged! As you say yes to Christ, He will reward your obedience! Know that in every sacrifice you make to obtain a closer walk with Him, there is nothing that can compare to the awesomeness of that intimate relationship you desire deep within.

 God, thank You for the ultimate sacrifice of Your Son, Jesus. Because of Him, I can experience the rewards of following Him obediently. Help the things of this world to grow less desirable as I strive in higher pursuit of You! Amen.

Mario and Meagan Hood, Great Commandment Network

Week 36, Weekend
Be a Bethany

His secret counsel is with the upright.

Proverbs 3:32

Bethany was a small town, two miles outside of Jerusalem. The city was the home of Christ's friends Mary, Martha, and Lazarus, but aside from that fact, the town of Bethany was pretty insignificant. It didn't have great historical, political, or even religious importance, but Jesus seemed to go out of His way to get there. He was intentional about going to Bethany, but why?

Bethany was a place of refuge for Jesus. It was a place where people He loved wanted to share moments of intimate fellowship with Him. Bethany was the place where Mary chose to sit at Jesus' feet and hear the vulnerable things of His heart. Jesus must have loved being in Bethany because it was a place where He could both give and receive loving care. (See Luke 10:38–42.)

Bethany was also a place of divine power and comfort. Jesus saw Mary and Martha's pain and felt their grief over their brother's death, and He wept. The human part of Jesus couldn't help but be moved by His friends' sadness. And then, on that same day, Jesus brought divine restoration and life to Lazarus. Christ raised His friend from the dead, demonstrating His ultimate power and provision.

Jesus has the same desire for His relationship with you. Imagine that Christ has these words to say, just for you:

> Dear one, I am hoping that your life and your heart would be My Bethany. I am hoping to have a special, one-of-a-kind friendship with you. I want to share My joy with you. I want to share about the things that sadden My heart with you. Just like in Bethany—I want to lavishly give and receive from you.
>
> Just like Bethany, I want to comfort you when you hurt, because your pain moves My heart. I want to bring restoration to your life, just like I did for Mary and for Martha. I want to see your family and your relationships revived, renewed, and full of life.
>
> And just like Bethany, even though I am your Savior and I am your God, I long to receive from you and spend time with you. I am ready to share closeness and intimate friendship with you.

God, I want my life to be like a "Bethany" for You. I'm grateful You want this kind of relationship because . . . Amen.

Terri Snead, Great Commandment Network

Week 37, Monday
When the Cup Won't Pass

"O My Father, if it is possible, let this cup pass from Me; nevertheless, not as I will, but as You will."

Matthew 26:39

This prayer was prayed by Jesus just a little while before He was to be crucified. In fact, Jesus prayed something similar two more times (see verses 42 and 44). Any of us who know the Gospel know that the cup did not pass. Christ was later crucified in the most gruesome way we could ever imagine.

We must realize as followers of Christ that, like Christ, we will be tested. This portion of Scripture, which takes place in the Garden of Gethsemane, reveals what it really means to truly follow after Him. After praying three times, the will of the Father did not change, but neither did the obedience of Christ. He later walked the road that led Him to the hill called Calvary, and He completed the will of His Father after being mocked, beaten, and betrayed.

Consider this: when the cup won't pass, it's there to drink. Just as Christ did, we must be obedient in carrying out the will of the Father no matter the cost or pain.

Meditate upon Hebrews 10:35–39 and then pray the following prayer:

Lord, help me to remain confident that in every test I will have a testimony. As I pass through tests, help me know the test is not about my credit but about Your glory. Help me be obedient just as Christ was obedient. Amen.

Mario and Meagan Hood, Great Commandment Network

Week 37, Tuesday
Baby Steps

My beloved brethren, let every man be swift to hear, slow to speak, slow to wrath.

James 1:19

While doing the dishes one day, I realized that every other time I turned to rinse a dish and then place it in the dishwasher, silverware or dishes were missing from the dishwasher. Because of the loudness of running water and the garbage disposal, I wasn't hearing my eighteen-month-old daughter come into the kitchen, reach into the dishwasher, and take dishes into the family room. I finally caught her and the stash of dishes and silverware. Walking back into the kitchen, I quickly noticed the floor leading out of the family room was carpet and the flooring in the kitchen was laminate and both were separated by a silver strip. I instantly knew I had an opportunity to teach my daughter self-control by setting a boundary she was not to cross while I was doing the dishes. It took awhile but she now knows she is not to "cross the line." I've seen in the last few weeks more patience and self-control developing within her.

Because my daughter is only eighteen months old, there is so much she has yet to learn. Everything I teach her is a process, and as she grows I see the principles becoming evident without me having to remind her. Our spiritual lives aren't much different. The verse above is encouraging a display of the fruit of the Spirit. Just as a child was once a baby and a baby once a fetus, a fruit was once a seed in the ground. It took time to be planted and rain to make it grow. We are no different in our spirits.

As we grow spiritually, the more fruit we will bear. It is a sign of maturity and growth and wellness. This verse, found in James, will help us not say things we will later regret and also encourage times for reflection after listening.

Reflect upon Galatians 5:22–23. In what areas does your life show growth and maturity by ripe fruit? In what areas have you yet to see the harvest of planted seeds?

Lord, in all I do, help me to bear much fruit in You. May others be blessed by the harvest in my spiritual life. Help me to be open to the nurturing of Your Spirit as I grow more in You each day. Amen.

Week 37, Wednesday
The Joy of Knowing

"I am the good shepherd; and I know My sheep, and am known by My own."

John 10:14

This passage of Scripture is so beautifully assuring for all of us who follow Christ. The chapter speaks of the relationship between sheep and their shepherd. When the sheep know their shepherd's voice, they do as He says and follow Him. As with anyone's voice, it takes time to learn. Before caller ID, my family lived in a one-story home with a black telephone that hung on the wall. When certain people would call and I would answer, they wouldn't have to tell me who it was; I would know because of their voice. For instance, when my grandmother would call I would know instantly it was her!

After growing in the Lord for many years, His voice is no different. I immediately know that still, small voice that is so gentle, yet so powerful. I love that this passage says in verse 4 that the sheep follow Him because they *know* His voice.

How well do you know God's voice? When was the last time He spoke to you?

A few weeks ago, I was having a rather difficult day with my son. Dalen is a very smart four-year-old who can just about talk his way out of anything if you let him. We are trying to teach Dalen that every thought is not meant to be spoken, but he hasn't quite learned this completely yet. On this particular day, my son was voicing every thought his mind produced, including some very disrespectful objections to some things that I needed him to do. Eventually I had to sit him down, and he explained to me that the devil was telling him to say these rude and harsh things. I immediately asked him how he knew it was the devil. He very confidently explained that it was because Jesus doesn't say bad things.

As you learn the voice of God, you must familiarize yourself with His character. He will always speak truth and love. My four-year-old is already learning this overcomplicated principle. The more you read His Word, the more you will discover about Him and be able to decipher His voice over all others.

God, allow me to know Your character through Your Word. As I learn more about You, may I learn to be more obedient in following You as You speak. Amen.

Week 37, Thursday
"I" in Team

So then each of us shall give account of himself to God. Therefore let us not judge one another anymore, but rather resolve this, not to put a stumbling block or a cause to fall in our brother's way.

Romans 14:12, 13

Have you ever heard the phrase "There is no I in team"? What If I told you there *was* an "I" in team? No, it's not literally in the word *team*, but in the concept that word is portraying.

When we are part of a team there is an I involved, and that I is you. As a matter of fact the team is made up of individuals, so in reality there are many Is that make up a team. Challenges arise on a team when one wants to stand out above the rest. This is when the team is not seen anymore, but only that one I.

As an individual you are a disciple of Christ, but you are also a part of the body of Christ, or the team of Christ. We each have to give an account for ourselves, for our actions, and for our decisions, but it doesn't stop there. Just as one bad player can affect how an entire team plays, in our walk with Christ we have to examine how our decisions are affecting other believers.

Paul tells us not judge, but rather to try to not be a stumbling block to others. Simply put, there comes a point in your walk with Christ where you mature to see past the faults of others and become a stepping-stone instead of a stumbling block. You have to take responsibility for your actions and make sure that you (the I) don't overtake the team. This will ensure that the team wins in the end.

God, I know that You are the righteous Judge and that all people will have to give an account of their actions to You. I am thankful that the blood of Jesus Christ covers my sins and enables me to live in right standing with You. Lord, I pray that You help me to be an encourager to other believers in the faith. As David prayed, I also pray that You search me and know my heart, try me and know my thoughts, if there is anything wicked in me, lead me to the way that is everlasting. Amen.

Mario and Meagan Hood, Great Commandment Network

Week 37, Friday
Me, Myself, and Others

Let nothing be done through selfish ambition or conceit,
but in lowliness of mind let each esteem others better than himself.
Let each of you look out not only for his own interests, but also for the interests of others.

Philippians 2:3, 4

Today on average you can expect to be exposed to around 3,000 ads per day. That's right, 3,000! A global corporation can spend over $620 billion each year to try to make their product seem desirable to you. With those kind of statistics, it's no wonder our culture is so "me" driven. Everywhere you look, someone is trying to get you to buy something or do something for yourself. I'm not saying you can't or shouldn't do things for yourself, but as a disciple of Christ our lifestyle should be one that reflects the fact that we care about others as well.

In the Christian life selfishness has no place. If our lives are to reflect Jesus, then the one thing we should display is selflessness! Jesus lived to serve people and He died to save people! He was all about giving His life away, and at the same time Jesus didn't want to build His own reputation (Philippians 2:7). He only wanted to do the Father's will (John 6:38). If we want to be like Jesus, then we, too, should live to give our lives away to others. The cause of Christ in every Christian's life should include ways in which we can serve other people. Not so that we can build a name for ourselves, but so that the Gospel is advanced and the name of Jesus is lifted up.

Again, in the world that surrounds us today, it easy to think of only "me" and not others. We as disciples are not called to be like the world but to change the world (John 15:9; Romans 12:2).

Jesus, You lived a selfless life, putting others before Yourself and displaying the love of the Father for all people. I want my life to mirror Your life and display this same selfless love. In a world that teaches me to think of only myself, I pray that You renew my mind to put others first. Show me how to serve others in such a way that Your name will be magnified above all other names. Amen.

Mario and Meagan Hood, Great Commandment Network

"Be holy, for I am holy."

1 Peter 1:16

This verse in 1 Peter might seem a little bossy or unrealistic. Is God really asking us to reach a goal that will never be attainable? Is God seriously demanding our perfection? Why would God want our holiness? Why is He telling us to be like Him?

Our God, the real God, isn't bossy or demanding. He isn't holding out an impractical standard. Peter is letting us know that because God is holy, He wants us to live out our lives always striving for holiness and maturity … because the more we are like Him, the closer we will be to Him. God's motive behind His hope for our holiness is that He deeply longs for a closer and more intimate relationship with us.

What might it look like to be a maturing follower of Jesus?

- Children frequently go to great lengths to justify their poor choices, but as maturing followers of Jesus, we are called to be accountable to God and to take responsibility for our actions (Romans 14:12).
- Children tend to talk a great deal and often have trouble listening carefully, but as maturing disciples of Jesus we are called to speak less and listen more both to God and to other people (James 1:19).
- Children are often intensely selfish and focused on their own desires, but as maturing disciples of Jesus, we are called to abandon self-preoccupation and to direct our energy toward loving and serving God and others (Philippians 2:3–4).
- Children generally have a very limited, simplistic understanding of most subjects, but as maturing disciples of Jesus we are called to pursue detailed knowledge and understanding of God's Word and to live with wisdom and discernment that comes from time spent with Him.

How does it make you feel as you consider God's motive for your spiritual maturity? The reason why He wants you to mature and grow spiritually is because God deeply desires a closer relationship with you.

When I consider God's motive for my spiritual growth, I feel _____ because … Tell Him about your gratitude and willingness to grow.

Father, my heart wants to be mature in all that I do and say. Help me to see any of my childish ways and help me to trade them for more mature choices, because I want to be closer to You. Amen.

Week 38, Monday
Grace Alone

Having predestined us to adoption as sons by Jesus Christ to Himself, according to the good pleasure of His will, to the praise of the glory of His grace, by which He made us accepted in the Beloved.

Ephesians 1:5, 6

In the South, it seems that no matter what restaurant you choose to eat breakfast, grits comes as a side item—no matter what you order! Grits are a dish of coarsely ground corn kernels boiled in water or milk. Now, that doesn't sound too delicious on paper, but add a lot of butter, salt, and pepper, and it always tasted great.

I remember as a new believer having breakfast one morning with a mentor of mine, and he was trying to explain the grace of God to me. Finally, after several times I still wasn't getting the point clearly. He grabbed my bowl of grits and said, "Grace is like grits; it just comes with the deal!" Looking back, it may have been unorthodox but it stuck with me.

This Scripture tells us that the Father, according to His pleasure and will, brought us into His family through His only begotten Son to the praise of His glorious grace. How wonderful is it to know that you have been freely given His grace! In fact, for us to become His son or daughter, we need this free grace because we cannot earn our own way into a relationship with the Father. Knowing this, it was His pleasure to provide a way for us, that is, through Jesus, to enter into His family as adopted sons and daughters.

As disciples of Jesus Christ, we must understand that it is by this grace and this grace alone that we have a relationship with the Father. We have done nothing to earn our status as sons or daughters, but through the obedience of the Son and our belief in Him, our sins are forgiven and the status of sinner separated from God becomes son or daughter connected to the Father. Grace is the deal. By it we have a relationship with the Father.

Gracious Father, I thank You for providing a way into a relationship with You through Your Son, Jesus. I praise You for the grace that is freely given to me. Help me to extend that same grace to others. Amen.

Mario and Meagan Hood, Great Commandment Network

Week 38, Tuesday
Now You See Me, Now You Don't

For you died, and your life is hidden with Christ in God. When Christ who is our life appears, then you also will appear with Him in glory.

Colossians 3:3

Bang! You're dead. Not physically, but spiritually, or at least you're supposed to be. As a kid I remember that some of the best times I had playing were when the other kids and I would role-play. We guys would pretend to be superheroes or action figures, and the girls would pretend to be a princess or Tinkerbell. As kids we pretended to be someone else; as Christians we don't play pretend. We are to be Christlike.

Think about this: When Jesus died on the cross, He took our place. He physically died for our sins and when we receive Him as Lord and Savior we accept this spiritually. The challenge to all believers is to allow our lives to be hid in Christ so that when others see us, they actually see Christ.

The writer in Romans encourages us to walk in the newness of life (Romans 6:4). Jesus Himself said, " I have come that they may have life, and that they may have it more abundantly" (John 10:10). Jesus is not the center of the believer's life; He is the fullness of the believer's life. Every dream, every goal, every aspiration for the believer should be to glorify Jesus.

For the believer the question is not, Am I going to live for Christ or for myself? The question for the believer is, How can I display Christ today through the life I now live? When you see me, I hope you see Christ.

Jesus, I thank You for living Your life in full obedience to the Father's will and for dying on the cross for my sins. I recognize that You lived a life that I could never live and died a death that I should have died. Jesus, teach me through Your Word how to live in such a way that I display You to others on a consistent basis. I want my life to be so hidden in You that everything I do brings glory to Your name. Thank You for this new and abundant life that I have in You. Amen.

Mario and Meagan Hood, Great Commandment Network ·

Week 38, Wednesday
Made in God

For we are His workmanship, created in Christ Jesus for good works, which God prepared beforehand that we should walk in them.

Ephesians 2:10

Usually on the bottom of everything that is made you will find a stamp that says made in (insert name or place or country). The country in which the product was made or by whom the product was made will often determine the value of the product. Why? Because depending on who and what the product was created for, it may not need as expensive parts or labor to construct it.

Have you ever really thought about how the God who created the universe is your Creator? That you are the workmanship of God? In today's modern era, with all the advancements in technology, we lose the essence portrayed in the word *workmanship*.

At one point in society, everything was made by hand. Yes, that's right. There were no computers or machines to build any products. Everything was created by someone's dedicated skill in a particular craft. Today you might see these products as antiques and valued at a high price, because someone spent hours and hours to make a single product and workmanship of that type is hard to find anymore.

Consider this: You were made by God in Christ to do a good work. You were created on purpose for a purpose. The most valuable thing that man has ever created does not come close to the value you have in God. You are the very image of God (Genesis 1:27). You are fearfully and wonderfully made (Psalm 139:14). You are destined to succeed (Jeremiah 29:11). You are chosen, you are royalty, and you are set apart as a possession for God alone (1 Peter 2:9). You are the workmanship of God.

The very fingers of God created you, and He knows you intimately (Psalm 139). You are made in God!

Lord, words cannot express the gratitude in my heart for creating me. I am in awe that You have thought of me even before I was knit together in my mother's womb. Lord, thank You for all the blessings that You have placed on my life; I do not take them for granted. I thank You for the amazing gifts and talents that You have given me. Show me how to use what You have given me to do the good work You have already prepared for me. Amen.

Mario and Meagan Hood, Great Commandment Network

Week 38, Thursday
With Everything

So he answered and said, "'You shall love the Lord your God with all your heart, with all your soul, with all your strength, and with all your mind,' and 'your neighbor as yourself.'"

Luke 10:27

Growing up playing sports, I heard the phrases "Give it all you got," or "Leave it all on the field," or "Don't hold anything back" a lot. I especially remember hearing it near the end of a game.

Why at the end of a game? Because that's when you are at your weakest and feel like giving up. The thought was that if you left everything "out there," then no matter what the outcome, you had given it your best. No matter if you won or lost, in victory or defeat, if you gave it everything you had, then you had done your job.

Our journey with God is no different. God wants us to give Him everything we have. We are to love God with all our heart, with all our soul, with all our strength, and with all our mind—basically to love Him with everything we have. Not just at the end of the game (or our life) but right now!

If you are feeling weak, if you are feeling down, if you are feeling like you're on your last leg, there's not a more perfect time to live for God with everything you've got. For God declares, "When you are weak, then I am strong" (2 Corinthians 12:9–10)! God's strength is made perfect in your weakness and He has provided the right amount of grace for you to receive the victory in every situation. I challenge you to be determined to live for God with everything you've got!

God, today I come before You with all that I am and say that I will live for You with everything that I have. The love You have shown to me deserves this kind of response, and I am determined to show this same love to others. I pray that my heart will always beat after You. I pray that my soul will always long after You. I pray that my strength will always be grounded in You. I pray that my mind would always focus on You. And in my times of weakness I pray that Your strength would rise in perfection. Amen.

Mario and Meagan Hood, Great Commandment Network

Week 38, Friday
Don't Talk About It, Be About It

Therefore, from now on, we regard no one according to the flesh. Even though we have known Christ according to the flesh, yet now we know Him thus no longer. Therefore, if anyone is in Christ, he is a new creation; old things have passed away; behold, all things have become new.

2 Corinthians 5:16, 17

Have you ever ridden in a new car? How about a used car that was new to you? At the time you may have thought, *I have never seen this model before anywhere*, but by the time you leave the car lot or your friend's house you have seen the exact same car five times! Now, I'm pretty sure five people didn't go out a buy those cars at that moment; instead, you had most likely seen the car before but you didn't recognize it. That's because your experience determines your perspective.

Our experiences shape us. They leave an imprint that's either negative or positive. The challenge for believers is to see past our past and to live for the future. Paul encourages us to regard no one according to the flesh, which is his or her sinful nature, but to see him or her in the Spirit as a new creation in Christ. This is not to excuse or support behavior that goes against Scripture. He is simply urging us to see the potential of Christ that resides in every believer. To change our perspective of others, we need to change our experiences with them.

No matter what dictionary you use, *new* is *new*. What I mean is this: you can't take something old and make it new. Yes, you can refurbish something that is old, but no matter what clever word you used to describe the old product, at best it is only "like new." In Christ, all old things have passed away, therefore it's not "like new"; it is brand new!

 Father, I am so grateful that You see me in Christ as a new creation. Help me to see beyond the old things and to focus on the new creation You have made me to be. Let my life become a testimony to others that You are able to redeem anyone at any time. Father, I pray for opportunities to have new experiences with others in order to gain a new viewpoint of them. Amen.

Mario and Meagan Hood, Great Commandment Network

Week 38, Weekend
He Believes in You

"If anyone serves Me, let him follow Me."

John 12:26

A disciple is someone who has chosen to be with a mentor in order to become like them. A baseball player chooses to become a disciple of his professional hitting coach in order to become a better player, while a pianist chooses to become a disciple of an expert music teacher in order to master the instrument. By the same token, in order to become disciples of Jesus, we must commit to being with Him in order to learn how to be more like Him.

How about you? Have you committed to follow Jesus and become His disciple?

Yes, I have chosen to be a follower of Jesus and have yielded my life to Him. I'm confident of this decision because...

(If you are not confident of this decision or are not sure what it means to receive Christ's gift of salvation, be sure to talk to a pastor or an adult who can help.)

During Jesus' time on earth, He made disciples out of all kinds of people. Jesus obviously didn't choose disciples based on their status or influence because some of His disciples were fishermen and tax collectors. Christ looked for disciples whose hearts were ready to yield to Him and follow Him.

When Jesus called His disciples to follow Him, it was the custom for religious teachers to mentor young apprentices. When a rabbi gave the privilege of becoming His disciple, that meant the rabbi believed in you. He believed you had what it took to become like him.

What about you? Jesus, believes in you. He believes that you have what it takes to become like Him!
- Jesus is ready to mentor and disciple you. Just like the music teacher who's ready to practice with you every day, Jesus wants to be with you daily. Will you join Him?
- Jesus is ready to reveal Himself to you. Just like the coach who's ready to share the secrets of becoming a great baseball player with you, Jesus is ready to reveal the secrets to being like Him. Are you ready to hear Him and read His words?
- Jesus is ready to listen to you and join you in worship and in prayer. Will you be there, too?

God, I desire to be closer to You and follow You daily. Thank You for believing in me. Amen.

Terri Snead, Great Commandment Network

Week 39, Monday
Generations Shaped by the Word

By faith we understand that the worlds were framed by the word of God,
so that the things which are seen were not made of things which are visible.

Hebrews 11:3

As we look at Hebrews 11:1–3, we are awestruck at the courage and impact of these heroes of faith. They've impacted their own generation and the generation of today. The whole chapter of Hebrews 11 is a lesson of one life making a generational impact. For example the word "worlds" in Hebrews 11:3 is the Greek word *anions*, which means "ages, or generations, or a reference to time, such as a lifetime."

This is not a reference to the planets being created, but to a generation of life or time, an age or opportunity for a person to impact their generation.

The rest of chapter 11 demonstrates person after person who received a word from God that changed them and their generation.

We must learn to hear the voice behind the verse. We must know the God of the Bible, not just the Bible. When they heard His voice, they had faith to act, to stand with conviction, to pass on to the next generation the God of Abraham, Isaac, and Jacob. Hear His voice in the Word. Let it go deep within you. It is His voice for your lifetime. You are a generation-changer.

His voice gives you today what you need to reshape and reconstruct the time, age, and day in which you live. We cannot accept things as they are. Ask what you can do, with the faith you live, to change your generation. Read the list of generation-changers in Hebrews 11; they are listed there to inspire us to hear His voice for our day.

Jesus, I am overwhelmed as I consider my generation. What part do I play? How can I make a difference? Lord, speak to me this day so that I may hear Your voice and hear Your will for my life. Help me to impact this generation today and forever. Jesus, You said Your Word is the truth, that Your Word is Spirit and Life. Today I set my heart to hear Your voice, and no other will I follow. Empower me to pass my faith to the next generation. Speak to me today about my generation. I want to hear Your Voice in the verse! Amen.

John B. Lowe II, Great Commandment Network

Week 39, Tuesday
Whom Do You Want to Be Like?

*And Paul said, "I would to God that not only you, but also all who hear
me today, might become both almost and altogether such as I am, except for these chains."*

Acts 26:29

Have you ever wished you were someone else, anyone else? Anywhere else, besides where you were at that moment of pressure? Maybe you thought, *I just want to disappear!*

Acts 26:12–32 tells the story of the apostle Paul in trouble again. His life is on the line this time. He is in a room surrounded by enemies. This would be a good time to disappear, to be anyone or anywhere other than who and where you are!

The people in the room are there to condemn him to death. To pick his life apart. To inspect, to make him an example to others. He answers and tells his story; things are going normal for a hearing of this sort.

Then the conviction, the security of being loved and knowing who one is, and the purpose for one's life is pushing to come out of Paul. *Enough of this pressure to condemn me! I am here to save you!* (Note Acts.26:27–29.)

In verse 29, Paul made a statement that no one in the room had heard from a person who was on trial for their life: "I wish all of you were like me, except for these chains." Paul declares, "I am loved, accepted, unconcerned for my own life. I do not wish to be you, lost in the presentation of power, pomp, and prestige. I would to God you were like me." What confidence in one's self!

So I ask you today: Do you know how completely and deeply you are loved? Are you secure in Him? Is your relationship based on your performance or on popularity? (See Romans.8:31–39.) Dwell on the everlasting, deep love Jesus has for you. Then you, too, will want to pass it on to all in the room.

Jesus, there are people in my life, in my room who need to experience the deep, sincere love I have experienced in You. Help me to love as I have been loved. Help me, under pressure, to take the opportunity to tell others of how free I am, to be confident in my relationship with You, to say, "I would to God you were like me." Amen.

John B. Lowe II, Great Commandment Network

Week 39, Wednesday
You and You Only

Now you Philippians know also that in the beginning of the gospel, when I departed
from Macedonia, no church shared with me concerning giving and receiving but you only.

Philippians 4:15

I taught this lesson to my children, family, and church: you and you only. Let it be said of us. The church of Philippi was an extended family of Paul's. Paul was writing while he was in prison. It was a painful time in his life in more ways than one. (Read Acts.16.) These people became his extended family, church, and friends.

Paul reminds them of their meeting and reminds them that no other church but "you and you only" had shared with him so much. I think of this often, out of all of the churches he had begun, only one supported him faithfully financially.

Here, it is obviously finances he is speaking of. Yet we know money is not given to people we don't love, believe in, and respect. Freely, they chased him down to give offerings to him; Paul had no post-office box to mail it to. They chased him across Europe. Why? They loved him; they loved the message of salvation; they were convinced by Paul's actions that he loved them, too.

He took the wrongful beating and imprisonment. He did not leave when the prison doors opened. He stayed to share salvation with a household that became a church, an extended family. They did not forget the price he had paid to share his life, love, and salvation with them.

Perhaps someone in your life has been there for you. Remember that sense of security. The knowledge of being loved and cared for. Is there a spouse, a child, or a friend that you and you only can love?

 Jesus, I want to be the kind of person that while I live my life, others will say of me, "you and perhaps you only loved me and supported me." Lord, help me to live my life as an extension of Your family. Help me to love first! Amen.

John B. Lowe II, Great Commandment Network

Week 39, Thursday
Defined in a Word—*Faith*

...and being fully convinced that what He had promised He was also able to perform.

Romans 4:21

In a world filled with such uncertainty, I wanted my children to have a firm conviction as to who Jesus is and who they are in Him. I wanted them to have confidence in their prayer life. So I taught my children that Abraham was not perfect, but the God in whom he believed is holy.

Abraham was not the Father of Faith because he had no struggles coming to faith. He was the Father of Faith because he simply believed God. He believed God, and therefore it was counted to him as righteousness. His works or circumcision did not justify him. Perhaps like us, in the time of developing his faith. Abraham was learning to not consider himself, but it was God he was to consider.

During these times of struggle, like us Abraham and Sarah were looking at the issue wrong. As they continued their faith journey, they came to understand it was not them but God who would bring the promise to pass.

Satan loves for us to think that somehow, some way, God needs us to be a super-human person, instead of us depending on a supernatural God. The focus is wrong. When it is corrected, we are free: free like Peter to step out of the boat, while we steadfastly look unto Jesus. We walk carefree, but the moment we become self-conscious we begin to sink. Let us learn from Peter and call out to the One who can and has saved us. Live free with no fear of failure. Faith is strong when our focus is on Jesus and not ourselves.

Jesus, it is the surety of Your unchanging character in which I trust. Your holiness requires You to be consistent and unchangeable. Therefore I can depend on Your eternal Word and Your character to be the same. I can be fully persuaded that You will fulfill every promise to me; therefore my faith finds rest in You, Jesus. Jesus, it is faith that pleases You, faith that establishes me in righteousness, faith that imparts conviction to my soul. Help me to see You clearly that I might stand in unstable situations. Amen.

John B. Lowe II, Great Commandment Network

Week 39, Friday
Forgiveness, an Act of Violence

I have forgiven . . . lest Satan should take advantage of us;
for we are not ignorant of his devices.

2 Corinthians 2:11

We forget that Satan has a perfect will for our lives. John 10:10 states it plainly, that Satan came to steal, kill, and destroy. Unforgiveness is a great weapon of Satan to do all three of these things.

What devices does Satan use to take advantage of us? In the context of our Scripture, it is unforgiveness he is speaking of. Let us not be ignorant or blinded by offense. Forgive.

When we receive forgiveness for salvation, we know the difference in our heart, the freedom that comes from the release of the bondage to sin. We are forgiven!

We also have watched people struggle with darkness, depression, and hurt while holding tightly to the injury, then love comes, soaking, oh so deeply inside, touching areas that had been hardened for a long time. Freedom of self comes by releasing others? Yes, it is true.

There is yet a deep freedom to be experienced. Satan loves for us to harbor grudges; we call them hurts or painful experiences. It is Satan's plan to hold your life captive by the chains of unforgiveness.

Ephesians.4:32 encourages us to forgive as we have been forgiven—completely. When we release forgiveness, it is an act of violence against the plan of hell for your life.

Satan loses the access he has been privy to. We are not ignorant of his devices, so we will not be willing to hold on to hurt when we can be so easily healed. By freeing others we ourselves are set free.

Jesus, You are the One I want to follow. I follow Your example. While You were on the cross, You said, "Father, forgive them; they know not what they are doing." I believe those who have hurt me really do not know they are being used by Satan's kingdom. I choose to forgive _____. For _____. I release them, as well as myself, from Satan's plan; I choose an act of violence, forgiveness. Amen.

John B. Lowe II, Great Commandment Network

Week 39, Weekend
To Protect and Provide

Forget not all His benefits.

Psalm 103:2

You have a God who has written down His laws to live by because He wants the best for us. He's not a God who wants to ruin your fun or control your life. He's a God who wants to provide and protect. You have a God who deeply desires to bring good things to your life and save you from harm.

Remember a few of the times when you've seen God provide for you as you've chosen to live according to His laws. Have you ever chosen to live by God's laws and sensed His peace, experienced the relief of a clear conscience, the joy of a job well-done, or the gratitude of living a life with wise choices?

God, I am grateful that You've provided _____ as I choose to make choices that align with Your Word.

Now, remember a few of the times when you've seen God protect you as you've chosen to live according to His laws. Have you ever escaped negative consequences, been relieved of guilt or shame that may have resulted from poor choices, or been protected from the pain of difficult relationships because you lived a life that aligned with God's laws?

God, thank You for Your protection from _____, as I made decisions that align with Your Word. I am especially grateful for the time when . . .

Spend the next few moments telling God about your gratitude for how He has provided for you and protected you. Thank Him for being the kind of God who is trustworthy and wants the best for you.

God, thank You for being the kind of God who wants the best for me. I know You've given Your laws as a protection and a guide for me. That's one of the great benefits of my relationship with You! Help me to live out my convictions. Empower me to stand strong because of my trust in You! Amen.

Terri Snead, Great Commandment Network

Week 40, Monday
Plan for Your Future Marriage

. . . submitting to one another in the fear of God.

Ephesians 5:21

As a married person, I did not and do not want to be married and miserable. As I read the Bible, I saw a recurring theme: Love your spouse as you have been loved.

Three times we are instructed to love others as Christ loved the Church.

Ephesians 5:25: Love as Christ gave Himself for the Church. "Husbands, love your wives, just as Christ loved the Church and gave Himself up for her."

Ephesians 5:28: Love as you would your own body. "In this same way, husbands ought to love their wives as their own bodies. He who loves his wife loves himself."

Ephesians 5:33: Love your spouse in particular as you love yourself. "However, each one of you also must love his wife as he loves himself, and the wife must respect her husband."

We learn that loving others well means loving like Jesus, but it also means love for one's self. Love today as if everything you said or did was for you. Practice loving others like you would want to be loved. Practice these skills now so that when you marry, those skills will be second nature.

Sometimes I have encouraged couples to speak to one another as if they were talking to strangers. Why? They would never talk to a stranger in the ways they speak to their spouse. Practice submitting yourself to these same guidelines. Talk to others the way you'd talk to a stranger that you want to impress.

Try this as well. Ask the people you care about to answer this question: What does it look like to love you well? Each of us has different needs, entry points to our hearts. Find other's needs and entry points and love them there.

Lord help me to love others, deeply and freely. I want to be happy and satisfied in life, so help me to love as I have been loved by You.

John B. Lowe II, Great Commandment Network

Week 40, Tuesday
Obedience

Children, obey your parents in the Lord, for this is right.

Ephesians 6:1

The ever-increasing pace and influence of others on our families creates enormous pressure in raising children today. How unique it is that fathers are instructed not to be angry with their children. A father's anger can go so deep.

Parents have such an opportunity to impact their children and create memories, both good and bad, that will last a lifetime. The Word of God teaches that the heroes of faith made mistakes. All of us make mistakes.

Once when we were at dinner, one of my boys had been asked to move his milk. He didn't. Of course he spilled his milk. I let him have it for the mess. Five minutes later I knocked my own milk over. Silence fell over the room.

The angry dad had committed the same crime; humbly I repented and asked for forgiveness. My children tell me that my humility and repentance opened their hearts again to me.

Read the book of First John. Meditate on the love and we should have for others. We are instructed to handle the Word of God carefully.

John 1:14 says that the Word became flesh and dwelt among us. Sadly, it's true that we don't often follow the Word that dwells among us.

Jesus, help me to follow the Word and apply it to how I handle and love my family. Holy Spirit, Acts 1:8 says that we have been given power to be witnesses. Help me, Lord, to be a loving witness to the most important people in my life—my family members. Amen.

Week 40, Wednesday
Beware of Satan's Trap

"The thief does not come except to steal, and to kill, and to destroy.
I have come that they may have life, and that they may have it more abundantly."

John 10:10

Most people believe God has a plan for their lives. What people forget is that Satan also has a plan. Jesus pointed this out very clearly.

Yes, it is a plan—Satan's plan—a strategy to destroy your life. We are encouraged to not be ignorant of Satan's devices (2 Corinthians 2:11). We are to be aware of Satan's traps: "Then, when desire has conceived, it gives birth to sin; and sin, when it is full-grown, brings forth death" (James 1:15).

Satan builds desire which, as it builds, leads one into Satan's trap of unforgiveness. You are a child of God, born of His Holy Spirit. You have the ability to resist and defeat Satan, avoiding sin before it is even conceived.

Someone once described unforgiveness as a person who drinks poison then expects the other person to die. Forgiveness is an act of violence; it is not passive. Forgiveness is a act of faith and love for oneself as well as the other person.

Forgiveness is one of the greatest ways to shut the devil down in your life. By setting others free, we liberate ourselves. No one can hold you in a state of bitterness but you alone. Choose to let the offense go; refuse to rehearse it and spread the offense to others.

It is said of Mother Teresa that when someone reminded her of a particular offense, she answered, "I remember forgetting that." Remember to forget. Forgiveness is an act of violence against Satan's plan for your life. Don't participate in holding grudges. Forgive and live freely of offense.

Holy Spirit, help me to be sensitive to Your leadings, to avoid the trap of offense. I resist Satan and submit to God. I walk in holiness with Your power in my life. I choose to forgive. Amen.

John B. Lowe II, Great Commandment Network

Week 40, Thursday
Fight for the Relationship

"Be angry, and do not sin": do not let the sun go down on your wrath.

Ephesians 4:26

I was visiting with an elderly couple who had celebrated sixty years of marriage. I asked them what their secret was to have been married, happy and satisfied, after sixty years. They shared several stories, the most interesting of which was how they were secretly married and no one knew for two months. They lived at home with Mom and Dad while meeting secretly when they could. They laughed freely as they reminisced about travel, the Depression, wars, job changes, and family life.

They had always been attendees of church and kept close ties with friends who were healthy for their marriage. They were never drinkers or smokers. They stayed within their budget, living in the same house for forty years. After a good laugh they thought that the best thing they did was to never go to bed angry, just as the Bible teaches. They went on to explain how their decision was tested one night.

One morning, they were up until 3:00 a.m. fussing over a difference of opinion. Then he finally said, "I agree with you, that you are wrong." She looked at him shocked, and then burst into laughter. They went to bed happy, and without strife or anger, finished their discussion the next day.

As I reflected on their conversation, I counted the number of times they used the simple phrase, "like the Bible says." In a two-hour conversation, I could recall at least twelve times that comment was made. "Like the Bible teaches"—so simple, yet so powerful. James 1:22 says, "But be doers of the word, and not hearers only, deceiving yourselves."

As Christians we assume that knowing what the Bible says is the same as doing what the Bible says. It is in the doing of Scripture that we flesh out the truth of Scripture. It is a challenge not to let the sun go down on a disagreement, but it is healthy when we do like the Bible says.

Jesus, help me to live by the simple loving truth in Your Word. Help me to not only know it, but to be a doer of it—to love and live like the Bible says. Amen.

Week 40, Friday
A Carnal Christian

. . . for you are still carnal. For where there are envy, strife, and divisions among you, are you not carnal and behaving like mere men?

1 Corinthians 3:3

The true test of a carnal Christian here is strife and division, which demonstrates immaturity. Paul wrote to the church that is unable to receive solid truth, "You are acting like mere men." They were acting as if they were not saved, as if they knew nothing of love, forgiveness, or the power of the Holy Spirit to bring unity.

Strife is not about unity, but about who is right. Strife opens up doors for Satan to then begin to find fault in other areas, as well. Friends become enemies over the same situation that at one time brought excitement. Now it has become a power struggle.

It is obvious from Scripture that the power of God is manifested when God's people are in unity. It's no wonder Satan loves strife.

James 3:16 says, "Where envy and self- seeking exist, confusion and every evil thing are there." Wow! Now there is a reason to keep strife out of our lives!

Even medical science has confirmed that strife is a contributor to depression, disease, and many other ailments of the body. We were not designed for strife. Make the choice to forgive and not to be offended.

Psalm 119:165 says, "Great peace have those who love Your law, and nothing causes them to stumble." Agreement takes work; it takes giving of one's self for a peaceful resolution. Seek peace, prefer others, and depend upon the Holy Spirit to empower you to agree.

Holy Spirit, I give You control over my mind and my emotions. I ask You to help me not be prideful or insecure about myself, to seek peace and not strife. Amen.

Week 40, Weekend
At All Costs

Even a child is known by his deeds, whether what he does is pure and right.

Proverbs 20:11

If you've ever been in love, you know what it means to go out of your way to please another person. If you love someone, you're careful not to do anything that would jeopardize the relationship; at all costs you avoid things that would hurt the other person.

Our convictions concerning what is right and wrong are to be grounded in this same framework. Because of our deep love for Jesus, we want to be careful not to do anything that would jeopardize our relationship with Him. Because of our deep love for Jesus, we'll want to avoid doing things that would hurt Him.

Take the next few moments and remember how Jesus has loved you. How has He provided for you? How has He cared for you? How has He been attentive to you, forgiven you, supported you, or accepted you?

Jesus, I am so grateful that You loved me by . . .

I am particularly glad about the time when You . . .

Now, take time to express your love to Him—specifically regarding your commitment to live out your convictions. What are the convictions that you want to live out because you want to please Him?

God, I am committed to living out my conviction to . . .

What are the convictions of things you want to avoid because at all costs you don't want to hurt your relationship with Jesus?

God, I am committed to living out my conviction to avoid _____ *because I know that to do these things would hurt You.*

Jesus, I know that my ways are not always the right ways. I want to live out my convictions because You always know what's best for me. You love me and I'm grateful. Help me to remember that my doing what's right pleases You and I want to do that because I love You. Help me to remember that doing what's wrong, hurts You. And at all costs, I don't want to hurt the One who has given His life for me. Amen.

Terri Snead, Great Commandment Network

Week 41, Monday
I Wish Everyone Was Like Me

"King Agrippa, do you believe the prophets? I know that you do believe." Then Agrippa said to Paul, "You almost persuade me to become a Christian." And Paul said, "I would to God that not only you, but also all who hear me today, might become both almost and altogether such as I am, except for these chains."

Acts 26:27–29

Have you ever found yourself in a place that you wished you were not? Perhaps you found yourself in a setting where you say, "I wish I was anyone but me right now." It seems that many of us want to be anyone except who we are—athletes, stars, rappers, even people whose lives are falling apart.

In Acts 26:27–29, the apostle Paul was standing in a judgment hall. His life was on the line. He was surrounded by guards, pomp, and power, as well as bound by chains. His very life was hanging in the balance. Even in the air of condemnation and judgment, the truth of who Paul was in Christ, his love for Jesus, and the knowledge that he was loved by Jesus swelled in his heart. Paul presented his case and his defense. Then he boldly pressed the issue of eternity to King Agrippa: "King, do you believe the prophets? I know you believe."

Agrippa shouted, "You are mad with learning." With poise of certainty as to who he was and to whom he belongs, Paul said in Acts 26:29, "I wish everyone within the sound of my voice was even as I am, except for these chains."

When Christian men and women wish to be anyone except who they are, we see a key to our identity: *love*. When one is held so securely by the love of and for Jesus, nothing else matters. King Agrippa and Festus were so used to people begging for their lives, it was unnerving for them to see this man look them in the eyes, vacant of the fear of man.

Perhaps today we could see how deeply we are loved, that nothing is worth throwing away the security we find in His acceptance. (See Romans 8:31–39.)

Today, Father, like Jesus and Paul, I ask for the understanding of how completely and deeply You love me, so that I will be immovable in Your love. Jesus, help me today to experience the support of Your Spirit when I am under pressure so others will desire to be like me, deeply loved and fearless. Amen.

John B. Lowe II, Great Commandment Network

Week 41, Tuesday
No One Like Timothy

But I trust in the Lord Jesus to send Timothy to you shortly, that I also may be encouraged when I know your state. For I have no one like-minded, who will sincerely care for your state. For all seek their own, not the things which are of Christ Jesus.

Philippians 2:19–21

When you study Paul's life, you will notice he traveled with many people on his mission trips. As I was reading the scriptures one day, it struck me as odd that after a lifetime of preaching, traveling, and raising up sons in the faith, Paul finally had one, Timothy, who would care for the people the same way he did.

Let's take a closer look at Philippians 2:19–21.

Verse 19: But I trust in the Lord Jesus to send Timothy to you shortly, that I also may be encouraged when I know your state.

Verse 20: For I have no one like-minded who would sincerely care for your state.

Verse 21: For all seek their own, not the things which are of Christ.

Verse 22: But you know his proven character, that as a son with his father he serves with me in the gospel.

Perhaps we could be such a one to care for people as the Lord Jesus would have cared. There were many who had been instructed, many whom Paul had set in ministry. Yet only one of all the people over all of his years was trusted in the way that Timothy was.

But God only needs one in each situation to step up and be His hand to touch the untouchable. To be His arms to hug and hold the broken. To be His voice to speak a kind, encouraging word to the person who is about to throw their life away.

I believe you can be the one today in someone's life to care for them as Paul or Jesus would have cared for them. Give just a little time, sprinkled with love.

Jesus, I need Your help today to be aware of the hurting people around me. They want to seem as if they are okay. But help me to sense their need and care for them with love and action. Amen.

Week 41, Wednesday
Truth Is a Person

There was a certain man in Caesarea called Cornelius . . . a devout man and one who
feared God with all his household, who gave alms generously to the people, and prayed to God always.

Acts 10:1, 2

Cornelius, a centurion of Rome's powerful military, had been watching nation after nation be conquered by Rome. In Rome there were gods for nearly everything and everyone. But Cornelius had stopped praying to these man-made gods long ago.

He had watched as other nations were conquered. The empire of Rome rolled over them as they cried to their gods for help. He could not help but notice there was no help, no intervention of any kind from their gods. Then came the replacement of their gods with Rome's gods. There were different names, different attributes, but the people seemed to accept the change and continue to worship man-made, hand-crafted Roman gods the same as their own easily enough.

Until Israel was conquered. These people would worship no God other than Jehovah! One God, indeed. Their devotion struck Cornelius; they would not compromise even under death. Cornelius was curious by their total devotion to this one-God concept.

He investigated and asked questions of servants, leaders, anyone who would enlighten him as to why they loved and honored this God. He was impressed that they had no graven images, nor would they entertain the thought of creating any. He was hungry to worship the Truth. As he watched and learned, he prayed. Acts 10:2 says that he prayed always. Cornelius was a truth seeker. His search for God was met by an angel, which gave him instructions to send for a man, Peter, which he did. Cornelius was about to hear words that would bring true salvation to him and his household! When Peter arrived, he shared about Jesus—the way the truth, and the life.

Perhaps today you are seeking truth, or you will meet a Cornelius, someone who has paid attention to the realities of the world. They are seeking the truth, and the truth is a Person, Jesus Christ. Truth seekers always encounter the true living God in Jesus Christ.

Jesus, men pray to know the truth. They have witnessed all kinds of imposters and false philosophies, and yet a hunger remains in them for the truth. They need to know the Person, You, Jesus. Help us, Lord, to know You, to share You with all who are truly seeking today. Amen.

John B. Lowe II, Great Commandment Network

Week 41, Thursday
Judge Not

"Judge not, that you be not judged."

Matthew 7:1

The word *judge* is also condemned. Many times in life we are hurt, or sometimes we are the one who hurts others. Forgiveness is the answer for either situation, not judgment or condemnation. King David made a harsh judgment once.

Second Samuel.12:5–6 tells us, "So David's anger was greatly aroused against the man, and he said to Nathan, 'As the LORD lives, the man who has done this shall surely die! And he shall restore fourfold for the lamb, because he did this thing and because he had no pity.'"

David, in his anger, passed judgment on himself. Nathan answered, "You are the man." No doubt that was an "epiphany moment" for David. His sin, his anger, led unknowingly to his own sentence to a lifetime of hurt and pain.

In a moment of anger, David sentenced himself with no mercy or grace.

Nathan said, "The sword will never depart from your house." (See 2 Samuel 12:10.)

And it never did. David experienced the tragic death of children, and his wives were violated publicly just as he had violated Bathsheba privately. He lived a lifetime of war and trouble with other nations.

David's anger, a moment of destructive emotion, led to judgment, and harsh condemnation of others, for judgment is without mercy to the one who has shown no mercy. Mercy triumphs over judgment (James 2:13).

We have experienced mercy, grace, and love from the Lord Jesus, forgiveness for our sins. Should we not extend the same to others today every day?

People do sin, they do hurt us, yet their sin blinds them. Let not our sin blind us to our need for forgiveness and our need to forgive.

Jesus, while hanging on the cross, You did not curse or pass judgment; You forgave. Help me to allow the Holy Spirit to soften my heart when I am offended. Mercy is the word for my life. MERCY for others and for me! Amen.

Week 41, Friday
Resilient Faith Stands the Test

Therefore, my beloved brethren, be steadfast, immovable, always
abounding in the work of the Lord, knowing that your labor is not in vain in the Lord.

1 Corinthians 15:58

Jesus said that trials and tribulations would come, yet we act surprised when they come to our house. When I read the Bible, I am amazed at how the Church thrived in a hostile environment.

According to Acts 8:1–3, great persecution was facing the Church. People were dying, and funerals were going on. People were being imprisoned. Saul was wreaking havoc against the Church. Yet the people grew stronger.

Perhaps your environment, your world, is filled with hurt and havoc. I know mine has had some times when the pain was so great I wanted to walk away from everyone and everything. I found, however, that in the confusion of hostility there can be peace, love, and power to right the wrongs.

Luke 7:23 tells us, "And blessed is he who is not offended because of Me."

Luke.7 records several miracles taking place as John the Baptist sat in prison waiting to be executed. He sent disciples to Jesus to ask, "Are You the One or do we look for another?"

John had announced that Jesus was the Lamb of God; he saw the dove settle on Jesus. He knew that Jesus was the Messiah. But the trials, the pressure, had caused a shift of doubt in John. When we are alone and hurting, it gives Satan an advantage to have accessto our hearts that he normally would not have access to.

When there is a crisis in your life, do not change your opinion of Jesus! Remember, He has not changed! Everything else may change, but Jesus does not change. Blessed is he who does not get offended in a crisis.

Jesus, help me to see You as the unchanging Lord. Events do not reflect
Your love for me or Your holy character; Your unchanging nature reflects
Your love for me. Jesus, help me to be steadfast and immoveable. Amen.

John B. Lowe II, Great Commandment Network

Week 41, Weekend
Whom Do You Believe?

There is a way that seems right to a man, but its end is the way of death.

Proverbs 14:12

All of us have had some amount of mistaken beliefs as children. At one time, we've all believed in the existence of imaginary figures like Santa Claus, the Easter Bunny, or the Tooth Fairy. Our shift from childish beliefs to correct ones came about through the influence of other people—our family members or other childhood caregivers. In other words, most of us stopped believing in Santa Claus not because we were given conclusive, scientific proof that he does not exist, but because someone whom we loved and trusted told us that he does not exist and we believed them. Our willingness to trust our parents and abandon our childhood beliefs reveals an important principle concerning convictions—most of the time, what you believe is heavily influenced by whom you believe.

The writer of this proverb is drawing a contrast between convictions that are based merely on human understanding and convictions that are based on a deep, loving relationship with God. According to the writer, some beliefs that seem perfectly correct to many humans actually lead to death (whether physical or spiritual). We need a more reliable standard on which to base our beliefs—a standard that is only to be found in the Word of God.

Even when it comes to our Christian convictions, the answer to the question, "What do you believe?" depends greatly on the answer to the question, "Whom do you believe?" In other words, we do not believe the teachings of Scripture simply because they make sense to us. We believe them because they are the words of One whom we love and trust. Similarly, we do not obey the commandments of Scripture merely because they seem like sensible principles for living. We obey them because they serve as guidelines concerning the proper way to relate to One whom we love and trust. It is first and foremost our relationship with Jesus that is to inform our spiritual convictions, just as it was first and foremost our relationship with our parents that shaped our basic beliefs about the world.

 God, thank You for being Someone I can trust. Thank You for providing Your Word that allows me to know the Truth and base my life upon it. Amen.

Week 42, Monday
Change of Heart

"Believe Me that I am in the Father and the Father in Me,
or else believe Me for the sake of the works themselves."

John 14:11

Jesus invited His disciples to consider a means by which they could establish a foundational conviction for their belief. The proof of the union of Jesus and His Father is threefold. They should believe Jesus (a) because of His character ("I am in the Father and . . . the Father is in Me"); (b) because His words are the Father's ("The words I say to you are not just My own"); and (c) because the miracles reveal God's working through Him ("the Father, living in Me . . . is doing His work . . . believe on the evidence of the miracles themselves).

Jesus once more stresses the intimate connection between the Father and Himself. In the Scripture passage today He invites us to "Believe in God, believe also in Me" (John 14:1); and believing on His Word will have a profound meaning in each of our lives regarding the formation of right and wrong.

Our convictions can be defined as "being thoroughly convinced that Christ and His Word are both objectively true and relationally meaningful." From today's passage my question for you is, What influence shapes and defines your beliefs? "Believe Me that I am in the Father and the Father in Me, or else believe Me for the sake of the works themselves" (John 14:11). Jesus today is still extending that same invitation for you to establish your belief in Him. My dear friend, Scripture tells us "The works of the Lord are great, studied by all who have pleasure in them. His work is honorable and glorious, and His righteousness endures forever. He has made His wonderful works to be remembered; the Lord is gracious and full of compassion (Psalm 111:2–4). I want to encourage you to believe on Jesus for the sake of works themselves.

Dear God, as I rest from this day, may I have yielded my will to the leading of the Holy Spirit. Lord, direct my path as I acknowledge You in all of my ways. I pray that You will receive glory and honor from my life. Lord, I now ask Your blessing as I seek Your will. Lord, direct my steps and guide me in the path of Your righteousness, I pray. Heavenly Father, thank You for this wonderful and awesome privilege I have experienced in the abundance of Your provision. Thank You for Your amazing grace that has kept me throughout this day. Lord, I pray that I will always have a changed heart filled with gratitude for You each day of my life! Amen.

Ron and Casey Warford, Great Commandment Network

Week 42, Tuesday
Our Conviction

"I am the true vine, and My Father is the vinedresser. Every branch in Me that does not bear fruit He takes away; and every branch that bears fruit He prunes, that it may bear more fruit."

John 15:1, 2

The idea of conviction is a major theme throughout all Scripture. God's Word consistently challenges us: "And you shall know the truth, and the truth shall make you free" (John 8:32).

The agent of conviction is the Holy Spirit; and the means of conviction is either the Word of God or God's general revelation of His demands through nature and of our inborn consciousness regarding a sense of right and wrong.

Jesus instructed His disciples on three vital relationships. Disciples are to be rightly related to Jesus: "I am the true vine"; to each other: "every branch"; and to the world: "That bears fruit and may bear more fruit". As Christians our lives, too, should mirror that same relational connectedness. We're to remain (abide), to love each other, and to testify or witness. Dear friends, today take joy in this general truth "Finally, brethren, whatever things are true, whatever things are noble, whatever things are just, whatever things are pure, whatever things are lovely, whatever things are of good report, if there is any virtue and if there is anything praiseworthy—meditate on these things" (Philippians 4:8).

Heavenly Father, I thank You for this day with gratitude and thanksgiving. Lord, I pray that I will discover more of Your truth! May I seize the opportunity to bring You honor and give You praise. Lord, I acknowledge Your truth. You are the God of all truth and Your Word is everlasting. Without You I am nothing. I praise You for another day of experiencing Your divine truth. May Your truth guard my mind and heart I pray. Amen.

Week 42, Wednesday
Relationally Meaningful

*"Most assuredly, I say to you, he who believes in Me, the works that I
do he will do also; and greater works than these he will do, because I go to My Father.
And whatever you ask in My name, that I will do, that the Father may be glorified in the Son."*

John 14:12, 13

What an amazing thought for you and me to embrace relationally: "He who believes in Me, the works that I do he will do also. . . . Greater works than these he will do" (John 14:12). From this passage the apostle would not necessarily do more miracles than Jesus did (e.g., feeding 5,000), but rather their outreach would be greater (e.g., Peter in one sermon had 3,000 converts). This was possible because Jesus had gone to the Father and had sent the Holy Spirit. Yes, miracles are important, but some evangelists have done even greater things than these by preaching the Good News to many more thousands of people in prior centuries and up into the twenty-first century.

It is to this end that Jesus on His throne in glory will do everything we ask in His name: "Whatever you ask in My name, that I will do" (John 14:13); this is not a magical formula, but it is the prayer of every believer as Christ's representative. So it is necessary that you and I love one another and daily live our lives in relationship with Christ: "If we say that we have fellowship with Him, and walk in darkness, we lie and do not practice the truth. But if we walk in the light as He is in the light, we have fellowship with one another, and the blood of Jesus Christ His Son cleanses us from all sin" (1 John 1:6–7). Today live relationally with the God of creation!

*Heavenly Father, help me this new day to better relate to those You will
place into my life. Lord, may I love them as You have loved me. Help me to
feel with Your heart and to touch with Your hands. May I relate to others
with compassion and gentleness. Lord, all that I am and hope to be is found
in my relationship with You. Lord God, I thank You for the abundant provision You have bestowed upon me this day! Amen.*

Ron and Casey Warford, Great Commandment Network

Week 42, Thursday
Believing in Christ

And this is His commandment: that we should believe on the name
of His Son Jesus Christ and love one another as He gave us commandment."

1 John 3:23

A confident and effective prayer life is founded on obedience to God's command: "and whatever we ask we receive from Him, because we keep His commandments" (1 John 3:22). Believing in Christ and His Word has a profound and relational meaning in each of our lives. The convictions of my faith provide for me a foundation upon which I build a better self-worth. And yet, as I grow in grace and enter more deeply into union with Christ and abide in Him, I have learned that to pray in the name of Christ also means to pray in His Spirit. A name is a word by which we call to mind the whole being and nature of an object. When I speak of a lamb or a lion, the name at once suggests the different nature peculiar to each. The name of God is meant to express His divine nature and glory. Therefore, the name of Christ means His whole nature, His Person and work, His disposition and Spirit. To ask in the name of Christ is to pray in union with Him.

Heavenly Father, it's my desire to live a committed life of serving You. Lord, equip me for the journey as I share with those You give me opportunity to serve. Anoint me with the power of the Holy Spirit and grant to me the boldness to speak unashamedly of Your goodness. May the witness from my life bring You honor and glory. Lord, I am thankful for Your love that You show to me daily! Amen.

Ron and Casey Warford, Great Commandment Network

Week 42, Friday
Believing His Word

Since you have purified your souls in obeying the truth through the Spirit
in sincere love of the brethren, love one another fervently with a pure heart, having been born
again, not of corruptible seed but incorruptible, through the word of God which lives and abides forever.

1 Peter 1:22, 23

I remember as a young man struggling with the idea of living a pure life because of my belief in Jesus Christ. For me there were so many temptations and things that I wanted to do. Many of my desires were not pure, nor were they pleasing to God. As I matured in my Christian walk, I came to an understanding that my life was no longer to be lived to please myself. Holy living demands purification. A positive result of obeying the truth is a purified life. The New Testament teaches believers to "love one another fervently with a pure heart" (1 Peter 1:22). Having convictions rooted in believing God and His Word gives you the ability to live a life that is pleasing to Him. While everything else in life will pass away, "'The word of the LORD endures forever.' Now this is the word which by the gospel was preached to you" (1 Peter 1:25).

Having a belief in His Word, the Good News, can start today. God wants to teach you the way in which you should go. He wants to bring fruitfulness and prosperity to your life. Prayers are answered because of believing the Word!

Lord, I thank You for Your Word to guide me and change me. Help me make time every day to read and meditate on Your Word. Lord, I thank You that You are faithful and just to bless me. Lord, I pray that I will obey and trust You because You are God alone! May I trust in Your Word forevermore. Amen.

Ron and Casey Warford, Great Commandment Network

Week 42, Weekend
Great Reward

*The law of the LORD is perfect, converting the soul; the testimony of the
Lord is sure, making wise the simple; the statutes of the LORD are right, rejoicing the heart;
the commandment of the LORD is pure, enlightening the eyes; the fear of the Lord is clean, enduring
forever; the judgments of the LORD are true and righteous altogether. More to be desired are they
than gold, yea, than much fine gold; sweeter also than honey and the honeycomb. Moreover
by them Your servant is warned, and in keeping them there is great reward.*

Psalm 19:7–11

When we move from knowing the Word to actually allowing our choices to be shaped by the Word, we are promised significant benefits. David tells us that when we live in accordance with the Word of God, our souls are restored, we receive wisdom and enlightenment, and we are filled with joy—in short, "there is great reward" (v. 11). In addition, the Psalmist notes that God's Word serves to warn us, helping us to avoid choices that might have tragic consequences. When we live out God's Word in our everyday actions and decisions, we enjoy a clean conscience before God, are enabled to pursue right relationships, are filled with the joy and peace that come from knowing that we are making wise choices, and are protected from many of the difficulties that result when people make choices without reference to the Word of God.

Can you think of an occasion when you made an important choice that was influenced by the Word of God? What was the outcome? Did you experience any of the rewards mentioned by the Psalmist (such as increased wisdom or joy)? How might the outcome have been different if you had made a choice that was not influenced by God's Word?

How does it make you feel to know that God's motive behind His desire for you to live out your convictions that are aligned with His Word is so that you will have great reward? What does that do to your heart to know that God's ultimate desire is for your good?

I feel _____ when I consider that God wants me to live out my biblical convictions because He wants great reward for me.

    *God, direct the steps of my life and help me live out my convictions. Let
me be reminded that You only want what's best for me. Amen.*

Week 43, Monday
What Is Truth?

Pilate said to Him, "What is truth?"

John 18:38 a

We are often in search of the facts … truth about the best answer … truth to the specific concerns we have. Imagine the conversation between Pilate and Jesus: "Are You the King of the Jews?" Followed with Jesus' response: "Is that your own idea or did others talk to you about Me?" Faced with the position of a decision that he, Pilate, must make regarding the fate of Jesus: "What is Truth?" Pilate may have been jesting and meant, "What does Truth matter?" Either way there are times when you must be your own person, you must take a position on what you now know is truth. Pilate was not just discussing the truth in his Jerusalem palace the day he met Jesus; he was literally looking at it: "Have I not just told you? I came to bring truth to the world." Pilate was looking at the answer to his own question: "I am … the truth" (John 14:6).

Today's lesson serves as a moral indicator for everyone's life regarding the position of acceptance or rejection of the truth when faced with it. Moral and spiritual truth isn't so much a concept as it is a Person: "And this is eternal life, that they may know You, the only true God, and Jesus Christ whom You have sent. I have glorified You on the earth" (John 17:3–4).

Pilate's decision determined life or death for Jesus; your decision determines life or death for your own soul: "There is a way that seems right to a man, but its end is the way of death" (Proverbs 14:12). Having displayed a lack of interest in truth, Pilate revealed a lack of commitment to justice. He lacked the courage of his convictions. If Jesus was innocent of all charges, then Pilate should have set Him free. Instead, Pilate began a series of compromising moves to avoid dealing with truth. Is it possible that you and I will go to the same extreme as Pilate regarding matters of truth? He went out again to the Jews, and said to them, "I find no fault in Him at all" (John 18:38). Truth is found in the Person of Jesus Christ. Will you accept Him as Lord and Savior of your life today?

Dear Lord, thank You for loving and caring for me! Heavenly Father, I rejoice in the truth of Your Word. I am grateful to have experienced the victory over sin that has resulted from trusting in You and Your Word. Now Lord, may I continue to rely upon You in all that I do. Amen.

Week 43, Tuesday
Moral and Spiritual Truth

"For God so loved the world that He gave His only begotten Son, that whoever believes in Him should not perish but have everlasting life. For God did not send His Son into the world to condemn the world, but that the world through Him might be saved."

John 3:16, 17

Moral and spiritual truth isn't so much a concept as it is a Person. It isn't so much something we believe as it is someone we relate to. Jesus wanted His disciples to recognize the relationship He has with the Father. "For God so loved the world that He gave His only begotten Son, that whoever believes in Him should not perish but have everlasting life. For God did not send His Son into the world to condemn the world, but that world through Him might be saved" (John 3:16–17).

Here we have the very essence of God's truth being revealed to us in the person of His Son, Jesus Christ. "There is no other name ... by which we must be saved" (Acts 4:12).

God so loved the world; this is the great truth that motivated God's plan of salvation. All people on earth— or perhaps all creation—were given His one and only Son. "A Son is given" (Isaiah 9:6): "For unto us a Child is born, unto us a Son is given; and the government will be upon His shoulder. And His name will be called Wonderful, Counselor, Mighty God, Everlasting Father, Prince of Peace."

My thoughts today are about establishing a relationship with the Person of Jesus: "With all lowliness and gentleness, with longsuffering, bearing with one another in love, endeavoring to keep the unity of the Spirit in the bond of peace. There is one body and one Spirit, just as you were called in one hope of your calling; one Lord, one faith, one baptism; one God and Father of all, who is above all, and through all, and in you all."

Lord Jesus, thank You that I have come to know the purpose and plan You have for my life. I praise You for loving me so much that You gave Your Son for me. May I with gratitude commit my life to always serve You with my whole heart all the days of my life. Amen.

Ron and Casey Warford, Great Commandment Network

Week 45, Wednesday
Who Is This Man?

*Jesus answered, "You say rightly that I am a king. For this cause I was born,
and for this cause I have come into the world, that I should bear witness to the truth.
Everyone who is of the truth hears My voice."*

John 18:37

Who is this man? Perhaps this was the thought or question that rushed through the mind of Pilate. He was faced with making a decision regarding Jesus. Jesus' accusers did not have the wherewithal to convict Him of a crime He was not guilty of. Face-to-face the prisoner and the governor study each other: "Pilate said to Him, 'What is truth?'" And Jesus' thought: *Have I not told you? I came to bring truth to the world.* Pilate realized in the consciousness of his inner man that he was looking at the answer to his own question.

At specific periods in our life we are faced with the dilemma of making critical choices concerning what is truth. Just as Pilate did, we also go out to seek the counsel, advice, and even the sanction of others, all the while knowing that the answer to our question is right before us!

We believe the truth that Jesus as the sinless Son of God atoned for our sin through His death on the cross. And the offering of His blood as a sacrifice for sin redeems us so we are forgiven—set free—and raises us to new life in Him. On our own we cannot understand the truths of God: "The natural man does not receive the things of the Spirit of God, for they are foolishness to him; nor can he know them, because they are spiritually discerned. But he who is spiritual judges all things" (1 Corinthians 2:14–15). Allow the Holy Spirit to reveal Himself, His purposes, and His ways to you today!

Lord Jesus, help me to know the truth and may I accept that truth for my life. Lord Jesus, there is no fault in You and Your ways lead to everlasting life. May I find that peace and security that is found in serving You! Amen.

Ron and Casey Warford, Great Commandment Network

Week 45, Thursday
God-Honoring

"And this is eternal life, that they may know You, the only true God, and Jesus Christ whom You have sent. I have glorified You on the earth. I have finished the work which You have given Me to do."

John 17:3, 4

Eternal life, as defined by Jesus, involves the experience of knowing the only true God through His Son. "All things have been delivered to Me by My Father, and no one knows the Son except the Father" (Matthew 11:27). It is a personal relationship of intimacy that is continuous with the Father and the Son. Our lives reflect glory and honor to God through everything we do: "That they may know you …" the Word ***know*** here, in the present tense, is often used in the Greek New Testament to describe an intimate personal relationship with Him (God). And that relationship is eternal, not temporal. For a believer eternal life is not simply endless existence. Everyone will exist somewhere forever: "And these will go away into everlasting punishment, but the righteous into eternal life" (Matthew 25:46).

The question is, in what condition or in what relationship will they spend eternity? Will you consider the relationship you have with honoring God? Does your relationship with your mother, father, sister, brother, husband, wife, son, or daughter bring glory and honor to the Father? To develop God-honoring convictions is to relate intimately to Jesus, the One who is truth. In the troubled times of my life, when life has felt overwhelming and difficult, I have learned that God is with me (praise God!). He cares about me: about my struggles, my doubts, my worries, even my failures, my hopes and dreams and desires, through the joy and confusion of my days, to comfort me in the dark hours, to challenge me when I make the wrong decisions, and to strengthen me to make better ones.

Why would you not want to serve, honor, and worship a God who cares for you in such a myriad of ways?

 Heavenly Father, I have come to know You will never leave me or forsake me, this You have promised in Your Word. Lord, I seek to honor You in everything I do and in all my ways as You give me opportunity to share with others Your great love toward me. Lord, I pray that my light shines bright for Your glory and honor. Amen.

Ron and Casey Warford, Great Commandment Network

Week 43, Friday
And the Word Became Flesh

And the Word became flesh and dwelt among us, and we beheld
His glory, the glory as of the only begotten of the Father, full of grace and truth.

John 1:14

Jesus Christ is the eternal Son of God, who is perfect in all His ways. Jesus is at the same time fully God and fully man, providing the bridge between an all-holy and righteous God and sinful humanity. God has always been speaking to His people. Today, He speaks by the Holy Spirit. The Holy Spirit will use the Bible, prayer, circumstances, and other believers to speak to us.

"And the Word became Flesh" (John 1:14). Jesus Christ is the very embodiment and essence of absolute moral and spiritual truth itself. "And the Word became flesh and dwelt among us, and we beheld His glory, the glory as of the only begotten of the Father, full of grace and truth" (John 1:14). Though Jesus was with His disciples, even some of them failed to clearly see the Truth (Jesus) before them.

Learning to trust requires the activation of your faith, embracing what you don't see while maintaining the evidence of what you're hoping for: "And we beheld His glory, the glory of the only begotten of the Father, full of grace and truth" (John 1:14).

Heavenly Father, thank You for caring for me and thank You for Your unconditional love shown to all mankind by giving Your only begotten Son for us. Lord, I pray that I will live my life to reflect Your glory throughout my life time. Amen.

Ron and Casey Warford, Great Commandment Network

Week 43, Weekend
Our Only Hope

I say then: Walk in the Spirit, and you shall not fulfill the lust of the flesh.

Galatians 5:16

None of us are perfect. We'd don't like to look at ourselves this way, but every one of us is a sinner. We each go our own way, making wrong, sinful choices. The good news is that Jesus chose to go to the cross and give His life because of our sins. The Savior chose to take our sins upon Himself and receive our punishment. Here's the mysterious contrast: God is a God who is both rich in mercy and ultimately holy. He is so holy that He cannot relate to sin in any form. So rather than lose relationship with us, God restored the possibility of relationship by sacrificing His Son.

Because Christ gave His life on Calvary for you and me, we must face the truth that our sins have a direct connection to His death. He died because of *my* sins. He had to die because of *yours.* Our sinful choices are a part of what hurt Jesus at Calvary. And in fact, the sin of our lives hurts God's heart. He is saddened as He sees us suffering the consequences of our sin. It pains His heart to watch us make choices that are against His Word.

How do you feel as you consider the personal connection of your sin and Christ's death? Your sin and the pain it causes God's heart?

I feel _____ as I reflect on the truth that my sins have a personal connection with Christ's death.

I've come to realize that God's heart hurts when I make wrong choices. That truth makes me love God even more because . . .

Our only hope of making right choices in line with His thoughts and His ways is to live our lives yielded to the direction and prompting of the Holy Spirit.

Our only hope is to declare our helplessness to live a life that is pleasing to God, apart from the Holy Spirit's guidance and power. Claim the promise that, in your humility, God will guide you with His Spirit (James 4:6).

> *Father God, I am helpless to make right choices without Your Spirit's help. There is no hope of my embracing Your ways instead of my ways unless Your Spirit empowers me. Guide me and help me. I need You every day. Amen.*

Terri Snead, Great Commandment Network

Week 44, Monday
The Power Behind the Bible

All Scripture is given by inspiration of God, and is profitable for doctrine,
for reproof, for correction, for instruction in righteousness, that the man of
God may be complete, thoroughly equipped for every good work.

2 Timothy 3:16, 17

Paul had just noted that the Scriptures are able to make one wise with regard to salvation, a lesson Timothy had learned long before. But now Paul wanted to reemphasize to Timothy the crucial role of God's revelation in his present ministry. Paul reminded Timothy that all Scripture is God-breathed (inspired), that is God's Word was given through men superintended by the Holy Spirit so that their writings were without error. Paul asserted the "usefulness" of the Word. For each aspect of Timothy's ministry, whatever it might be—teaching (instructing believers in God's truths), rebuking those in sin (1 Timothy 5:20), correcting those in error (2 Timothy 2:25), and training in righteousness—for all of these and more the written Word of God is profitable. With it the man of God (one who must provide spiritual leadership to others) is complete, capable, and proficient in the sense of being able to meet all demands.

Though Paul stresses the importance of dependence upon the Word, every believer has their trust and dependence rooted in the Word of God. Our power to witness and live a committed life of faith is based in the Word alone. Every denomination and faith-centered group has or developed their doctrine from the Word. Pause and ask God to lead you often in Scripture that deepens your love for Him!

Heavenly Father, from the rising of the sun until the going down of the same, Your name is to be praised. Lord, the power of Your Word is what leads to salvation, and I rejoice in the hope of Your Word for everlasting life. Lord, increase my faith to trust in Your Word more. Amen.

Ron and Casey Warford, Great Commandment Network

Week 44, Tuesday
What God's Word Says

*Jesus answered and said to them, "You are mistaken, not knowing
the Scriptures nor the power of God."*

Matthew 22:29

The Sadducees' problems arose from what Jesus said . . . because they did not know the Scripture or the power of God. This was a strong denunciation of religious leaders, for of all the people certainly they should have known God's Word and His power. You must know the Word of God for yourself. The importance of knowing the Word of God as the instruction on how you're to live life is consistent with the Scripture: "All Scripture is given by inspiration of God, and is profitable for doctrine, for reproof, for correction, and for instruction in righteousness, that the man of God may be compete, thoroughly equipped for every good work" (2 Timothy 3:16–17). As a believer, once you have committed yourself to study and ongoing communion with God lived out by a yielded life to the Holy Spirit, you become a mature Christian available for God's use.

To be "instructed in righteousness" is to be "raised" or "matured" through our intimate relationship with God. It's not enough to go on what someone else tells you about the Word of God, but it matters most what you know and become obedient to. Read God's Word and study it for yourself!

 *Dear Lord, I thank You for Your Word that gives me direction and pur-
pose. Lord, help me to live my life faithful to pleasing You, and as You give
me opportunity I will be diligent in sharing with others "What Your Word
Says." Amen.*

Week 44, Wednesday
All the Teachings of Scripture

Knowing this first, that no prophecy of Scripture is of any private interpretation, for prophecy never came by the will of man, but holy men of God spoke as they were moved by the Holy Spirit.

2 Peter 1:20, 21

Scripture should be interpreted only in context, that is, a prophecy cannot stand alone without other prophecies to aid in its understanding. Scripture should not be interpreted according to one's own individual liking, either. Scripture cannot be correctly interpreted without the aid of the Holy Spirit. The Scripture did not stem merely from the prophets themselves; their writing came from God. All the teachings of Scripture, whether in the form of an instruction, parable, admonition, percept, ordinance, or command, are intended to show us the right way. The Bible describes God's complete revelation of Himself to humanity. It is a record of God's dealing with humanity and His Word to them. God speaks to you through the Bible. Have you ever been reading the Bible when suddenly you are gripped by a fresh, new understanding of the passage? That was God speaking. And when God's Word says, "Follow this way"; "Avoid those places"; "Abstain from those actions"; or "Embrace those thoughts," it is not trying to restrict us or bully us. Gods' Word is simply providing guidance to your life in ways that you have not yet become accustomed to.

As Christians desiring to follow the direction of God, would it not seem likely that we should gain a better understanding and appreciation of how God manifests His divine purpose and will for our lives? God speaks to you and me by the Holy Spirit to reveal Himself, His purpose, and His ways. God speaks to individuals, and He can do it in any way He pleases. As you learn to walk in an intimate relationship with God, you will come to recognize His voice. Jesus compared the relationship He has with His followers to the relationship a shepherd has with his sheep (John 10: 3, 27). Perhaps the questions you would ask is: How does God speak to me? And how can I know when God is speaking? When you spend time in God's Word, you get to know His voice. Then, when God speaks to you, you will recognize His voice and follow Him.

 Father God, thank You for the privilege of calling You Father. Thank You for all of the directions, guidance, and comfort found in Your Word. Help me to always have that relationship with You, to hear and know Your voice. Amen.

Ron and Casey Warford, Great Commandment Network

Week 44, Thursday
To Be "Instructed in Righteousness"

My little Children, these things I write to you, so that you may not sin, and if anyone sins, we have an Advocate with the Father, Jesus Christ the righteous. And He Himself is the propitiation for our sins, and not for ours only but also for the whole world.

1 John 2:1, 2

To be "instructed in righteousness" is to be raised or matured through an intimate relationship with God. Being honest brings blessings because God is true. Staying sexually pure brings blessings because God is just. God's commands for us to act in certain ways flow out of who He is and how He Himself acts. His ways simply reflect who He is—perfectly right—and that way of living brings blessings. Our convictions form an influence regarding our view of right and wrong. Godly convictions will always lead a Christian believer to pattern his or her life after the One who is righteous: "For the LORD is righteous, He loves righteousness; His countenance beholds the upright" (Psalm 11:7). "Righteousness and justice are the foundation of Your throne; mercy and truth go before Your face" (Psalm 89:14).

Continue to be "instructed in the righteousness of His Word"!

Heavenly Father, I thank You for Your great love toward me that yet while in my sins You still loved me. By Your sending an Advocate for my sins I am forgiven. I honor and serve You with my whole heart. Amen.

Week 44, Friday
The Bible's Fundamental Purpose

Yes, and all who desire to live godly in Christ Jesus will suffer persecution.
But evil men and impostors will grow worse and worse, deceiving and being deceived.

2 Timothy 3:12, 13

It was important for Timothy, as for all Christians including you and me, to realize that persecution awaits everyone who wants to live a godly life in Christ. From this Scripture today we learn that Timothy could actually expect the situation to get worse and the pressure to intensify. False teaching would increase as evil men and impostors (magicians) were deceiving and being deceived. This becomes a vivid perspective of what we as Christians may experience.

"But you must continue in the things which you have learned and been assured of, knowing from whom you have learned them, and that from childhood you have known the Holy Scriptures, which are able to make you wise for salvation through faith which is in Christ Jesus" (2 Timothy 3:14–15). Scripture brings salvation only when you places your faith in Christ Jesus. The Bible is the ultimate authority for faith and life. The fundamental purpose of the Bible goes even deeper than providing us with rules and guidelines that can bless our lives, while the convictions He leads us in through His Word are "for our good"—just as Moses instructed the nation of Israel: "Keep the commandments of the LORD and His statutes which I command you today for your good" (Deuteronomy 10:13). The authority and power of Scripture to protect us and provide for us derive from the Author of the Book – God Himself. God is the power behind the Book. Pause and ask God to lead you often in Scripture that will deepen your love for Him!

Heavenly Father, thank You for Your Word that guides my way. I pray that You will deepen my commitment to the study of Your Word. Lord, I find in Your Word the essentials for life's purpose. Amen.

Ron and Casey Warford, Great Commandment Network

Week 44, Weekend
Don't Forget

I will delight myself in Your statutes; I will not forget Your word.

Psalm 119:16

The Bible can truly be an amazing blueprint for our lives. When we make a priority of discovering the truths of God's Word, and remember (not forgetting) His specific plans for living, we will come to the same conclusion as the Psalmist: we will delight or find joy in the Bible because it works!

How has God's Word brought good things to your life?

Perhaps your choice to follow God's Word prevented you from experiencing harm or maybe you've followed Scripture's direction and that brought help to your relationships, more clarity to your life, direction, or hope in the face of life's challenges. Has there been a time when your choice to follow the teachings of the Bible brought blessings for your life? To get you started, here are a few verses to consider:

- Give and you will receive (Luke 6:38).

- Give all your worries and cares to God, for He cares about you (1 Peter 5:7).

- Honor your father and mother. Then you will live a long, full life in the land the Lord your God is giving you (Exodus 20:12).

- Trust in the Lord with all your heart; do not depend on your own understanding. Seek His will in all you do, and He will show you which path to take (Proverbs 3:5–6).

- But if we confess our sins to Him, He is faithful and just to forgive us our sins and to cleanse us from all wickedness (1 John 1:9).

Which biblical truths have you lived out and were consequently blessed with good things?

I'm grateful to God for using _____ (specific Bible verse) in my life to protect me/bring good things like . . .

God, thank You for giving Your Word to guide me. Thank You that Your Word is a good blueprint for me. I am especially grateful for how Your Word says _____. I am delighted that Your Word brought blessings to my life. Amen.

Terri Snead, Great Commandment Network

Week 45, Monday
Get To's

*How then shall they call on Him in whom they have not believed? And how
shall they believe in Him of whom they have not heard? And how shall they hear
without a preacher? And how shall they preach unless they are sent? As it is written: "How
beautiful are the feet of those who preach the gospel of peace, who bring glad tidings of good things!"*

Romans 10:14, 15

Most of us have heard or read verse 13 of Romans 10: "For whoever calls on the name of the Lord shall be saved." We often forget that God uses us to bring the Good News to our friends and family members. Right before Jesus left the planet, He gave specific instructions, a mission to the disciples and to all who would follow Him. He said, "Go and make disciples." God surely does not need us, but He chose to use us. We think sometimes that we should see a bright light come out of heaven. Well, guess what? God did send a bright light; it was the people He used to influence you to Christ.

Your decision to follow Christ was a result of the Holy Spirit of God drawing you but also using people and circumstances. Think about the people whom God used in your life to influence you. You were drawn to these people even though they were not perfect. Aren't you glad that they were sent to you?

You live where you live and go to the school you go to because God put you there to be an influence to the people you are around. It is hard sometimes to drag yourself out of bed to go to school. Today, look at it from another perspective. "I get to go to school because God has sent me. I am on a mission to influence the lives of my friends, and today I will bring glad tidings of good things."

*Jesus, help me see people as You see them. Help me today to be light to a
dark world and let others be drawn and attracted to the Holy Spirit in my
life. Amen.*

Mark Roberts, First Priority

Week 45, Tuesday
Your Circle of Influence

I thank my God, making mention of you always in my prayers, hearing of your love and faith which you have toward the Lord Jesus and toward all the saints, that the sharing of your faith may become effective by the acknowledgment of every good thing which is in you in Christ Jesus.

Philemon 1:4–6

There is a reality show where obese individuals learn to exercise and eat healthily. They compete to see who can lose the most weight. Some contestants arrive needing to lose more than half of their body weight. This often means they must shed more than 150 pounds.

At first, losing 150+ pounds seems an impossible task. The thought of losing the weight of "an entire person" is overwhelming to most of the contestants. However, they quickly learn that healthy and lasting weight loss is accomplished one pound at a time (with the goal of losing two to three pounds a week), and if they work together and encourage one another along the journey, they can be successful.

When you step back and look at your school as a mission field, it is easy to become overwhelmed at the thought of sharing the Gospel with your entire campus. After all, how are you going to get hundreds of people, most of whom you don't know, to listen to you talk about God?! But just as healthy and lasting weight loss is accomplished one pound at a time over an extended period, healthy and lasting evangelism is accomplished one person at a time. Sharing the Gospel at your school must be done through personal, one-on-one relationships, and it must be done together as the Body of Christ.

Instead of being overwhelmed by the "big picture," focus your attention on the handful of people whom God has placed within your circle of influence. Your circle of influence includes the people whom God has placed around you at school. For instance, who sits next to you during science class? Who often shares a table with you at lunch? Whom do you stand around with waiting at the bus stop?

Who around you at school needs to experience God's love? God put them in your life for a reason. Begin helping them lose the weight of their sin by sharing God's Good News of salvation!

God, please help me to see the people around me with Your eyes. Give me the courage to begin a relationship with them, discernment to know how I can minister to them, and the wisdom to know when and how to share Your Good News. Help me to broaden my circle of influence and make the sharing of my faith effective so that You may broaden your Kingdom. Amen.

Haley Wherry, First Priority

Week 45, Wednesday
Far from Perfect

Though He causes grief, yet He will show compassion according to the multitude of His mercies. For He does not afflict willingly, nor grieve the children of men.

Lamentations 3:32, 33

It doesn't take long to realize that life is far from perfect. There are things that can happen to us that cause a deep amount of pain, such as parents getting divorced, someone you know who is diagnosed with cancer, a best friend betraying you, or having someone you love die.

Many of these circumstances are beyond our control, so we sometimes have the tendency to blame the one Person we know who could have prevented it from happening: God.

When we are in the midst of these circumstances it is so easy to get angry and to want to know why God is allowing it to happen to us. Since we can't always find the answer to that question, we often come to the conclusion that God gets pleasure out of watching us suffer. However, that is the furthest thing from true. Instead of trying to figure out why you are going through the pain, the important thing to remember is that God is perfect and He is still in control of your life. He loves us with an unconditional love. We won't always understand why bad things to happen to us, but what we do know is that God shows us compassion and comfort, and He gives us the strength to make it through those hard times.

He is a God who is faithful to bring beauty from our pain, and if we keep our trust in Him, He will use both the good and the bad circumstances in our lives to bring glory to His name.

 Heavenly Father, I know that this life is going to let me down and that I am going to go through seasons of pain. Help me always remember that You love me and that You promise to comfort me and carry my burdens so that I don't have to. Allow me to see the good through the bad, and trust that You have my life in Your hands! Amen.

Laura Beth Beghard, First Priority

Week 45, Thursday
A Sower of Seeds

Behold, a sower went out to sow. And as he sowed, some seed fell by the
wayside; and the birds came and devoured them. Some fell on stony places, where
they did not have much earth; and they immediately sprang up because they had no depth
of earth. But when the sun was up they were scorched, and because they had no root they withered
away. And some fell among thorns, and the thorns sprang up and choked them. But
others fell on good ground and yielded a crop: some a hundredfold, some sixty,
some thirty. He who has ears to hear, let him hear!"

Matthew 13:3–9

This is an amazing passage and an encouragement to us as Christians. It reminds us as believers that every day we get up, we get to be sowers of the Gospel. We can choose every morning once our feet hit the floor to become sowers for Christ. It reminds us to look at our schools differently—not as a place we dread to go but as a place we go to sow God's seed.

The passage also reminds us that as we sow, some of that seed falls on different soils. Some falls on the wayside and doesn't take root; some falls on stony ground; some in the thorns. It is easy to get discouraged when we see this happen. We should not get focused on where the seeds fall because that is not in our hands but God's. We should focus on our willingness to share or, in Jesus's terms, sow His message.

It is encouraging when we get to rejoice with those who do receive Christ and are saved. This passage is a great reminder for us to stay obedient to Christ in sharing His message. This passage also encourages us to pray for the different types of soils of "our classmates" and even for some of our closest friends. Every seed we sow counts!

Lord, help me today be sensitive to those around me. Help me to share
Your loving grace and help others to see how much You care about them.
May the seed we sew bring honor and glory to Your name. Amen.

Week 45, Friday
Sound the Alarm

Blow the trumpet in Zion, and sound an alarm in My holy mountain!
Let all the inhabitants of the land tremble; for the day of the LORD is coming, for it is at hand.

Joel 2:1

I was in the airport when someone opened a door that should not have been opened, and an alarm went off. I was at first annoyed, but then I thought, *The alarm is going off! I need to tell someone about it! The door is open, and it needs to be shut.* The alarm that is sounded in Joel is telling us something, something more important than a door in the airport is open. It tells us that the day of the Lord is coming, and that we need to repent. Even more than that, others need to know that they need to repent. God wants to use you, wherever you are today, to sound the alarm! He is in control of all things, but within His control He has given us a responsibility, an assignment. That assignment is to tell others about the God who has and is changing us from the inside out. We really do believe in the God of the Bible, and we believe that all He says is true. We hold the power of salvation in our hands, and God is wanting us to blow the trumpet and to sound the alarm as we go through our day today!

Father God, please help me today to see how important You are in my life, to see that You have given me an assignment today. Help me make Your message the most important part of my day. Please give me the strength and courage that it will take to forget about my selfish needs and to put Your message first. Give me the strength to step forward when You give me the opportunity to blow the trumpet and to sound the alarm in love to everyone I come in contact with today. Amen.

Shannon Popp, First Priority

Week 45, Weekend
A Problem and Solution

And the Lord *God said, "It is not good that man should be alone."*

Genesis 2:18

The book of Genesis reminds us that Adam had a seemingly perfect life in the Garden of Eden, but there was one problem: he was alone. Adam had a perfect, unspoiled relationship with God, but he still needed a relationship with another person.

This need for other people is part of our God-given makeup. We are designed to need a relationship with God and with other people. When our relationships are broken, disconnected, or missing, we understandably feel alone.

Do you ever ignore your feelings of aloneness and try to find something other than God-given relationships as a temporary fix?

Sometimes when I am feeling lonely, instead of going to God, family, or supportive friends, I will . . . *(For example: Sometimes when I am lonely, instead of going to God or friends, I will escape into video games, drink too much, go for a drive, listen to music, get angry and take it out on my brother, etc.)*

There is nothing that can substitute for healthy relationships with God and other people. So acknowledging our aloneness can move us into the community that God has provided.

Think about the relationships that God has provided—just for you. Has He provided a parent, grandparent, teacher, pastor, coach, or other adult who cares for you? Has God provided a friend, cousin, sibling, or neighbor who knows you and enjoys being with you? God has definitely provided a relationship with Himself—He knows you intimately, understands you perfectly, and unconditionally cares for you.

Here's the basic idea: God was so concerned about you that He provided a relationship with Himself and other people. He knew that feeling alone was one of the most painful experiences that we could ever endure, so He didn't just announce our problem of aloneness, He solved it!

 God, thank You for being concerned about my aloneness and thank You for providing for me. Amen.

Week 46, Monday
What's in a Name?

"Nor is there salvation in any other, for there is no other
name under heaven given among men by which we must be saved."

Acts 4:12

What's in a name? Words and names have lost their meaning in today's culture. Just ten years ago if someone walked up to you and asked you about your iPad or iPod, you might have pointed them to a bathroom! When we hear names like Cal Ripken, we think of the ironman of baseball. When we hear the name Jose Conseco, well, our thoughts are not so positive. The point is that we have a given name from our parents, but what we do with that name either points people to Christ or away from Him.

No other name can offer you eternal life and abundant life but the name of Jesus. You have a relationship with the heavenly Father because of His Son, Jesus. You have taken on the name *Christian*. Does your being a Christian really make a difference to the folks God has placed around you?

It will never be popular to stand up for Christ. Putting the needs of others above your own, loving your neighbor, doing good to those who would do evil to you, exercising humility, suffering with those less fortunate, and doing it all with a pure heart can only be done when you die to self and follow Jesus.

Someone in your school needs to know the love of Christ today. Whose name has God placed on your heart?

Jesus, help me love others the way You love them. Help me die to myself.
Help me live today so others will be drawn to the One whom I live for, Jesus.
Help me make Your name famous. Amen.

Dr. J. D. Simpson, Jr., First Priority

Week 46, Tuesday
On These Things

Finally, brethren, whatever things are true, whatever things are noble, whatever things are just, whatever things are pure, whatever things are lovely, whatever things are of good report, if there is any virtue and if there is anything praiseworthy—meditate on these things. The things which you learned and received and heard and saw in me, these do, and the God of peace will be with you.

Philippians 4:8, 9

Every day, we face hundreds if not thousands of choices. What we eat for breakfast, what we are going to wear to school, and even what things we will fill our heart, mind, and soul with as we start our day. We even have to choose what we will meditate (or think) on before we take on the rest of the day.

I believe this text is clear that if we are going to walk into the arenas God has called us to influence, we can only do that when we set our hearts on His ways, on things that are praiseworthy or full of God's light. Such things would include the truth found in His Word and Spirit, the noble idea of God knowing whom we will affect this day, then preparing us for it, and especially the love He has for us.

Consider today, in a world where people face so much turmoil, what have you thought on as you prepare for the day ahead? In these things, what you received, heard, or focused on, the peace of God will be with you. In a world so over whelmed by darkness and turmoil, your choice to think on light or praiseworthy things is sure to provide opportunities for you to share that peace with others.

Take a moment to think on such things and then use this prayer as a starting point . . .

Father, You are true, You are noble, You are good, and through Your Son, Jesus, You have put such things in me by your Spirit. As I walk today into the arenas that You have prepared me for, please help me to walk in Your peace so that others around me may see my life as a reflection of You. Amen.

Steve Cherrico, First Priority

Week 46, Wednesday
In Due Season

And let us not grow weary while doing good, for in due season we shall reap if we do not lose heart.

Galatians 6:9

In today's culture, "doing good" is not popular. In fact, the tide has even turned to suggest that "doing bad" is the better way to go. It certainly seems more popular in the world around us to not only live for the moment but to live for ourselves. For the Christian this can be challenging to our faith and commitment as a believer and follower of Christ.

More often than not, doing good isolates the Christian and overwhelms us with feelings and thoughts that what we do really doesn't matter. Do-gooders are often labeled and even rejected by their peers and the culture. One writer of scripture even asked the question, "Why do the wicked prosper?" (see Jeremiah 12:1).

I'm sure you have often thought that those around you engaged in doing bad things seem to be doing just as well or even better than those who consider their ways. At the moment this may seem a reality, but there is a final chapter to this thing called life. We must not lose heart and allow Satan to deceive us into believing that what we do really doesn't matter because what we do today impacts our tomorrow.

If the farmer looks across the field right after planting the crop, the reward is nowhere to be seen. It is buried underneath hours of hard work, commitment, and faith that in due season his work will yield a reward. If the farmer based his commitment to the harvest on the immediate results and what he could see in the natural, his work would appear to be in vain. It is what's underneath the dirt that will eventually bring out the reward, and this takes time.

For the teenager today, one of the most difficult challenges is to see the end from the now. It is hard to stay reminded that life is full of seasons and that doing good has its season of reward as well. Part two of Galatians 6:9 says that in "due season" we will get what is coming to us. The Christian life is a journey. It is about God working on our eternal being and shaping us into people He will hang out with in eternity. So do not lose heart in doing good—it will pay off!

Jesus, help me to realize that even though doing good is not always popular and often seems pointless, in the end it pays off. Let me live each day with the understanding that what I give out will be given back to me in the end. Teach me to see the end from the now. Amen.

Mark Robbins, First Priority

Week 46, Thursday
Worship Well

Therefore, brethren, be even more diligent to make your
call and election sure, for if you do these things you will never stumble.

2 Peter 1:10

What!? Did you hear that? God gives us the answer! He tells us how to get to the thing we've been striving to achieve our whole lives: perfection. Aaahhh, to live a day without any regrets, worry, immorality, or envy, but instead to have steady and faithful joy, peace, patience, kindness, gentleness, and self-control. No drama! Sounds good! So what is the secret to being perfect? It begins with knowing who we are in Christ, based on 2 Peter 1:3–5. Verse 5 says, "But also for this very reason, giving all diligence, add to your faith virtue, to virtue knowledge."

Faith is the basic view that the "way" of Christ is more satisfying than the "view" from the world. With faith in Christ established, be diligent in adding to your faith: virtue. Virtue is the quality of doing what is right and avoiding what is wrong. Jim saw the alcohol that was offered him at the party but believed that by passing up the fun tonight, he would have more fun in the morning without being sick or needing to lie to his parents. Add to your virtue: knowledge. Knowledge implies experience because when you do right and avoid wrong, you start to know why God has given us right and wrong. For example, Jim experienced true freedom from guilt, shame, and lying by not drinking, and he had a very enjoyable day with his friends Saturday afternoon fishing. All the while, his friends talked about who got caught the night before and who didn't. Once you have that knowledge (that following Christ is fulfilling and brings joy), you are better able to have self-control. We add to self-control a steadfastness that is loyal in the face of trouble and difficulty. In America, a "habit" typically describes the bad we do all the time. Scripture uses the word *steadfastness* to describe the good habits we gain from self-control, knowledge, virtue, and faith.

When steadfastness endures, the Scripture uses the word *godliness,* which means "to worship well." When godliness describes you, "brotherly affection" overflows from your heart.

Lord, help me worship well this day. Amen.

Week 46, Friday
Stay Connected

"I am the vine, you are the branches. He who abides in Me,
and I in him, bears much fruit; for without Me you can do nothing."

John 15:5

Oftentimes we attempt to do things on our own, and more often than not we fail at what we were trying to accomplish. For the most part, our intentions are pure and not for personal gain. So why is it that we still cause earth-shattering messes that seem like have no escape?

Have you ever seen a limb from an apple tree grow an apple after being ripped right off of the tree? Of course not; that's why the vine is so important to us. Galatians 5:22–23 says, "But the fruit of the Spirit is love, joy, peace, longsuffering, kindness, goodness, faithfulness, gentleness, self-control." If we want to abide, or remain, in God, we must stay connected to the vine.

What do I need to do to stay connected to the vine? Well, reading this devotional is a good start. It sounds difficult but it isn't. Jesus is the vine and staying connected to Jesus is as easy as communicating with Him. Get to know Him. Reading the Bible is a great way to learn who Jesus was and is today, and not only understanding Him but also His expectations for us. Prayer is another way for you and me to communicate with Jesus. We speak to Him and He speaks back.

Staying connected to the vine isn't difficult. However, it does require a commitment to communicate with the Creator who continuously gives us life.

 Lord, thank You! You are the Vine and I am a branch. You give me life. Give me the strength I need to remain in You. I pray that Your fruit in me will be visible to my friends who need to know You. Please help me to reach my friends with the love that You have placed in me. Lord, use me! Amen.

Gary Pennington, First Priority

Week 46, Weekend
He Is Good

Teach me good judgment and knowledge,
for I believe Your commandments.... You are good, and do good.

Psalm 119:66, 68

The Bible is more than a set of rules and regulations. It's more than a collection of nice stories and parables. The Bible is a love letter from God. God has written His letter and He's hoping that we'll read it and respond.

- We know that God's Word shows us what to **believe** about life.
- We hear how the Bible reveals **how we should live** our lives.
- But the often-missed (and sometimes most critical) role of God's Word is that it invites us into an intimate relationship with the Savior.

Here's a prime example: we all know that Church leaders regularly emphasize the importance of the Ten Commandments. Remember those? Here are five of them.

- You shall not murder.
- You shall not steal.
- You shall not commit adultery.
- Honor your father and mother.

We're challenged to live according to the Ten Commandments and believe the critical insights about God's character and holiness. But when we study the Ten Commandments and don't experience the heart of the compassionate Father who gave us those commandments, we don't see the God who is love. We miss the message of love behind the Ten Commandments when we see only the "thou shalt not's" without recognizing the heart of love that lies behind them. Why did God give us these commandments? Was it to raise a standard of moral behavior? Yes. Was it to give testimony of a righteous God? Of course. But Deuteronomy 10:13 also speaks of these commandments being given "for our own good." Evidently, our loving Father gave us these commandments because He didn't want His children to hurt themselves or one another.

God, thank You for giving us Your love letter in the Bible. Thank You that everything that's contained in Your Word has been written because You want what's good for me. Amen.

Terri Snead, Great Commandment Network

Week 47, Monday
Confidence

For I am not ashamed of the gospel of Christ, for it is the power of
God to salvation for everyone who believes, for the Jew first and also for the Greek.

Romans 1:16

Many times we as Christians don't share our faith because we feel inadequate, like we don't know enough or we won't be very good at it. We don't have enough confidence in ourselves, our knowledge, or our ability, and therefore we remain silent for fear of failure.

I remember when I was in about the fourth or fifth grade, we took a family vacation with several other families to the beach. One night several of us guys were out on the beach playing football when a group of older guys asked if they could join. During the course of the game one of the older guys picked me up and slammed me to the ground. I never have been a big guy, especially in elementary school when I could have hidden behind a stick of bamboo, but I jumped up with tears in my eyes threatening to beat the guy up. Of course he laughed, as did everyone else, and gladly invited me to try if I liked. Fortunately, wisdom got the better part of me and I declined the invitation, but I did not hesitate to let him know that my dad was up in our condo and he would do my bidding for me. I had no doubt he would be victorious.

Just as my confidence was not in my own ability to defend myself, but in that of my dad, so should be our confidence in the Gospel. God does not ask us to be evangelism superheroes, but to be confident in the message of the Gospel and trust that in it is the power to change lives. It is Him, not us, who will be victorious.

Paul reminds us in 1 Corinthians 2 that it is not by our own wisdom or persuasive speech that we share Christ with others, but by the power of the Holy Spirit.

God, would You give me confidence in the power of the Gospel. Help me to trust in the power of Your Word, not in my own speech. Give me a burden for those around me who need to hear the Gospel. Help me to not be ashamed, but to be confident in You. Amen.

John Carruth, First Priority

Week 47, Tuesday
Open and Obedient

So Philip ran to him, and heard him reading the prophet Isaiah,
and said, "Do you understand what you are reading?"

Acts 8:30

And he said, "How can I, unless someone guides me?" And he asked Philip to come up and sit with him. The place in the Scripture which he read was this:

"He was led as a sheep to the slaughter; And as a lamb before its shearer is silent,
So He opened not His mouth. In His humiliation His justice was taken away,
And who will declare His generation? For His life is taken from the earth."

So the eunuch answered Philip and said, "I ask you, of whom does the prophet say this, of himself or of some other man?" Then Philip opened his mouth, and beginning at this Scripture, preached Jesus to him. Now as they went down the road, they came to some water. And the eunuch said, "See, here is water. What hinders me from being baptized?"

God recently used this story in my life. I am reminded that by being obedient and sharing the Gospel gives us an opportunity to be a part of God's great plan to redeem humanity. Experiencing God on earth gives us a small glimpse of what heaven will be like in the future.

Philip was having remarkable success in cities in Samaria, where revival seemed to be breaking out. God wanted to use Philip to reach one. Philip was obedient and went south to Gaza.

The Ethiopian eunuch was like many people we know today. They are searching for the answer but do not know how to find it. The Ethiopian had traveled to Jerusalem to find the "one true God," and he was introduced to him through Philip on his way back to Ethiopia. God used this Ethiopian's testimony to reach thousands throughout Africa.

If we are open and obedient, God will use us to intersect the lives of people who are searching for something spiritual. We can introduce them to Jesus Christ. The Gospel message is powerful, and when it is presented, it always demands a response.

Lord, keep my heart open and obedient to Your leading so I can be ready
to tell others about You. Amen.

Scott Avriett, First Priority

Week 47, Wednesday
My Legacy

O God, You have taught me from my youth; and to this day I declare Your
wondrous works. Now also when I am old and grayheaded, O God, do not forsake me,
until I declare Your strength to this generation, Your power to everyone who is to come.

Psalm 71:17, 18

What do we leave behind? What will be your legacy? Our lives are full of transitions where we move on to what is next. Whether you are in middle school, in high school, or are an adult, the one constant is change. Before we quickly move to our new stage in life, I think it is appropriate to ask, What of me will be remembered?

In a world full of change, God's story in your life is constant. It is the one thing that you and I can leave that will continue to have impact when we are gone. You may have set new records in sports or academics, but the truth is, someone will eventually break them and set new ones. These things are good, but in the scheme of eternity what real impact does the best grade point average or most touchdowns make?

As followers of Christ, you and I have been given the most amazing story ever, and we are not just called, but commanded to pass it on. Whether you are eleven or ninety-one years old, the story of God in your life is the one thing that will follow you into eternity. You are remembered by people you leave behind and the impact you have made. Declare His power, His strength, and His story, and that will be a legacy that will continue long after we have moved on to the next thing.

Father God, give me the strength, the courage, and the opportunity to-
day to declare Your story to all who are to come. May my legacy be a life of
knowing You and making You known. Amen.

Tony Hevener, First Priority

Week 47, Thursday
Power of a Changed Life

For Christ did not send me to baptize, but to preach the gospel, not with wisdom
of words, lest the cross of Christ should be made of no effect. For the message of the cross
is foolishness to those who are perishing, but to us who are being saved it is the power of God.

1 Corinthians 1:17, 18

How many times have you had the opportunity to share with your friends about Jesus and didn't? As Christians, we all experience this in our lives. We may feel like we don't know enough Scripture, we don't feel like we can express ourselves eloquently enough, or we may just think that people would laugh at us for believing that what Jesus did for us on the cross has life-changing power. The truth is that the cross of Christ has the power to change your friends from the inside out!

It's not all about being a Bible scholar or having the ability to articulate your thoughts in a manner that will "wow" your friends, and not everyone is going to fall in love with Jesus the first time you share His message with them. But what people cannot argue with is the power of a changed life.

When questioned about being healed by Jesus from blindness in John 9, a man told the Pharisees, "Whether He is a sinner or not I do not know. One thing I know: that though I was blind, now I see" (verse 25). He gave testimony to the life-changing power of Jesus! This man didn't have a lot of wisdom to share. All he knew was that Jesus had opened his eyes and given him sight.

You do not have to be intimidated in any situation you are given to share Christ with anyone. Knowing that Christ lives inside of you and that the Word of God is a powerful tool that can be used to open the spiritual eyes of your friends and those you come into contact with on a daily basis, you can be confident in knowing that He will give you the words to say in whatever situation you may face.

Jesus, give me the strength and confidence to boldly share Your Word and
message to those I come into contact with today. Amen.

Darin Peppers, First Priority

Week 47, Friday
What's Worship?

Therefore by Him let us continually offer the sacrifice of praise to God, that is, the fruit of our lips, giving thanks to His name. But do not forget to do good and to share, for with such sacrifices God is well pleased. Obey those who rule over you, and be submissive, for they watch out for your souls, as those who must give account. Let them do so with joy and not with grief, for that would be unprofitable for you.

Hebrews 13:15–17

What is worship? This question has somehow confounded the Church over the past few decades. When I was young, people fought over whether worship songs should be "contemporary" or "traditional" and paid little attention to worship as mission. Worship is not just a style of music, or a meeting at church, just for Sundays, and it doesn't start or stop. You worship God every second of every minute of every day with your lifestyle and actions.

In Hebrews 13 we clearly see three defining aspects of worship as mission: First, worship is the proclamation of truth. In verse 15 we see the sacrificial praise of God is the verbal proclamation of His name. The "fruit of our lips" mentioned here reminds us it is the Holy Spirit that enables and directs us to speak up to tell our friends and family about the love of Christ.

Second, worship is sacrificial service. The model of sacrifice was Jesus, and we are commanded to live in light of what He's given to us. Serving others should distinguish Christians from the world around us. In verse 16 we are warned to "not forget" because in doing so we give in to our fleshly desires and neglect the transformation of lives.

Finally, we are called to humble submission. It takes great humility to submit to the leaders God has placed in our lives. As we grow in humility, we grow in leadership. Leadership is a weighty task; we are told in verse 17 our leaders should keep "watch out for your souls."

Jesus, help us become a generation on mission to worship You through the proclamation of truth, sacrificial service, and humble submission.

Dean Ross, First Priority

Week 47, Weekend
Give a Courageous Testimony

"You shall be witnesses to Me."

Acts 1:8

Living out a passionate love for God and embracing our identity as the ones who are loved by God will supernaturally produce a love for others. As we continue to sense God's love in our lives and deeply experience His care, we won't be able to keep the Good News of the Christ to ourselves. When we encounter people who don't know Jesus, we'll be motivated to be a witness of God's Good News that:

- Love comes from God and God (actually) IS love (1 John 4:7–8).

- God is caringly involved with every part of our lives (Psalm 139:3).

- God can't wait to show us grace and compassion (Isaiah 30:18).

- God, in Christ, has made complete provision for our sin that keeps us alone and separated from Him (Romans 3:23; 6:23).

- The incredible life that God has planned for us can be real for us now and for all of eternity (John 10:10).

- Whoever chooses to call upon the name of the Lord will be saved from their separation from God and become a member of His family forever (Romans 10:13).

Reflect on the truths of God's Good News. Which part is the most meaningful to you now and why?

As I consider all that God has done so that I can have a relationship with Him, I am most grateful today for . . .

Let this be a part of what you share with people around you today. Be a witness of all that Christ has done for you. Ask God to give you opportunity to be a witness for Him.

God, please give me the opportunity and the boldness to be a witness for You today. Help me see and take advantage of the open doors You provide for me. I want the chance to tell others what You have done in my life. Make me a courageous witness for You. Amen.

Terri Snead, Great Commandment Network

Week 48, Monday
How Do You Smell?

Now thanks be to God who always leads us in triumph in Christ, and through us diffuses the fragrance of His knowledge in every place. For we are to God the fragrance of Christ among those who are being saved and among those who are perishing. To the one we are the aroma of death leading to death, and to the other the aroma of life leading to life. And who is sufficient for these things? For we are not, as so many, peddling the word of God; but as of sincerity, but as from God, we speak in the sight of God in Christ.

2 Corinthians 2:14–17

How do you smell? Do you smell like victory? We have victory though Jesus. He conquered death, hell, and the grave. You know how you feel after a win or a victory? It is amazing. There is a refreshing feeling of accomplishment that comes with being victorious. As Christians we should have that feeling every day. Bad days will come, but we should always have the perspective of God, so that His smell is on our clothes, in our hair, and on our lives.

God has given us a wonderful job, to help Him share the truth in Christ! We should be approachable by anyone in our school. How do you smell? Do you have the fragrance of His knowledge in every aspect of your life? We are not merely peddling God's Word, we are living it out loud every day for those who haven't trusted Christ yet. It is a matter of life or death. What will you smell like today? Remember students reach students!

Father God, we humbly come to You today. We thank You for the sacrifice of Jesus on a cross for our sins. We thank You for allowing us to help You complete Your mission. God, we ask You to strengthen us spiritually, mentally, and physically in order to share Your love or fragrance with all of our classmates. Please help us not to get so wrapped up in our lives and daily routines that we forget those around us who smell nothing good in life. God, help us smell of You in all that we do! Amen.

Tim Bargo, First Priority

Week 48, Tuesday
Our Way vs. The Right Way

When a man's ways please the LORD, He makes even his enemies to be at peace with him.

Proverbs 16:7

We live in a generation when everything around us encourages us to "do it your way." Even restaurants are all geared to give us more and more choices. Instead of fries and a Coke with your meal, in fast food restaurants you can choose milk and fruit or onion rings and juice. Not to say that having so many choices in life is evil or bad. But we have become so accustomed to having things "our way" that we ***think*** that it is the "right way."

God has given us the ability to decide if we want "our way" or His plan for our lives. God's way is where there is happiness and fulfillment. If you believe that God is not really all that He said He is, then you will choose your own way. But if you really begin to understand and accept the unconditional and unfailing love of God, you must yield to a new way of thinking. It's called *faith*.

If you choose this new way of thinking, it will show in your actions and in the very essence of who you are. The choice to follow Christ will not be a bed of roses, without opposition or criticism. Many have made the choice to follow Him and have been ridiculed by friends, even family. But for those who stay strong and continue to follow, God's love will show through, too!

Ask yourself these things: Has there been a time when you felt your choice made more sense than the path God had chosen for you? When you evaluate your Christian walk, is it active or passive? Do you blend in easily?

God, help me depend on You more each day. I want to walk in Your ways and not my own. Help me live in such a way that Your love shows through my life. Amen.

Week 48, Wednesday
How's Your Vision?

Philip said to Him, "Lord, show us the Father, and it is sufficient for us." Jesus said to him, "Have I been with you so long, and yet you have not known Me, Philip? He who has seen Me has seen the Father."

John 14:8–10

In John 14, Philip asked to see the Father, which means he wanted to actually see God. Philip wanted to see the God who created the universe. He wanted to see the God who led Israel out of Egypt after overthrowing Pharaoh. He wanted to see the God whom no man can see without dying. He wanted to see the God whom he had read about and heard sermons about his entire life. Jesus' answer to Philip was awesome and absolutely amazing. He told Philip that He was the very God that Philip wanted to see. He told Philip that Philip had been walking with this God for "all this time."

And who was this God Philip saw? Jesus fed everyone around Him who was hungry. Jesus protected the condemned and offered them a way to glory. Jesus touched those whom the very law said were so unclean that even touching them could make others unclean and lawbreakers. Jesus ate with the biggest sinners of society. Jesus even got on His hands and knees and washed Philip's feet. Lastly, Philip saw this omnipotent God lay His life down on a cross for even those who nailed Him to it.

The Bible says that Jesus Christ is the Word of God in the very flesh. It says that Jesus is the exact representation of God and the fullness of His being. Jesus Himself said that He was God's will in heaven being manifested on earth. Jesus said He did nothing without seeing the Father do it first. If we desire to truly know who God is, we can look at the life of Jesus. If we do, we will see a God who gave up everything that made Him God in order to redeem us.

Jesus Christ is who God has always been and who God will always be. He could be anything and He chooses to be the God who washes our feet.

    Lord, help us to see who You truly are and to share this love with all around us. Amen.

Al Allen, First Priority

Week 48, Thursday
Be Still

Be still, and know that I am God;
I will be exalted among the nations,
I will be exalted in the earth!

Psalm 46:10

This world is loud, crazy, and busy. Many of us don't know how to sit still, much less be quiet. Don't you find it interesting that the Bible says, "Be still, and know I am God"? Everything in our culture seems to go against the very thought of taking time out to spend time with God. We have so many "distractions," like Facebook, Twitter, text-messaging, and the media that is always at our fingertips!

So, if our culture is pulling us away from having a relationship with Christ, what can we do to remove distractions from our lives? What if we just set aside a few minutes every day to sit and be still in silence and solitude? No noise, no talking, no distractions, just listening—listening to God and to what He desires for you. To do this you will have to get by yourself and for a few minutes, turn everything off and tune out all other distractions. The hardest part will be controlling your thoughts and keeping them focused on God.

How much time can you set aside each day to spend with God in silence and solitude? A fast is one of the best ways to temporally remove a distraction or other things to focus more attention on your relationship with God. A fast normally lasts for just a short designated period of time. What could you fast from to find that silence in your life?

Take time to read more about people who did this in their live. One example is Daniel. He said, "Then I set my face toward the LORD God to make request by prayer and supplications, with fasting" (Daniel 9:3).

 Lord, help me today to pause and be still and recognize the distractions that keep me from You. Amen.

Week 48, Friday
To Live Is Christ

For to me, to live is Christ, and to die is gain.

Philippians 1:21

Paul sums up his life's purpose in this short but powerful verse! "For to me, to live is Christ, and to die is gain" period.

If Paul was living, breathing, and active on this planet, then his purpose was Christ. But to really understand this verse, we must take a look at where Paul came from.

Paul was a bright, up and coming Pharisee who persecuted followers of Christ. As a matter of fact, Paul was present at the stoning of the first follower of Christ ever martyred for his faith, Stephen. The Scripture states that Paul, at this time Saul, was holding the coats of the people who were murdering Stephen. It goes on to say that Saul even consented to this murder, meaning that he was one of the ones in the crowd cheering them on. Then, while on the road to persecute more followers of Christ, Paul encountered Christ in a way that would forever alter the course of his life. God then spoke to a man named Ananias and told him to deliver a message to Paul. God said to tell Paul that he would be God's instrument to take the Gospel to the Gentiles and that he was going to suffer greatly for the Lord's name. This is where Paul's life and ministry began.

Everywhere Paul went, his passion was proclaiming the Gospel. It even got him in hot water one day. One day, while Paul was in a city called Lystra, he began proclaiming the Gospel and a crowd formed around him. They began to pick up stones and fling them at Paul. As the stones hit Paul, he began to cower down and the crowd moved in closer until eventually Paul was motionless on the ground. The crowd then dragged him outside the city gates to leave him for dead. As some of Paul's cohorts were standing beside him wondering if he was dead or alive, Paul began to move. Paul then did the unthinkable! He walked right back into the city!

Are you living with a Christ-centered passion? Are you passionate about proclaiming the Gospel in the greatest mission field of your life—your school's campus?

God, help me to wake up every day with a passion for Your name that far exceeds anything else in my life! Amen.

Ricky Breazeale, First Priority

Week 48, Weekend
You're His Beloved

"As I have loved you, that you also love one another."

John 13:34

With this one verse, Jesus was both reminding the disciples about all of the ways that He had loved them, as well as foreshadowing His upcoming display of love on Calvary. Christ's reminder of how He loves is without comparison. And in this same verse, Jesus also gave us a clue about how His love is supposed to impact our lives. He wants us to soak up His love deeply and personally and then— demonstrate that same love to others. The basics of Christianity are revealed in the verse: receive His love and then show it to others.

How has Jesus loved you? Take a moment to reflect on just a few aspects of His love:

• God has shown His love to you by sending His Son to die for you. While you were still going your own way and an enemy of God, He sent Jesus to die just for you. His love is without condition, demand, or expectation. It is freely given because you are the "loved of God" (see Romans 5:8).

• God has shown His love to you by being present with you at every moment of every day. Nothing can separate you from His love. Nothing you do can change His love. His love cannot be lost, lessened, or diminished. It is forever yours because you are the "loved of God." It's who you are because of what He has declared as true of you (see Romans 8:38–39).

• God has shown His love to you by sending His Spirit to live inside of you. The Scriptures say He has poured out His love to you. Like a fountain or a spring of living water, a relationship with God means daily refreshment, eternal well-being, and a continual filling of His love because you are His "beloved" (see Ephesians 3:18–19).

Which of these truths are most meaningful to you at the moment? Reflect on who God has declared you to be and what His gift of love has made true for you. How does His love make your heart glad?

I am especially thankful for the truth that God loves me by _____ because . . .

God, I want to deeply experience Your love for me. I want to fully embrace my identity as Your "beloved." Let my love for others be a reflection of how You have loved me. Amen.

Week 49, Monday
You're an Overcomer

And do not be conformed to this world, but be transformed by the renewing of your mind, that you may prove what is that good and acceptable and perfect will of God.

Romans 12:2

Ever been called a hypocrite? Ever known one or thought you were one? God's children are not hypocrites. They are a work in progress; saintly sinners who are on an epic journey, being transformed into the likeness of Christ. It would be an arrogant ambition if it were not begun by the invitation of Jesus through the will of God Himself! Failure to be like Christ is not hypocrisy. Hypocrisy is pretense—acting. A Christian is not pretending, neither when they are being like Christ or when they sin. Both activities are very real.

Everyone has a bad day on occasion. Sometimes a bad day can turn into a bad year. If professionals—football players, baseball players, doctors, teachers, etc.—have a bad day or year, does that make them a hypocrite (a pretender)? Certainly not! They remain genuine professionals even though bad days happen.

This is true with God's children, too. Even though there will be bad days, one remains genuine. No one is perfect. And sinning occasionally does not make a Christian a hypocrite. Your competence might say something about effort, maturity, or discipline, but it does not mean that you are pretending.

Are there pretenders among us? Yes. Sometimes guys or girls will pretend to be Christian to get close to someone. Sometimes they'll pretend for their family, friends, or boss. It happens. Likewise, sometimes Christians will pretend that they are not in trying to fit-in, impress someone, or excuse their behavior. Pretense happens.

So the next time you hear the word *hypocrite* ask yourself, "Was it pretense?" If it was Christ living in you, it was genuine, and if it was you living in sin it was genuine. This is the difference between being an "overcomer" and being "overcome." Both are real and God wants us to be real, especially with ourselves.

God, continue helping me to be a genuine Christian, having no pretense with myself, my family, my friends, or anyone. Transform me by the renewing of my mind, that I may spend my days becoming more like Jesus. I want to be a genuine example of faith. Amen.

Jim Keck, First Priority

Week 49, Tuesday
Shine On

"You are the light of the world. A city that is set on a hill cannot be hidden. Nor do they light a lamp and put it under a basket, but on a lampstand, and it gives light to all who are in the house. Let your light so shine before men, that they may see your good works and glorify your Father in heaven."

Matthew 5:14–16

The Scripture often uses illustrations to help us understand how to live the Christian life more clearly: one of those is a light. You may remember in John 8:12 Jesus said, "I am the light of the world. He who follows Me shall not walk in darkness, but have the light of life." He called himself the light, then interestingly He called *us* the, light of the world. Wow, how cool it is that that we are called the light of the world! We carry the same task as Jesus, to lead others to the Father.

As followers of Christ, we are called to "shine." As pointless as it would be to turn on a light and then cover it up, it is crazy for us to have the true light of God in our lives and then not allow it to be evident.

The way you live your life tells others around you that Christ lives in you. Do you live your life allowing others to be pointed to Jesus or pushed away from Him?

Every day you have countless opportunities to be a light for Jesus. Take advantage of them! As you step on your campus, look for ways to "shine," whether you are in the class room or the locker room, at lunch or on the bus, or maybe at an after-school event. There are students around you who are searching for something. They are walking in darkness and you have the light. They may be watching you. How we treat others, how we react to circumstances, the words we speak, and the company we keep are often when we hide our light. Remove the stuff that covers your light and choose to "shine"!

Jesus, You are my light and You have called me to be a light to others who are in darkness. Help me to show them Your light every day by how I live my life for You. Amen.

Week 49, Wednesday
The Extra Mile

And when they could not come near Him because of the crowd, they uncovered the roof where He was. So when they had broken through, they let down the bed on which the paralytic was lying. When Jesus saw their faith, He said to the paralytic, "Son, your sins are forgiven you."

Mark 2:4, 5

When you read this in context, an unbelievable true story unfolds. We see four friends who really desired to see their paralyzed friend have an encounter with Jesus. They had to overcome many obstacles, distractions, and maybe even doubt. But we see that in the end Jesus saw their faith (v. 5) and touched the paralyzed man's life. He was forever changed (both physically and spiritually).

Undoubtedly they knew that if they could get their friend to Jesus, he could be healed—his life would be changed forever! What about you? Do you have a friend who needs to be introduced to Jesus so their life can be changed? I am guessing you do.

Well, what are you doing about it? Have you given up? Do you feel like there is no hope? In reading the entire passage (vv. 1–12), you can see that they overcame many obstacles to get their friend to Jesus. Are you willing to do what it takes?

It takes a compassionate faith (one that sees our friend is lost without Jesus), a convicted faith (knowing that Jesus can bring forgiveness), and a committed faith—one that goes the extra mile to bring a friend to Jesus!

Lord, thank You that You have life-changing ability and in You there is forgiveness. Help me to be a friend who has a compassion for the lost that will lead to conviction and a committed faith that will in turn bring others to You. Amen.

Chris Lane, First Priority

Week 49, Thursday
Be a Gate

As for the Parbar on the west, there were four on the highway and two at the Parbar.

1 Chronicles 26:18

What, you've never read this before in the Bible? Bet you didn't even know that it's considered the "John 3:16" of the Old Testament! No . . . not really. But it is in there, and if "all Scripture is given by inspiration of God, and is profitable for doctrine, for reproof, for correction, for instruction in righteousness" (2 Timothy 3:16), then these verses should be able to connect with our lives somehow, right?

Consider this: in context (considering who and what this is about), this passage describes the placement of guards at certain gates of the Temple, the place to connect with God. It's one of several assignments that King David passed along with regard to the construction and staffing of the most significant structure in the entire nation. If the king thought this was important, then it must have carried some weight in the scheme of things.

Here's the deal . . . these guards/gatekeepers were placed there with a purpose. They were responsible to make sure certain people (Gentiles) didn't go into the Temple and that the stuff that was in the Temple didn't "grow legs and walk out" (get stolen). But there is no Temple now because Jesus came to be the way, the truth, and the life for us to connect with God. And Jesus has placed (called) us to live our lives as a gateway to His love and mercy in our homes, schools, and places of work. Our purpose is to serve Him and to make sure that those around us know that God offers salvation to all people through faith in Jesus Christ. This is the Gospel . . . to abide in Christ and let our lives splash on everyone around us with His love, grace, and generosity.

Though we'll never be mentioned in the Bible (even in an obscure fashion), we can embrace the spirit and passion of the Parbar!

 God, help me to appreciate and accept the placement and purpose of my life. Help me understand that You have given me everything I need in Jesus Christ to fulfill Your calling. I need Your strength to keep watch in my home and school, always looking for the opportunity to be an open gate for family members and friends to encounter the Gospel. Amen.

Fred Revell, First Priority

Week 49, Friday
Feet Time

Now it happened as they went that He entered a certain village; and a certain woman named Martha welcomed Him into her house. And she had a sister called Mary, who also sat at Jesus' feet and heard His word. But Martha was distracted with much serving, and she approached Him and said, "Lord, do You not care that my sister has left me to serve alone? Therefore tell her to help me." And Jesus answered and said to her, "Martha, Martha, you are worried and troubled about many things. But one thing is needed, and Mary has chosen that good part, which will not be taken away from her."

Luke 10:38–42

Ever find yourself saying to friends: "Man, I am so tired these days from all the stuff I have to do? I don't think that's the way God intended life to be lived. In reality, it's Satan who tempts us to push our schedule to the brink. If he can't make us bad, he just makes us busy. Somewhere in our waking moments, we must take a spiritual time-out.

Martha had a smartphone, Facebook, a Twitter account! Martha defined herself by her busyness. Martha was so busy "doing" for God that she forgot where God was—right in her own living room! We gotta "be with" God before we can "do for" God.

Notice what Jesus said: "There is really only **ONE THING** worth being concerned about . . ."

Scripture (see Joshua 1:8; Psalm 1:3) tells us that each day we should schedule some "feet time" with Jesus . . . when we sit at Jesus' feet and let Him pour His Word, His love, and His power into us. I must warn you, though; it will come at a price. You might fall behind on *American Idol* or *Dancing with the Stars*, or even miss out on the latest half-cooked serving of reality TV.

The important thing to keep in mind is that every precious second invested in your relationship with Christ can *never* be taken away.

> *Father, my life is Yours. I've been bought by the cross of Jesus. Fill me with Your Spirit; use me and guide me to accomplish Your will and advance Your Kingdom today. Help me to never fall into the trap of thinking I am too busy to spend daily time with You . . . in Your Word, in worship, and in prayer. Amen.*

Phil Brown, First Priority

Week 49, Weekend

It's a Promise

"If you love Me, keep My commandments."

John 14:15

Why do you think God leaves us here, after we've come to know Him? He could have designed things so that once we become followers of Jesus, we would automatically be lifted to heaven. Apparently, God wants us here for a reason. Matthew 28:19 reminds us of one the main reasons that God has us here. In fact, it's a command: to help others see Jesus and follow Him.

Some of us hear God's commands, and because we view God as an inspecting God, we read this verse and imagine God shaking His finger as He speaks. This kind of God has a tone of expectation and demand in His voice. This kind of God looks at us with a stern look and expects a certain level of performance and measures our ability to bring others to Jesus.

Some of us may view God as disappointed in us. As you read the verse in Matthew 28:19, you may have heard a voice that seemed full of dissatisfaction. This kind of God might look down at you with arms crossed, shaking His head as He says, "If you really loved Me, then you would be able to follow these commandments. I'm not sure you really love Me because you're not proving it."

And others of us may see God as a distant God. As you read the commandment of making disciples, the voice you heard may have seemed cold or disinterested. A distant God would speak the verse while seeming preoccupied with other things or more important people.

Consider this: the real God is actually quite different from anything above. He knows that when we come to experience His love and feel it personally, we'll *want* to live out His commandments. In fact, John 14:15 can be read as a promise: "If you love Me, *you'll keep* My commandments."

Hear God's heart: *I'm longing for you to love Me. Knowing that as you love Me, you'll keep My commandments.*

> *God, help me to experience more and more of Your love for me, so that I can live out more and more of Your commands. Thank You for believing in me. Thank You for being the kind of God who longs for me to feel Your love, so that I can keep Your commandments and live daily for You. Amen.*

Terri Snead, Great Commandment Network

Week 50, Monday
Equipped for the Task

Then Jesus said to them, "Follow Me, and I will make you become fishers of men."

Mark 1:17

Preachers are called by God to share the Gospel of Christ. They usually attend college for years to become equipped for the task. It's their job. What about you? Are you called to share the Good News? Are you equipped to tell your friends about what Christ has done for you? Matthew 28:19 says, "God therefore and make disciples of all the nations, baptizing them in the name of the Father and of the Son and of the Holy Spirit." Jesus tells us to go! Jesus didn't say to go *if* you are old enough, *if* you are wise enough, *if* it's convenient, and *if* you aren't scared or shy.

One Thursday morning, I had the blessing of hearing a shy ninth-grader speak in front of more than one hundred fellow students at a club meeting. He knew he was equipped for the task. For months the student leadership, parents, teachers, and youth pastors had been praying for him. With notes in his hand, he took a deep breath and plainly told the students the truth about what Christ has done for us all. At 7:30 in the morning, in a noisy middle-school room, while sitting on the cold floor, three students became followers of Jesus themselves.

Students are sharing what Christ has done in their lives with their peers on the school campus. Student leaders *are* stepping out with great faith. They are sharing Christ's love with many students who don't go to church in order to hear what the well-equipped preacher says on Sunday morning.

I was witness to those three souls that were saved that day. God used a shy ninth-grader to share His message of love. I hope we all care enough to share the love of Christ.

Father God, I pray Your blessings on the students of my school. Fill them with Your Holy Spirit to speak boldly about Your love. Soften hearts to prepare our school campuses to hear the Gospel message. May Your presence bring peace to our schools. Amen.

Laura Davidson, First Priority

Week 50, Tuesday
Stay in the Tent

And it came to pass, when Moses entered the tabernacle, that the pillar of cloud descended and stood at the door of the tabernacle, and the LORD talked with Moses. All the people saw the pillar of cloud standing at the tabernacle door, and all the people rose and worshiped, each man in his tent door. So the LORD spoke to Moses face to face, as a man speaks to his friend. And he would return to the camp, but his servant Joshua the son of Nun, a young man, did not depart from the tabernacle.

Exodus 33:9–11

This passage of Scripture is so inspiring to read. You see the man of God, the leader of God's people, enter the tabernacle—the Tent—and when he does, God appears! You see the people of God watching Moses and the pillar of cloud, and in response to what they see, they worship! And then we discover that in the tabernacle, the Lord speaks to Moses face-to-face. How incredible!

Whatever you do, don't stop reading at this point in the passage. The next sentence is the most inspiring of all. After a face-to-face conversation with God the Father, Moses left the tabernacle and returned to the people. That must have been incredibly difficult! To have that in-depth of a conversation with the Father, and have to leave to return to the world as we know it. But look at what Joshua did. He "did not depart from the tabernacle." He stayed in the presence of God! "Moses, you may need to go back to the people, but as for me—I'm staying right here with the Father!"

Oh, that we would be a people who not only seek the presence of the Father, but stay in His presence. The gift of the Holy Spirit to the believer is an incredible gift! We don't have to stay in a tabernacle to be near the Father. We don't have to wait until Sunday morning to experience the closeness of the Father. For the believer, God is with us everywhere we go!

Father, today I want to be close to You. I want You to be close to me. Teach me to worship You and celebrate Your presence in me every moment of every day. Thank You for the gift of the Holy Spirit and salvation through my Savior, Jesus. Amen.

Week 50, Wednesday
Battle Cry

"Oh, that my words were written! Oh, that they were inscribed in a book!
That they were engraved on a rock with an iron pen and lead, forever!
For I know that my Redeemer lives, and He shall stand at last on the earth;
and after my skin is destroyed, this I know, that in my flesh I shall see God."

Job 19:23–26

Job's wish came true. God did write down his words in a book. Actually, God used many other people like Job and placed their words purposefully in His Bible so as to provide loving hope for the desperate.

When you read the story of Job, his life appeared hopeless. Not so with God. God used Job's story as evidence that Job wouldn't be abandoned. God loved Job and was well aware of his crazy situation. What really happened was that God allowed His amazing mercy and goodness to shine through Job's life. What's even more incredible is that Job was willing and embraced his circumstances.

In reality, all of us are one bad day away from having our own Job experience. If that ever happens, remember that Jesus lives! That was Job s battle cry. He said, "I KNOW that my Redeemer lives!" Will you make that your motivation and battle cry? I believe you have friends who feel that their situation is hopeless. I also believe that God is calling you to walk alongside those friends and share the battle cry that there is hope in the name of Jesus Christ.

Jesus, thank You for redeeming me. Because of Your great love, today it is my plan to allow You and Your love to shine through me. In fact, I'm committed to looking for opportunities to share the incredible news that through You, there is life! Please give me that chance. Thank You for redeeming me. Amen!

Paul Anglin, First Priority

Week 50, Thursday
The Best You Can Be

Therefore, my beloved, as you have always obeyed, not as in my presence only,
but now much more in my absence, work out your own salvation with fear and trembling;
for it is God who works in you both to will and to do for His good pleasure.

Philippians 2:12, 13

Salvation is free, but really *living* for God will cost you everything! It's important to understand that we have to constantly work on ourselves to be better. It's just a part of growth. Let's also make it clear that we don't have to do anything to *earn* our salvation. Jesus paid for that already on the cross and offers it freely to you.

This passage gives us so much to think about. It's clear to see that it is written *to* us and *about* us. This message was not written to your neighbor . . . it's talking to you! "Work out your *own* salvation . . ." We often hear the phrase, "Who you *really* are is the person you are when no one is looking." In the first part of this passage, Jesus talks about how we are to act in front of others and how we act by ourselves.

Is Jesus warning us that we are most vulnerable when no one is looking? He is telling us to focus inward and the outward will grow as well. Not vice versa. If we are weak on the inside, we can expect to fail. Don't all great seeds grow from the inside out? If you want God's plan to unfold in your life, then you have to work on the inside.

God wants the best out of you, so you can be the best YOU that you can be. That requires work. It's a part of growth, and in that growth we are becoming more of who we are supposed to be. God wants to use you the whole way through your journey, and He is showing you the awesome responsibility of doing the great things He has planned to do through YOU! God totally believes in you!

Jesus, thank You for my free salvation! Help me become the best me I can be so that You can use me at my fullest potential. Thank You for Your forgiveness and for believing in me. Help me as I continue to work things out! Amen.

Dan Maciuk, First Priority

Week 50, Friday
Be Ready to Reason

But when they did not find them, they dragged Jason and some brethren to the rulers of the city, crying out, "These who have turned the world upside down have come here too. Jason has harbored them, and these are all acting contrary to the decrees of Caesar, saying there is another king—Jesus."

Acts 17:6, 7

Wow, Paul and Silas showed up in Thessalonica and were staying with this guy named Jason. Paul and Silas were down at the local synagogue "reasoning" with the people, showing them that the Old Testament prophecies spoke of Jesus as the Christ. Well, the message hit home with some Jews and it says a large number of God-fearing Greeks and prominent women were also persuaded in what they heard. According to verse 5, some of the Jews got jealous and rounded up some bad characters from the marketplace, formed a mob, and started a riot. The mob was looking for Paul and Silas and cried out, "These men who have turned the world upside down are here in our city, saying there is another King—Jesus."

What a reputation! They had turned the world upside down. Are you turning your world upside down? Are you making a difference in your world? Does your world know because of you that Jesus is the King?

We all have opportunities every day to proclaim that Jesus is King. We are not talking about being weird, but "reasoning" with your classmates and showing them the Scriptures about Jesus.

Learn all you can about Christ and always be ready to proclaim Jesus Christ as the King of kings and Lord of lords. If we proclaim and reason with our friends and family and live a life pleasing to God, He will use us to persuade others and turn our world upside down.

Lord, thank You for the world You put me in. Help me know Your Word and proclaim it when I have the opportunity. Do a work in me so that I can, by deeds and mouth, proclaim You as King. Amen.

Hayden Roberts/Ryan Desort, First Priority

Week 50, Weekend
Worth Talking About

But I have trusted in Your mercy; my heart shall rejoice in Your salvation.

Psalm 13:5

One of the greatest truths we can share with those who don't know Christ is our gratitude for how we are loved unconditionally by a God of mercy and forgiveness. We can trust Him to show us underserved favor even though we all fall short of His holiness. If we are followers of Jesus, it is because we have trusted in His mercy and we can celebrate our relationship with Him.

Think about one of the times when you have messed up. Think about those times when you have failed, fallen short, or otherwise sinned against God. Remember those times. Think about the guilt or regret you felt. Remember the pain of consequences and the heaviness of your heart.

I remember the times when I have failed and fallen short; times like . . .

Now, take the next few moments and experience the unconditional love of Christ once again.

Imagine that you have gone for a walk. You're trying to clear your head and heart of the guilt, regret, hurt, and anger that you're feeling. You've messed up and it hurts.

Just as you round the corner and see your house, you notice that Jesus is waiting for your return. When He sees you in the distance, He is moved with compassion. He doesn't even wait for you to arrive . . . He runs to you! He leaps quickly and anxiously off the front porch because He can't wait to see you. He hugs you and whispers in your ear.

Jesus doesn't give a lecture or criticism. He doesn't fuss at you or remind you of how you've messed up. Jesus knows the consequences of your sin. He's fully aware of how things have gone wrong, but His voice is filled with care. Christ's eyes are kind and His body language is gentle and relaxed as He talks with you. Jesus tells you that He loves you and that His mercy is fully available to you.

As you consider Christ and how He has mercy in spite of your failures, how does that move your heart? And how might you share your gratitude and celebration with people around you?

 God, I celebrate how You have given me mercy in spite of my failures and sinful choices. Help me share about Your love with others. Amen.

Week 51, Monday
Two Kinds of Love

"He who has My commandments and keeps them, it is he who loves Me.
And he who loves Me will be loved by My Father, and I will love him and manifest Myself to him."

John 14:21

While we live in a time when it seems love is growing cold, we have received by way of the Holy Spirit's indwelling both the Father's love and the Son's love as the standard of all other love relationships.

You may have never considered this before, but our heavenly Father demonstrated love very differently from the Son. Throughout Scripture, God loves the Son by revealing all things to Him: "For the Father loves the Son and shows Him all things that He Himself does" (John 5:20). It is the Father who commands, sends, and commissions as He demonstrates His love for the Son by showing Him all things. At the moment of your salvation, the Holy Spirit placed within you this same self-disclosing love of the Father. You have within you One who is longing to reveal to you eternal things!

In response to the Father's revealing love, the Son loved the Father by yielding to His will. As a demonstration of His love for His Father, Jesus always yielded to His Father. "I can of Myself do nothing." (John 5:30). "I love the Father, and as the Father gave Me commandment, so I do" (John 14:31). In response to the Father's revealing, the Son's yielding was so complete that Jesus said, "He who has seen Me has seen the Father" (John 14:9). He perfectly represented His Father's will, ways and heart because He and the Father are one. You have within you the One who is inclined to yield, longing to please the God who has revealed Himself to us. You have within you the One who longs to express and extend God's glory through a yielded life.

The very same love that Jesus and the Father experienced with one another is now in us. What feelings do you have as you reflect on the powerful love that has been bestowed upon you? How does it make you feel to consider that God lives within you—and He wants to reveal Himself through you? That Jesus lives within you, empowering you to yield? Tell the Lord about your gratitude and humility today.

 God, I feel _____ when I consider that You live in me and want me to know You. I am especially grateful that . . . Amen.

David Ferguson, The Great Commandment Network

Week 51, Tuesday
How Might You Yield?

And Jesus cried out again with a loud voice, and yielded up His spirit.

Matthew 27:50

In His last words from the cross, Christ expressed both His identity and His legacy to us: He yielded! This is the key that unlocks the mystery of Jesus and the Father being One—whatever the Son did, it was only what He had seen the Father doing. In the same way, the key that will empower our living expression of God's glory will be our commitment to yield to whatever the Father reveals.

Consider some of these Scriptures that testify of how Jesus yielded. Ask the Holy Spirit to prompt your heart with any areas where you could further demonstrate your own love for the Father by yielding to Him.

Jesus yielded as He left heaven's riches and became a servant (Philippians 2:5–8). How might you yield to the Father and become more of a servant today?

Jesus yielded His actions to the Father. He did not seek to please Himself but desired only to please the Father (John 5:19; 5:30). How might you yield your actions to the Father today? How might you please Him with your life today?

Jesus yielded to the leadership of the Holy Spirit (Matthew 4:1). How might you yield to the leadership of the Holy Spirit today? How might you become more attentive to His direction and guidance?

Jesus yielded in order to be tempted as we are so that He might help us when we are tempted (Hebrews 2:18; Luke 4:1–13). How might you yield to the Father?

Jesus yielded to human authority (John 19:1–22). How might you yield to the Father and the human authorities that God has placed in your life today?

Now consider areas and issues in your life in which the Holy Spirit is longing to work. What do you sense will be the fresh work of yielding that the Lord is longing to see in you?

Lord Jesus, I wish to have an attitude of humility and look for opportunities to serve those who are leading me. Help me with my stubbornness because I tend to want things to go my way. Usually, I want to do my own thing and not follow the directions of my authorities. Help me to change that. Amen.

David Ferguson, The Great Commandment Network

Week 51, Wednesday
Transformed Priorities

Simon Peter answered and said, "You are the Christ, the Son of the living God." Jesus answered and said to him, "Blessed are you, Simon Bar-Jonah, for flesh and blood has not revealed this to you, but My Father who is in heaven. And I also say to you that you are Peter, and on this rock I will build My church, and the gates of Hades shall not prevail against it."

Matthew 16:16–18

We live in a day in which priority seems to be given to many things like material possessions and entertainment, while our important relationships are suffering.

Notice in the text above that when Christ affirmed Peter, He highlighted the Father's "revealing," and He affirmed Peter for hearing the Father's revelation. It was as if Jesus was saying to Peter, "You got it! And the reason you got it is because the Father revealed it to you." Both the Father's revealing and Peter's hearing are acknowledged. This foundational process of God revealing and His followers yielding— hearing and responding—is the "rock" upon which Christ is even now building His Church.

This foundational truth must shape our walk with Him. As we faithfully follow Him, our life priorities will change from what we are seeking to accomplish, acquire, or achieve, to a divinely prompted longing to hear Him and yield to Him. The longing to be nourished, prompted by the Holy Spirit within us, re-orders our priorities. Just as certainly as we must be nourished with physical food in order to mature physically, so also our spiritual nourishment must become a priority if we are to mature as faithful disciples and express His presence.

Consider your own priorities now. Are you more concerned about what you will accomplish, acquire, or achieve? Or is your heart longing to hear from the Lord and ready to yield to Him? Recommit yourself to hearing from God, yielding your heart to His plans and desires.

Dear God, there are many voices calling for my attention and often I'm not listening for Yours. I acknowledge that You do not have a speaking problem; rather I have an attunement issue. I want to recommit my ears to hearing Your voice, as You redirect me to focus on the important people and Kingdom issues in my life. Amen.

Week 51, Thursday
Hungry to Yield

But He said to them, "I have food to eat of which you do not know."

John 4:32

The "food" that nourished Jesus wasn't something that could've been served for dinner or ordered for breakfast. It wasn't a five-course meal or even a taste of Galilee's finest produce. Christ was strengthened, sustained, and nourished by yielding to whatever His Father revealed. Just as we also get hungry to be nourished by physical food, we must also become hungry to yield to God.

Perhaps this is what the Beatitude speaks of: "Blessed are those who hunger and thirst for righteousness, for they shall be filled" (Matthew 5:6). Could righteousness that produces satisfaction of hunger be the tangible expression of Christ followers yielding to what they have heard from God?

We have the opportunity to receive the same nourishment that strengthened and sustained our Lord. As God reveals Himself to us, He brings the opportunity to yield. We, too, can be nourished by the joy of knowing that we have yielded to the Father.

Just imagine, when the Father revealed Christ to you for salvation, you yielded to Him. You responded with trusting faith.

You may have come to see your hopeless state and yielded to Christ as your only hope.

You may have come to see Christ as life eternal and yielded to His abundant life.

You and I, like Peter, were challenged to yield to the reality of what the Father was revealing to us—that Christ was who He claimed to be and that we desperately needed Him.

Pause now and share a few words of gratitude with God. Thank Him for the marvelous revelation of Christ as your Savior. Thank Him for revealing Jesus and drawing you to Himself. Finally, express the joy that comes as you consider how you have already received His revelation, yielded to His Spirit, and are now an expression of His presence!

Heavenly Father, I'm grateful for salvation through Christ. And I appreciate the peace, joy, and satisfaction that comes from the nourishment of Your presence. May I impart life and hope to others as I remain yielded to You. Amen.

David Ferguson, The Great Commandment Network

Week 51, Friday
The Blessing of Solitude

Now in the morning, having risen a long while before daylight,
He went out and departed to a solitary place; and there He prayed.

Mark 1:35

Both the religious leaders and Christ's followers often misunderstood the Savior's priorities. Surely He would not want to be distracted by the children—and yet He rebuked the disciples and welcomed the children. Surely He would have nothing to do with "publicans and sinners"—and yet He was known as their friend. His entire life was a paradox, giving priority to those things that most others deemed unimportant, despised, or rejected. There's no clearer example of this paradoxical priority than His insistence on hearing from His Father: "I can of Myself do nothing . . ." (John 5:19, 30).

Christ prioritized hearing, and so must we. Mark 1 records that the disciples apparently had other priorities for the Savior. When they realized that Jesus had gotten up early and left the house, "Simon and his companions went to look for Him, and when they found Him, they exclaimed, 'Everyone is looking for you!'" (Mark 1:36–37). There were crowds to speak with, miracles to be performed, and sermons to preach, but Christ prioritized turning aside to a solitary place to pray. Did He spend time thanking His Father? Absolutely! Did Jesus pray for others during His times with God? Certainly! But of particular importance was that Jesus gave priority to hearing from the Father.

Setting aside time to hear the Father must become our pursuit and passion, just as it was for the Savior. Solitude moves us beyond His blessings to intimacy with the One who gives those blessings! When solitude—time alone with Jesus—become our priority:
• Prayer becomes listening as well as asking.
• Meditation on Jesus strengthens our relationship and nurtures our spirit.
• Withdrawal from the world and connection with Jesus frees us to set our minds on eternal things.

How does it make you feel to know that you have the privilege to hear from God, just as Jesus did? You have the chance each day to set aside time to truly know the heavenly Father! Tell Him of your gratitude for such a blessing. Listen to His Spirit and meditate on the image of a God who can't wait to relate with you each day.

God, I am grateful that I get the privilege of relating to You each day. Amen.

David Ferguson, The Great Commandment Network

Week 51, Weekend
Can You Hear Him Now?

In the year that King Uzziah died, I saw the Lord sitting on a throne,
high and lifted up, and the train of His robe filled the temple.

Isaiah 6:1

The prophet Isaiah's dramatic encounter with the Lord brought with it the need to put away the sin of "unclean lips." He confessed his sin: "'Woe to me!' I cried. 'I am ruined! For I am a man of unclean lips, and I live among a people of unclean lips'" (see Isaiah 6:5). Then God cleansed him by sending an angel with a live coal. The angel touched Isaiah's mouth and said, "Behold, this has touched your lips; your iniquity is taken away, and your sin purged" (Isaiah 6:6–7). Isaiah then heard the voice of God saying, "Whom shall I send, and who will go for Us?" The man of God then yielded to Lord: "Then I said, 'Here am I! Send me!'" (v. 8).

The story of this Old Testament prophet reminds us that cleansing often precedes clarity concerning God's voice and discernment about His will. Christ followers long to hear the Lord so that they, like Isaiah, want to put away anything that might hinder hearing from Him.

Do you need to put away:

• Particular areas of sin? Confess them to God and receive His forgiveness. Write about them:

• Unresolved emotions, like guilt, anger and bitterness, condemnation, and fear? Write about them:

• Childish things, such as finger-pointing or blame? Preoccupation with self? Idle chatter or gossip? Write about them:

Pause now and consider your own ability to hear from the Lord. Ask His Spirit to reveal anything that might need to be "put away." Sit quietly before the Lord and allow Him to speak to your heart. Be open to the gentle voice that urges you to purify yourself so that you might have deepened intimacy with the Creator.

Dear Lord Jesus, help me to put away these sins that are derailing me . . . I no longer wish to carry the burden of these unresolved emotions.. I'm embarrassed by my childish behaviors and want to renounce these. I wish to hear Your voice and no longer listen to the distracting noise of transgressions. Amen.

David Ferguson, The Great Commandment Network

Week 52, Monday
Obedience Redefined

Looking unto Jesus, the author and finisher of our faith, who for the joy that was set before Him endured the cross, despising the shame, and has sat down at the right hand of the throne of God.

Hebrews 12:2

We live surrounded by "relational inadequacies." We are uncertain how to be the best loving family member, dedicated coworker, or supportive friend. We struggle to relate well to our Lord Jesus.

Jesus scorned the shame of Calvary because of His joy in pleasing the Father. Christ's obedience to humble Himself to the point of death on a cross was rooted in this joy of pleasing His Father.

Would it have been genuine obedience if Christ had lived a perfect outer life, endured the cross, but felt irritated in having to do so? Outward obedience without this joy-filled longing to please may not be real obedience. Is it possible that our obedience is only pleasurable to God when it is motivated by this joy of pleasing Him?

Unfortunately, too often we can be "going through the motions" as Christians—outwardly complying with external standards of right and wrong, or saying the right things, all the while motivated by only duty or obligation. The Christian life is meant to be more than mere dutiful obedience; it must include a relational passion to please Him.

How about you? How will you know if you have been "going through the motions"? Are you:
• "Doing" Christianity rather than "being" Christ-like? Christ's disciples don't "do" Christianity, but rather express His presence through "being" Christ-like.
• Becoming prideful or self-exalting as you try to live out "right behaviors"?
• Becoming somewhat self-condemning as you fail to live out your beliefs, and now question if you are even "worthy of" God's blessings?

Pause now and consider your own walk with Christ. Has it been a growing, thriving relationship or mostly dutiful compliance? Consider how much more the Savior wants for you. He wants your life to be filled with His joy—the joy that comes from loving Him so much that you can't bear the thought of hurting Him.

God, I want to have this kind of relationship and this kind of obedience. Amen.

David Ferguson, The Great Commandment Network

Week 52, Tuesday
Cultivating Joy and Obedience

"But now I come to You, and these things I speak in the world,
that they may have My joy fulfilled in themselves."

John 17:13

We live in a day when strengthening relationships and deepening interpersonal connecting is lacking. Our world today is full of people who need the love and care of others. They are searching for someone to come alongside and share that love in a relevant, effective way.

Imagine Christ, as He stands with outstretched arms and prays to His Father. He prays on your behalf. The Gospel of John records His requests. Jesus prays the Father might protect you, sanctify you, and that you might be brought to complete unity with the Lord and with others. And all of these requests are motivated by His desire for you to experience His joy: "so that they may have the full measure of my joy within them" (see v. 13).

Christ loved the Father through His joy-filled yielding. We can also express our love to the Father in this same joyful way as we are prompted and empowered by the Holy Spirit within us. God wants us to experience more than willful, dutiful obedience. He desires that our obedience come out of the joyful wonder that we, the created, get to bring pleasure to the Creator!

But how will we cultivate this kind of obedience? How can we become this joy-filled believer? Take time to read this list of ideas. Allow the Holy Spirit to prompt your heart with one or more of these points of action.

- Give frequent praise and thanks to God that you have received in the Person of the Holy Spirit a yielding love to please Him.
- Make frequent declarations to God about how you long to please Him as you live in the fullness of His Spirit.
- Express joy for the simplicity of a life purpose that you are privileged to express His glorious presence and that He, through you, finds pleasure.
- "Exercise" yielding through submission in relationships with others.

 God, help me to complete one or more of these action steps. I want to yield in one of my relationships today, especially _____. Amen.

Week 52, Wednesday
How's Your Posture?

And Jesus answered and said to her, "Martha, Martha, you are
worried and troubled about many things. But one thing is needed,
and Mary has chosen that good part, which will not be taken away from her."

Luke 10:41, 42

Physical posture seems to be important for physical wellness. During our day-to-day life, it is helpful to frequently tune in to our body, reminding ourselves to keep our spine dignified, yet our other muscles relaxed. While we walk around, let the muscles in our face, jaw, and shoulders relax. When we relax our body, we find that our mind also relaxes. Likewise, spiritual wellness depends on our posture before the Lord.

In the above biblical passage, we see a contrast between Martha, a follower of Jesus who truly loved Him, but who made a priority of activity for Him, and her sister, Mary. Mary loved and followed Jesus but made a priority of hearing from Him.

Consider the following questions. Consider also the implications for your priorities:

1. What was Mary's posture? What is its significance to the principle of yielding even before you hear?
2. Which priority does Jesus say is more important? Listening to Him? Or doing even necessary things for Him?
3. The priority of hearing Jesus can guard us from earthly distractions:

- What emotions seem to have filled Martha's heart? Mary's heart? What emotions often fill your heart?
- Martha demonstrated a measure of self-centeredness. In what ways might you demonstrate self-centeredness?
- This story shows evidence of "comparisons that lead to division in relationships." What comparisons have you been making? What divisions have resulted?
- This story reveals a "demanding attitude." In what ways have you demonstrated a similar attitude?
- How have "things" and activities crowded your relationship with the Lord or with other people?

As you consider the implications for your own life, you will want to approach the Lord in prayer.

God, I want to sit at Your feet, listening, yielding, and loving You. Amen.

David Ferguson, The Great Commandment Network

Week 52, Thursday
Be Careful Not to Miss Him

"You search the Scriptures, for in them you think you have eternal life; and these are they which testify of Me. But you are not willing to come to Me that you may have life."

John 5:39, 40

While looking at a picture, have you ever discovered another image inside of it? Being transformed by our encounters with Him means much more than amassing knowledge about Christ, or mastering a systematic understanding of His life and teachings. The Pharisees pursued and accomplished great biblical knowledge—even memorizing the entire Bible, but they missed Him: "You have neither heard His voice at any time, nor seen His form. But you do not have His word abiding in you, because whom He sent, Him you do not believe" (John 5:37–38).

Consider these portrayals of Christ as they reveal the true person of Jesus. Ask the Spirit to stir your heart as you imagine . . .

- The tear-filled eyes of Jesus as He weeps at Lazarus's grave (John 11:35).
- The saddened and gratitude-deprived heart of Jesus as He inquires about the nine lepers (Luke 17:17).
- The supportive and encouraging Jesus as He foreshadows Peter's betrayal (Luke 22:32).
- The accepting words of Jesus as He looks past the sinful nature of Zacchaeus (Luke 19:1–10).
- The Jesus who intercedes for us and the concerns of our heart (Romans 8:33–34).

Pause for a moment and consider: Can you hurt for Jesus as you imagine the disappointment He must have felt as the lepers failed to say thanks? Can you imagine the kind of Savior who is able to defeat the sting of death and yet is sorrowed by a friend's emotional pain? Have you come to know the Savior who knows you're going to fail and yet loves you anyway? Finally, have you known the Christ who not only died for our sins on Calvary, but is now in realms of glory praying for our concerns?

Take the next few moments and reflect on this "kind of Jesus." Be careful not to miss Him! Now express your feelings for Him and to Him.

 Lord Jesus, I want to "fellowship with Your sufferings" (Philippians 3:10), for You are a "Man of sorrows and acquainted with grief" (Isaiah 53:3). I feel sorrow for Your pain. Amen.

David Ferguson, The Great Commandment Network

Week 52, Friday
Have You Come to Know Him?

Jesus said to him, "Have I been with you so long, and yet you have not known Me, Philip?
He who has seen Me has seen the Father; so how can you say, 'Show us the Father'?"

John 14:9

I magine the sadness that must have been in the Savior's heart as He uttered these words. Picture the scene in the upper room. The faithful followers surrounded Jesus: the ones who were the "closest" to Him encircled the room. He had already experienced the painful distraction of the disciples arguing among themselves; He heard them argue over who was to be the greatest in the Kingdom. He vulnerably shared how His body was about to be broken and His blood was about to be shed, only to be met with the dispute of His closest friends (Luke 22:17–26). Then as a testimony of humble servanthood, Christ took a basin of water and a towel and began to wash the feet of each disciple. He washed the feet of Peter, James, John, and even Judas. He washed the feet of the "betrayer," giving him one last chance for redemption. During the Passover meal, Christ even turned to Judas and said, "What you do, do quickly." Judas then departed to complete the terms of his betrayal (John 13:26–27).

As you read the account of this familiar story, pause now and reflect upon the heart of the Savior. What might the God-man have been feeling as He experienced the dread of crucifixion, the departure from intimate friends, the insensitivity of their response, and then the betrayal of one of His followers? What feelings might have been in Christ's heart in the upper room? Has your spirit connected with His Spirit on this level? Have you come to know Him in this way?

Allow the Holy Spirit to gently lead your heart into responding to the heart of Jesus as you hear Him say, "Have I been so long with you, and yet you have not come to know Me?" (John 14:9 NASB).

Jesus, my heart is moved with _____
_____ *as I encounter Your sorrow in a fresh way. I am moved with*
_____ *as I*
see You as the One acquainted with sorrow and grief. Amen.

Week 52, Weekend
He Rises to Show Grace and Compassion

For You, Lord, are good, and ready to forgive, and abundant in mercy to all those who call upon You.

Psalm 86:5

We live in a world full of people in pain. People have been wounded and scarred by violence and discrimination, family fragmentation, abandonment, rejection, materialism, addiction, and abuse. Tragically, when people have needed support and encouragement in their relationships, their pain has been compounded.

Pause and consider the truth that Christ longs to show you grace and is abundant in mercy. He is excited to show you favor and ready to forgive. He earnestly desires to shower you with undeserved, unexpected blessings.

Picture the Savior seated at the right hand of the Father. Use your imagination to paint the scene in the throne room of heaven. God the Father sits on His throne. Christ the Son sits to the right, the place of power and of honor.

The One who sits at the Father's right hand will be interceding for you as you go about your life today (Hebrews 7:25). And then at any and every point along the way, as you struggle to remain faithful or weaken from the stresses of this world, Christ will long to show you grace. Picture it now: Christ rises from His seat in the throne room. Jesus invites you close to Him, and with outstretched arms, He welcomes you to Him. With excitement in His eyes and graciousness in His voice, the Savior speaks a blessing over you.

Meditate on the Person of Christ, who, with outstretched arms and nail-pierced hands, welcomes you into His presence and is excited to bless you.

As I imagine Christ, and how He is excited to welcome and bless me, how He rises to show me compassion, my heart is filled with . . . (gratitude, joy, humility, confidence, reassurance, security) *because . . .*

  God, please let the blessing of this truth overtake my heart. Help me to remember it each day of my life. Amen.

Scripture Index

Scripture Index

Scripture Index

IMPACT: Student Leadership Devotional

Scripture Index

NOTES

NOTES

Notes

Notes